Praise for *Higher Calling*

"Scott Beardsley has always been an intrepid and inspirational leader—first at McKinsey, and now at the University of Virginia. In *Higher Calling*, Scott describes the current shift toward nontraditional academic leadership—told through his own personal experience transitioning from an exceptional career at McKinsey to his new role as dean of the Darden School of Business. His story is one that will deeply resonate with anyone interested in leadership in academia, and inspire everyone else who believes in the potential of a second career."

—DOMINIC BARTON, Global Managing
Partner, McKinsey & Company

"A very well-written and engaging narrative that is full of both quantitative and qualitative material into which Scott Beardsley gracefully weaves his fascinating personal story. A must-read for members of presidential search committees and those aspiring to a presidency."

—LAWRENCE SCHALL,
President, Oglethorpe College

"*Higher Calling* provides an extremely relevant look at the evolving requirements at the top of the academy. Scott Beardsley's personal account of his own deliberate entry into the hallowed halls of academia is supported by clear analysis of the trends and conditions influencing today's leadership profile. This study is both deeply personal and yet far-reaching. It offers invaluable evidence for anyone seeking to understand how the experience, skills, and perspective gained outside of higher education are becoming a source of change within."

—KENNETH L. KRING, Co-Managing
Director, Global Education Practice

"The increasing speed of change is transforming institutions everywhere, including in higher education. Scott Beardsley's own journey and analysis of hiring trends of university presidents illuminates important lessons applicable beyond academia. Great leadership talent is the ultimate asset and can be the ultimate variable in determining whether an institution fulfills its mission."

—TRACY WOLSTENCROFT, President
and CEO, Heidrick & Struggles

"This book should be read by everyone associated with selecting a college president, particularly those daring souls who might consider throwing their hat in the ring for the top job."

—STEVE REINEMUND, Retired Chairman
and CEO, PepsiCo, and Former Dean
of Business, Wake Forest University

"The increasing number of college leaders drawn from 'nontraditional' backgrounds has generated much debate and controversy within the academy, but the conversation has largely been anecdotal. Scott Beardsley's work takes a serious scholarly approach to this topic, drawing extensively on data drawn from case studies and interviews. This insightful book will advance the discussion about higher education leadership far beyond its current reliance on narrow stereotypical thinking."

—DAVID W. BRENEMAN, Professor Emeritus of
Education and Public Policy, University of Virginia,
and Former President, Kalamazoo College

"This is a must-read for both aspiring nontraditional presidential candidates and search committees considering those candidates. Beardsley has written a thoughtful analysis of the backgrounds of specific presidents, their experience of the search process, the unique challenges they face as presidents, and the advice they have for other aspirants. He has also provided a glimpse into the future leadership needs of the academy, which are changing daily."

—SHELLY WEISS STORBECK, Managing Director
and Founder, Storbeck/Pimentel and Associates

"Dr. Beardsley examines the factors that undergird the growth in the number of higher education leaders who come from nonacademic career paths. This is a timely book and should be read by search committees seeking academic leaders for their institution and those who aspire to such position, within and outside of the academic world."

—JOHN SIMON,
President, Lehigh University

"Scott Beardsley brings a refreshing approach to the conversation about traditional and nontraditional pathways to university presidential leadership. Not only is his personal experience of making a career transition from McKinsey to the University of Virginia relevant for any candidate considering leadership roles in higher education, but his insightful research also provides an excellent framework and playbook for a university board that is beginning to think about presidential succession. A must-read for any university presidential search committee."

—TODD STOTTLEMYER, Rector,
The College of William & Mary

"Scott Beardsley's book is that rare work in academia that strikes the perfect balance between personal, scholarly, and accessible. By the time one finishes the final chapter, one will understand both what inspires Scott and how this trend of nontraditional leadership in academe is more than a mere fad—it is here to stay. *Higher Calling* is an important and necessary contribution to the higher education landscape."

—MICHAEL SORRELL, President,
Paul Quinn College

"The promise and possibility of nontraditional academic leaders are at the forefront of Dean Beardsley's research. Stakeholders in the future of higher education, both nationally and internationally, should find this concept timely and exceedingly relevant."

—JOHN R. STRANGFELD, Chairman and CEO,
Prudential Financial, and Former Chair,
Board of Trustees, Susquehanna University

"Scott Beardsley has done all of us who work on presidential succession a great favor. Higher education has been tugged, by hard economics, and in its wake, by high-minded but intense constituents, each with different interests, and often different missions. Those tensions play out in searches, in disputes over the legitimacy of 'traditional' or 'nontraditional' candidates. The career paths of candidates become surrogates for a deeper struggle. Scott deftly explores the varied definitions in use and guides us all to understand that it is both the person and the experience, tailored to particular settings and particular challenges, that are critical, not the one path or the other."

—JOHN ISAACSON,
Chair, Isaacson, Miller

HIGHER CALLING

Higher Calling

THE RISE OF NONTRADITIONAL
LEADERS IN ACADEMIA

Scott C. Beardsley

University of Virginia Press | Charlottesville and London

University of Virginia Press

© 2017 by the Rector and Visitors of the University of
Virginia

All rights reserved

Printed in the United States of America on acid-free
paper

First published 2017

ISBN 978-0-8139-4053-3 (cloth)
ISBN 978-0-8139-4054-0 (e-book)

9 8 7 6 5 4 3 2 1

Library of Congress Cataloging-in-Publication Data
is available for this title.

To my grandmother "Nana,"
Margaret Harriet Whitcomb Beardsley,
an inspirational educator
and astrophysicist ahead of her time

.

All we have to decide is what to do with the time that is given us.

—Gandalf, in J. R. R. Tolkien's
The Fellowship of the Ring

CONTENTS

ONE OF THE more perplexing challenges facing college and university presidents today is the near unquenchable curiosity of all those worried about American higher education. There are worries about costs, graduation rates, and what some outside the academy perceive as student environments that are as toxic as they are dysfunctional. There are concerns about the men and women in charge of the institutions—worry that they are paid too much, that they spend too much of their time fund-raising, and, for some, that they are too beholden to big-time athletics. Then there are the scandals that have become the standard fare of both local newspapers and the news outlets that serve higher education more directly.

One of the ironies of the increased attention being visited on college and university presidents is that almost no attention is being paid to how these leaders are chosen—who gets to be a candidate, what voice either faculty or students have in the process, why the search committees charged with the selection process so often make safe rather than bold choices. Almost no one not directly involved in the selection of a new president has much appreciation of the complex and increasingly important king- and queen-making roles that a handful of national search consultants play in determining who gets considered for the job. The principal exception to this observation is a new awareness that an increasing number of institutions have chosen nontraditional presidents— men and women whose attractiveness to the appointing institution is that they are from outside the academy. They are not faculty—their successes and hence appeal do not derive from their standing as either scholars or teachers.

Scott Beardsley's *Higher Calling: The Rise of Nontraditional Leaders in Academia* helps fill that gap. And, of course, Scott is himself one of "them"— a twenty-six-year McKinsey veteran, a member of the firm's senior management, and eventually the senior partner responsible for educating new recruits in the McKinsey way. It is also worth noting that he is a competitive player on the senior men's tennis tour (he has played singles and doubles at the ITF World Senior Championships), testifying to his stamina and discipline, two traits characteristic of almost all McKinsey partners. *Higher Calling* first tracks Scott's rise in McKinsey, his interest in and commitment to training and education, and his introduction to the world of higher education recruiting as an unsuccessful applicant for the presidency of Dartmouth. It is a prologue that, in addition to serving as Beardsley's self-introduction, is an important contribution in itself, making the inner workings of McKinsey much less mysterious. En route to explaining his interest in the leadership of higher education, Beardsley pauses long enough to explain the process by which new McKinsey recruits are made—or are not made—partner. What the applicant endures is an up-or-out process managed by a host of interlocking committees that resembles nothing so much as the tenure processes at a major American college or university.

As Beardsley readily acknowledges, *Higher Calling* began life as his doctoral dissertation for the University of Pennsylvania's Executive Doctorate in Higher Education Management program. I chaired his dissertation committee. As he worked through the mound of data he had assembled on the careers of new and current presidents of American colleges and universities, I was reminded of the numeric skill and imagination an experienced McKinsey consultant brings to an intellectual engagement. Here he makes two scholarly contributions—he gets the numbers right, and that leads to a better understanding of just how varied the prior experience of institutional leaders has become. It also leads to an admission that the term "nontraditional" leader or president is not unambiguous, and, given the state of American higher education, that is probably not a bad thing.

The larger, more important lesson Beardsley teaches is the role search consultants have come to play. Beardsley was lucky to have become friends with a variety of top consultants, an experience most successful presidential candidates have had. In this realm, consultants become guides, interpreters of signals, and, when necessary, the deliverers of bad news. They are the screens on whom the institutional search committees come to depend, and, not unlike real estate agents, they must simultaneously serve both buyer and seller, search committee and candidate. It is, as Beardsley makes clear, important to understand the pool of nontraditional candidates from which they must recruit an active applicant, while at the same time damping the would-be-president's optimism that he or she will be the one chosen. Closely read, Beardsley's description of his participation in the Dartmouth presidential search gives a better understanding of what happens in a process that, for the most part, remains behind closed doors. In his hands the lives and interests of his king-makers come alive—they are real people who fervently believe what they do is essential. You also get the feeling that they are truly having a good time.

The ability to surround the reader with the people who have been important to him—family, McKinsey mentors and colleagues, fellow students (as for two years he traveled monthly from his home in Brussels to Philadelphia), search consultants, members of search committees, nontraditional presidents as well as traditional presidents and provosts—provides *Higher Calling* its most lasting contribution. Early on, Beardsley tells you the big lesson he learned at McKinsey: that people skills trump client skills almost every time. Take your time; don't accept his invitation to skip past the prologue to the meat of the book. Instead, get to know and appreciate everyone he introduces you to. It is, as Scott knows well, the people who make our enterprise important.

Robert Zemsky
Peach Bottom, Pennsylvania
January 2017

HIGHER CALLING

| Prologue

FROM MCKINSEY TO MONTICELLO

THIS BOOK MIGHT strike the reader as a curious amalgam. The core of it is the presentation of my research into an important and controversial trend: the rising number of higher education leaders who come from "nontraditional" backgrounds. But preceding those core chapters is a first-person account of how I found my own way to higher education leadership after a long career as a management consultant at McKinsey & Company, and I return to this mode of reflection at the end, in the epilogue. Don't these elements belong in two separate books—one to be stocked in a bookseller's education section and the other, perhaps, on the shelf in the self-help aisle that focuses on personal reinvention?

For me, of course, the topic of higher education leaders arriving in their offices via unaccustomed pathways *is* personal. But, more important, I have found that others are quick to erase the line between my statistical findings and my lived experience. Almost without exception, when I have talked with people about issues facing leaders in today's higher education context, the question has come up: "Why did *you* decide to make that career transition?" When I was actively interviewing for leadership positions, it was the most common question posed to me—edging out the second most common: "What is your vision for our institution?" And again, as work got under way on this book, conversations with editors invariably gravitated to my own journey. Perhaps it is no surprise that the human brain, having taken an interest in a topic, isn't content to stay at the level of abstract statistics. It wants to engage with stories. To honor that, I will devote most of this prologue to telling mine.

But first, I'll spend just a few introductory paragraphs conveying why it was important to pursue the line of research I did. To begin with, close your eyes for a moment and consider this question: When you hear the phrase "nontraditional leader," who comes to mind? As I embarked on my research, my use of that phrase sparked the other question people most commonly asked, and about which they often had their own strong, sometimes emotional, opinions: "How are you defining *nontraditional*?" Is it a category most defined by leadership style, background, values, or some other variable? Does being called nontraditional (or traditional) imply a potential strength or worrisome weakness? Is it a compliment or an insult? Think about who counts as nontraditional in other leadership contexts—for example, in the American presidency. If the emphasis is on career backgrounds, the "traditional" category would perhaps include Franklin Roosevelt, George H. W. Bush, and Thomas Jefferson, who largely spent their lives in politics before becoming presidents. By contrast, Ronald Reagan's long career as a movie actor, and Dwight Eisenhower's as a military general, would put them in the nontraditional set. In these terms, the U.S. public's recent choice between Hillary Clinton and Donald Trump was in part a referendum on traditional versus nontraditional leadership, with each voter personally defining just what that meant. But does the choice in higher education need to be so polarizing and black and white? I would like to think not.

In terms of how various presidents have actually governed and led, meanwhile, can it be said that a Reagan or Eisenhower did so in a less traditional way than, say, Roosevelt or Jefferson? If we're going to make a useful distinction with these labels, should the categories ignore background and instead refer to the way a leader goes about making decisions or chooses whether to adhere to traditions or certain cultural norms or values? The problem here is the introduction of more subjectivity. Some might describe someone they saw as old-fashioned or not technologically savvy as traditional, while others use the term to point to someone's deep well of relevant knowledge or strong moral fiber. In any case, the words are loaded.

Turning the focus to higher education, the term "traditional" has generally referred to a leader's career background—which, until around the 1970s, almost always (in the United States, at least) featured a rise through the tenured faculty ranks and then through the provost's office. For many institutions over the centuries, this also entailed promotion from within. These traditional leaders helped build a higher education system that has withstood the test of time and is the envy of most countries.

As this book explores, much has changed in higher education since the 1970s, and the number of nontraditional leaders—in whatever precise way that term is defined—has clearly risen. And, just as in U.S. presidential elections, debates over university president selections can elicit strong emotions. Traditional leaders have their ardent supporters and detractors. Proponents tend to see them as stalwart defenders of academic excellence and freedom who, as widely admired scholars themselves, will respect existing norms and culture, understand and protect tenure, and exercise shared governance judiciously. Detractors view traditional leaders as standing in the way of progressive change, reluctant to embrace new technologies, or unequal to the management challenges posed by higher education's increasingly complex economic realities. Conversely, nontraditional leaders have their own foes and fans. Their opponents stereotype them, especially if they come from business backgrounds, as top-down *dirigistes* who eschew consensus, are bottom-line driven, don't fully appreciate the value of the liberal arts or the core mission of higher education (or of a particular institution), and can't be trusted to pursue academic and research excellence. But supporters call them gifted in fund-raising, more able to embrace change and technology, and more capable of managing a changing economic model. As with all stereotypes, these assumptions might tend to be generally valid while being in specific cases very wrong.

Each leader is different and constitutes a segment of one. Thousands of higher education institutions in the United States present myriad challenges and cultures. I went into my research—and have come out of it—believing that branding someone as traditional or nontraditional is increasingly unhelpful. It also lacks nuance, since I have seen that it is entirely possible to have a traditional nontraditional leader, or a nontraditional traditional leader. For example, a university president who was formerly a CEO or lawyer might be a fervent defender of tenure, research, academic excellence, access and affordability, and the value of the liberal arts. He or she might successfully attract enormous amounts of philanthropy to support this mission while relying on a strong provost for the continuance of the traditional processes of shared governance. As this book explores, there are widely differing views on the definition of a nontraditional leader. Just as the terms "fit" and "diversity" mean very different things to different people, so do the terms "traditional" and "nontraditional." The use of the word "nontraditional" in a search to label a candidate or the style of candidate is not a neutral term and code word designed by the board or search committee to be a Trojan horse for a university agenda geared toward job-placement statistics, cost-cutting, reorganization, and state politics rather than academic excellence. Similarly, the choice of a traditional leader does not mean nothing will change.

When a higher education institution seeks a new leader, it typically appoints a search committee made up of representatives of important stakeholder groups—faculty, students, staff, and the board of trustees—and often facilitated by a consultant from a retained executive search firm. All these people—and I would expect all the readers of this book—bring their own cognitive biases to the deliberation. Dan Kahneman, whose behavioral economics research earned him the 2002 Nobel Memorial Prize in Economic Sciences, has probably done more than anyone to educate decision makers about the role of unconscious bias or System I bias, confirmation bias, and selection bias in influencing the "rational" choices they make, including in recruitment.[1]

My interactions with such committees made me highly aware that while at McKinsey I was considered to be a "nontraditional" leader by dint of my background in business. (However, given that I am a dean and professor, some might argue that now I am not clearly nontraditional.) Meanwhile, my awareness of the problem of cognitive biases makes me suspect that I might well bring my own "positionality bias" to my research, potentially encouraging me to be overly positive about or sympathetic to nontraditional leaders such as myself.[2] For that matter, some readers might be inclined to look for an agenda in any book published by a university press, written by a dean of its own institution, about higher education leadership. In the case of the University of Virginia Press, in particular, it does so in the aftermath of a very visible leadership crisis experienced by the University of Virginia (UVA) in 2012. I can quickly dismiss any hint that the latter affected my thinking in any way. The period in which the state-appointed University of Virginia's Board of Visitors pressured President Teresa Sullivan to resign over apparent disagreements on progress at the university, only to have the faculty and provost rise in protest to reinstate her, was well before my time at UVA or in higher education leadership; I was still employed at McKinsey & Company in Belgium in 2012. Learning about the incident subsequently only underscored for me the fact that leaders must operate and succeed in inherently and increasingly volatile and complex environments that include the various power brokers involved in shared governance.

As for any positionality bias I might suffer, to neutralize its effects, I focused on a subset of the higher education realm in which it would be possible to build a database of objective facts publicly reported across many years. Beyond doing the work to ensure that my findings, and ensuing discussions, were fundamentally fact-based, I also immersed myself in the extensive literature produced over the years by and about the many admirable traditional leaders who have built great institutions of higher education, and who continue to be prominent at their helms. Further, since the vast majority of higher education leadership searches today draw on the services of executive search firms, I interviewed highly experienced search firm consultants for their insights. Some might expect search executives to be inherently biased toward nontraditional candidates because the search executives themselves are for the most part not from the academy. My impression, based on many conversations and reviews of search outcomes, is that this is not generally so. As I will discuss, search firm executives have no professional incentive to favor nontraditional candidates; they are paid for completing successful searches and seek to create the happy clients that will mean repeat and referral engagements. From their perspective, the best candidate is often the one who presents the path of least resistance, who might well be a "traditional" one. Search firms, no less than the committees they serve, are having to come to terms with the fact that higher education and its associated leadership requirements are changing dramatically, as is the pipeline of interested and qualified candidates.

A distinguished scholar who has already been a provost and president elsewhere and demonstrated strong impact versus diverse challenges at a respected, comparable institution is always going to be an attractive candidate. But every search that attracts such a candidate creates a hole at the institution left behind. Traditional leaders in higher education will remain an essential source of leadership for decades to come. In many cases traditional leaders will be the best and right choices, but this is not simply because they were from the tenured faculty ranks. In many cases, nontraditional leaders may prove to be the right choices, but, as chapter 6 explains, they will have to overcome fears that they constitute threats, and part of this is demonstrating awareness of traditions and how to work with and learn from the faculty. Thus, having little business experience should neither be viewed as a strength nor a prerequisite to being selected as a traditional leader, and having little understanding of the faculty and higher education should neither be viewed as a strength nor a prerequisite for being selected as a nontraditional leader. This book is neither pronontraditional nor protraditional; it is proleadership. A university or college does not have a reproductive organ, and the development and sourcing of the next generation of leaders to take on the considerable challenges facing higher education enterprises is becoming difficult.

Now to my own story of transition—which I tell with the full realization that not everyone will consider the story of my past career, or the glimpse of the inner workings of McKinsey & Company it affords, to be such rich stuff. If it doesn't interest you, let me urge you to skip right to chapter 1. Throughout the central chapters, you will find plenty of other leaders' challenging experiences and distinctive voices adding insight to the analysis. But perhaps you are intrigued about how and why someone pursuing a career relentlessly in one sector makes a change to chase a dream—a calling—in another. Perhaps you yourself are contemplating such a career transformation. In that case, I invite you to consider my own multiyear, nonlinear, humbling, but absolutely fulfilling journey.

AUTUMN IS A generous season in Virginia, and even on a late afternoon in December 2014, it was a pure pleasure to be outdoors. As I stood on the steps of Monticello, the lovingly restored and preserved home of Thomas Jefferson, I watched the sun dip low on the horizon and felt the breeze from the mountain turn crisp. Somehow I was the only visitor on the grounds. But just as the 4:30 tour guide approached, a call I had been hoping to receive came through.

Hearing the voice of University of Virginia provost John Simon on the line, I shot an apologetic glance at the guide and turned my full attention to the phone. I learned I had made it to the last round of UVA's Darden School of Business's seven-month process to select its ninth dean. The next day, John said, we would travel together to Richmond for a series of one-on-ones with UVA's Board of Visitors. It would then be their job to decide between my competition, an accomplished scholar with previous dean experience at a top business school, and me—the "nontraditional" candidate.

In that moment, the leap I had been preparing so long to make suddenly took on the force of reality. The theory under which I had been operating—that my true calling was to work in higher education—might actually be put to the test. If I were invited to become the leader of the University of Virginia's Darden School of Business, it would mean a definitive break from my past twenty-six years at McKinsey & Company, and also from all the established habits of the life my family and I had built in Belgium.

The guide smiled as I concluded the call, and we began to walk. She might have picked up on the giddy agitation I was feeling, but she could not have known how my mind seized on details and stories she shared as it worked to find answers to newly pressing questions: Was I really the right fit for this place? And was it the best fit for me? I knew, of course, that Jefferson was the founder of the University of Virginia. There could hardly be a better place to contemplate what I might contribute to its stewardship.

Everything I saw and heard at Monticello resonated with me that day, from the careful cultivation of its gardens (which reminded me of my family's agricultural roots, and even my summer landscaping jobs as a college student in Anchorage, Alaska) to the various oenophilic and other mementos collected by an obvious Francophile (I am a French dual citizen), to the ingenious devices Jefferson used in his constant quest to be more productive. But it was the last thing I saw before leaving that offered the clearest message. Standing in front of Jefferson's gravestone, with the evening light fading fast, I made out what had, according to his wishes, been carved on it: "Here was buried Thomas Jefferson, author of the Declaration of American Independence, of the Statute of Virginia for Religious Freedom, and father of the University of Virginia." I had been told by my friend Tracy Wolstencroft, chief executive of the firm Heidrick & Struggles (and a former partner at Goldman Sachs who also transitioned to a second career chapter focused on leadership development), not to miss it. Now I saw why. Here lay a man who could not quite find room on his marker to mention that he had been president of the United States. As he looked back over his lifetime's achievements, his contribution to higher education had meant more.

The Job Everyone Wanted

Probably for most people, it is hard to read a carefully composed epitaph without thinking: How would I want my own to read? In my case, along with many colleagues at McKinsey, that question had been asked explicitly. It was a standard exercise in the firm's leadership development curriculum for senior leaders, part of a series of related questions: If you had one year to live, what would you do? If you had one day to live, what would you do? If you could be witness to your own funeral, what would be written on your tombstone? What would your colleagues say about you? What would your children say about you? Those might sound like risky questions for the firm to ask its partners to ponder. Would anyone's first thought in response be that they wanted to be remembered as a hard-charging management consultant? But McKinsey was confident that no tradeoff had to be made between what one would want to see on a gravestone and what one would have to be to ascend to its top ranks.

Certainly, the firm had and has no trouble attracting talent. In a recent year's recruiting season, more than two hundred thousand applicants vied for about two thousand positions. When I first sized up the consulting industry in the 1980s, I was in business school at MIT, and McKinsey's was the offer everyone wanted. About 200 of my 220 classmates applied there. Part of this was the era. We had all just arrived at the Sloan School when "Black Monday" hit, on October 19, 1987, and the stock market dropped by almost 23 percent. Some who had been thinking of financial services decided to change their plans. But strategic consulting was highly appealing in its own right—the work was intellectually stimulating, the lifestyle was heady (if often exhausting), and the pay was exceptional. My master's thesis advisor at MIT, Steven Starr (a great lawyer cum educator I was privileged to get to know before his life was suddenly cut short by a brain tumor, just weeks after grading my thesis), told me that I could not go wrong with McKinsey.

The fact that my first runs at the firm came up short only increased my resolve to join it. As a first-year MBA student, I applied for an internship and got a "see later" rejection. No matter—thanks to being selected for a scholarship, I was able to serve as editor of my school's *MIT Sloan Management Review,* which kept me busy that summer. The second year, I applied to McKinsey's office in Paris. But while my language skills were good enough for my wife, Claire—a French native whom I had met during an undergraduate summer abroad at the Tufts European Center at Talloires—they were not sufficient for my interviewers. Shifting my sights to McKinsey London, I made it through my seventeenth interview, only to be told (by my future colleague Nick Lovegrove) that there was "not a good fit between your profile and our needs." While he generously offered to forward my file to New York, I suspected I had struck out for good. It was only when my confidence was buoyed by some other offers—from McKinsey rival Bain & Company in Paris, from United Technologies' Leadership Development Program, and from Procter & Gamble to work as a financial analyst in Paris and Geneva—that I gave it one more try. Call it chutzpah, but I phoned McKinsey New York and indicated that, if my candidacy had a chance there, I would need to know very soon. As it turned out, the lead partner, Nancy Killefer, happened to be in Boston that very day and could see me. Within a matter of hours, I got the offer. I started as an associate of McKinsey & Company in New York City on August 19, 1989.

If career ambition and something of a competitive streak were responsible for my starting at McKinsey, there was something else responsible for my staying there. The way the firm talked about itself sounded like it was serving a higher purpose and making the world a better place. It was not about profit-maximizing. It was about mission. It was about values. Marvin Bower, the legendary builder of the firm, personified this. By the time

I joined, Bower was in his eighties but still keeping office hours. More evidence of my occasional audacity: I picked up the phone one day and dialed his number. I had heard his voice before; he narrated the short film that all new hires watched in orientation then about the firm's cultural values. To my great surprise, he answered the phone directly. Within minutes we were agreeing to have lunch. Knowing that everyone in the firm had an "obligation to dissent"—a dimension of the values that tried to save us from groupthink—I prepared for that lunch by thinking about how McKinsey could improve on a few (minor) people-related dimensions. Little did I know Marvin Bower would follow up by calling the New York office manager to discuss them.

One fact that everyone at McKinsey knows about Marvin Bower is that, at one point, he controlled the majority of McKinsey stock, yet he cashed out of it at essentially book value—a huge gift to the partnership—because his goal was for McKinsey to endure forever. With this transfer he created a structure whereby each senior partner had one vote, but he also put in place restrictions that make change of ownership excessively difficult. It became company lore especially because, several years later, Bill Bain, the founder of Bain & Company, went through a divorce that forced him to sell a large part of his founding stake back to the partnership at its market price. Soon after his colleagues took out debt to finance that stock purchase, a downturn hit, and, with no cushion, there were layoffs. Had I joined Bain—and I almost did—I would likely have been out of a job (although, to be fair, a few of my classmates went on to remarkably successful careers at Bain, and to this day it remains a great company).

Striving for Principal

Like the tenure track, McKinsey is an up-or-out organization, full of insecure overachievers. I am sure I was not alone in perpetually thinking I was one performance evaluation from being asked to leave, despite the seventy-hour weeks I was putting in. Only about half of consultants are promoted to engagement manager after two or three years; roughly one in seven makes it to partner; and one in fifteen or sixteen makes it to senior partner. Those not promoted at each stage are counseled out the door. Meanwhile, for those who make it to senior partner, the treadmill only runs faster. McKinsey is perhaps the world's best institution at providing quantitative, qualitative, and peer-reviewed feedback. Frequently and in detail, it points out any weaknesses that need to be addressed while also acknowledging strengths. For the academic thoroughbreds it hires, getting less than the equivalent of an A in any subject might be unthinkable, but when performance is broken down into dozens of separate categories, it is inevitable. Everyone discovers their relative weaknesses and eventually finds their limits.

Getting ahead in a firm like McKinsey is not only a function of billing hours and winning business. There is also an imperative to replenish the knowledge base that is the firm's whole value proposition. I could point to various similarities between McKinsey and a university (its distributed decision making, for example, makes governance as much of a cat-herding challenge as on any campus), but chief among these has to be its investment in research. Globally, McKinsey spends more than $300 million every year doing the research it needs to understand a huge range of economic sectors and management functions. It publishes the highly regarded *McKinsey Quarterly* as well as publishing through the McKinsey Global Institute, which rival top management and business publications in readership and top think tanks for economic perspective. If you think about it, a consultancy only earns its high fees if it delivers insights on which its clients can capitalize—ideally, before their competitors do. An important path to advancement at McKinsey, therefore, is to author research or develop an approach or framework or industry perspective that creates a platform for good advice and impact for many clients.

After I had been at McKinsey for two years and been promoted to engagement manager, I resolved anew to make my way to Europe. I floated the idea of a twelve- to eighteen-month posting there, emphasizing that I could leverage the experience in cellular telephony I had gained in New York to bring the first telephony and high-tech work to the Benelux practice. Peter Bisson was my "development group leader" (essentially an assigned mentor—something like an undergraduate faculty advisor), and he supported the request. He also predicted: "You will never come back." But even though the Brussels office manager, an American named Eric Friberg, gave me that chance and I joined his practice, it became clear over time that I would never gain the true insider status that is such an asset to any professional advisor in a local market. If I were going to continue to rise without coming back to the States, I would have to create a research-based platform that would support consulting assignments beyond Belgium.

Two analytical projects in those early years allowed me to do that. First was a study in 1993 called *The Future of Cable* (*Câbler l'avenir*), funded by a consortium of electricity providers that owned most of the cable television networks in Belgium. (Belgium also happens to have one of the highest cable television penetration rates in the world.) The study compared the forward-looking economics of competing broadband technologies such as ADSL, satellite television, cable, and microwave for applications such as voice over cable, high-speed Internet, and video on demand. It ventured to predict which would win out, where, and why. As further research yielded article after article, as well as internal research reports, I found myself well positioned in the midst of a global megatrend as one of McKinsey's global experts on the Internet and broadband.

Second was a failed proposal to the Belgian government, which had decided to privatize its phone company, Belgacom, and introduce competition to the mobile telephone market. I had worked on it for months, codifying lessons learned from similar moves all over the world. When McKinsey lost the work to Morgan Stanley and Arthur D. Little, I couldn't stand the thought that so much research might never see the light of day. So I flew to London and badgered the superstar partner who led both the telecoms and the privatization practices, Michael Patsalos-Fox, to help me turn it into a piece for the firm's *McKinsey Quarterly* publication. "Getting Telecoms Privatization Right" found its audience, and after completing some behind-the-scenes briefings for the CEO selected to lead Belgacom, John Goossens, I was on my way to creating a new platform for extensive client work.[3] As the era of mobile telephony dawned, McKinsey was the firm to talk to about the relevant regulations, market deregulations, and challenges for incumbent telephone companies.

Making partner in a professional services firm is a tremendous affirmation of one's contributions, and I was honored to become a McKinsey principal in January 1996, six years and five months after joining. By then, the opening of phone markets was sweeping the world, and far-flung opportunities presented themselves. My biggest client from 1997 to 1999 was a Venezuelan phone company. I flew across the Atlantic to and from Caracas close to a hundred times in those years. In 1999 I helped make the connection between Poland's phone company and McKinsey's new office in Warsaw. Before I knew it, another four years and six months had passed, and I was elected as a senior partner (director, in McKinsey's terms) in June 2000 — record time. For much of the next decade I helped to build McKinsey's emerging-markets telephone practice, introducing McKinsey's first telecom client service in fourteen countries. Much of this work was in the Middle East and Africa, but it took me to all the major continents, and to more than forty countries.[4]

My first foray into the Middle East was not long after September 11, when I flew into Dubai for an Organisation for Economic Co-operation and Development (OECD) conference on telecom deregulation.[5] Most of my colleagues, particularly the Americans, were surprised I would venture into the region. But I turned out to love it, and those early connections would go on to yield a decade of fulfilling work and deepening relationships with Emirati, Qatari, and Kuwaiti clients. Economic growth was happening in the Middle East and Africa (MEA) region at a blistering pace, supported by escalating oil and gas prices. In my decade working with clients there, I saw two of them grow from operating within one country and having market values of less than $2 billion into firms worth more than $20 billion and having footprints that spanned fifteen or twenty countries. The 1-billion-plus population of Africa needed to communicate, and expanding telephony boosted their productivity dramatically.

It was the kind of work that reinforced for me the messages I had heard since my first week at McKinsey: that the firm would rather point to having a meaningful impact on the world than to increasing its billings—but that there need be no tension between those. Reconciling social benefit with clients' success in competitive markets and with growing revenues for McKinsey was only a matter of the right mission and values.

A Business Entirely of People

People at McKinsey have all heard the firm's mission and most have memorized it: "Our mission is to help our clients make distinctive, lasting, and substantial improvements in their performance and to build a great firm that attracts, develops, excites, and retains exceptional people." That latter part of the mission became more central to my work as the years went by. Management consulting requires exceptional teamwork, and a senior partner can be only as successful as the teams he or she creates.

I saw that, for example, in my first team in Qatar. We kidded that we were less a band of brothers than a United Nations meeting. The newest consultant among us was Gassan Al-Kibsi, an MIT-educated Yemeni who taught me local customs and saved me when I tried to bring a bottle of red wine into the country. (He is now a senior partner and head of McKinsey Saudi Arabia.) Providing project leadership was John Tiefel, a former submarine officer from the Canadian navy with dual citizenship (also German), exceptional emotional intelligence, and a command of more than ten languages. (He went on to open McKinsey's Doha office and is now a senior partner in Zurich.) A second project leader was Luis Enriquez, a brilliant Chilean economist, regulatory strategist, and oenophile who had entered Harvard at age sixteen. (He became a senior partner in Belgium.) Kito De Boer, our senior partner, was an articulate and inspiring Dutchman raised in Venezuela who had risen to become the Middle East office manager yet didn't use a computer. (He has since worked with Tony Blair and John Kerry in their efforts to achieve peace in the Middle East.) Rounding out the team was another new consultant, Omar El-Hamamsy, an Egyptian-Canadian technologist fluent in French, English, and Arabic. (He is now a senior partner in the Middle East.)

Getting such diverse talent working together was exceptionally difficult, but when the team gelled, magic happened. And notice that all eventually made senior partner—a minor miracle. Watching that happen changed my source of motivation. My idea of pursuing success became to spell out all the people I wanted to help succeed, and to chart a plan with each of them to do it.

In 2000, then managing director Rajat Gupta called and asked if I would be interested in joining the Principal Candidate Election Committee (or PCEC), which recommends who should be elected to the McKinsey partnership. I enthusiastically accepted. Modeled after university faculty tenure committees, the global committee requires its evaluators to carve out six to eight weeks from their year to conduct intensive due diligence on nominated candidates from different offices, and to meet twice a year (in May and November) to make decisions. I joined an evaluation team led by Dominic Barton, who had just moved to Korea as a young senior partner (and is now McKinsey's managing director, equivalent to a CEO and chairman). A missionary's son and Rhodes Scholar who grew up in Uganda, in a household taken over by Idi Amin himself, Dominic is an avuncular, disarming, and gifted people leader with exceptional charisma and a prodigious work and travel ethic by any standard. He apprenticed me as an evaluator, and a long-term friendship was struck.

The peer-review process interviews all the existing partners who have had occasion to work with a partner nominee and creates a "support matrix" document capturing their assessments across multiple categories. The evaluator, who cannot have worked with the candidate or even be from the same

In front of my home, Pavilion I, in the Academical Village with my mentor Ron Daniel, former managing director (chief executive) and senior partner of McKinsey & Company. (Author's photo)

office or practice as the candidate, consults that and other quantitative and qualitative data, including "upward" feedback from lower-ranking staff and the nominee's self-authored "impact summary," to produce a summary of the case. Because various categories of election are possible, the evaluator's key responsibility is to form a recommendation of which, if any, is right for the nominee.

A minimum two-thirds vote in the committee meeting is needed for election—and if a candidate is not elected after two or three tries, he or she must leave the firm. As such, the process stirs up high emotions—certainly for the candidates but also for the people who know them. It has to be well managed for objectivity, and trusted as the best way to bind the McKinsey "one Firm" partnership to a global standard. In the review meeting, committee members read each case, and only the evaluator can respond to questions about it; others in the room cannot pipe up with personal opinions or stories. After discussion, the chair of the room appoints a third person to frame both the case for and the case against in terms of "what you need to believe" to vote in either direction.

In many ways, these committees brought out the best in McKinsey, testing tradeoffs in the values and showing the real character and personality of the evaluators themselves, who could not delegate any of the work. These were boardroom, not courtroom, deliberations. Sometimes there were moments of great levity. I remember a committee member asking about a candidate's executive presence: "But can he fill the room?" After a long pause and serious look of contemplation, the evaluator replied, "Yes. A very small room." In another case, a native German speaker told an evaluator in a strong accent, "If I listen to you, the candidate can walk on water. What I want to know is: Can she swim?" In both cases the room erupted with laughter.

I spent a dozen years serving on McKinsey's partner-review committees, also including the Principal Review Committee, or PRC, which evaluates younger partners, and then the Upper Tenure Principal Review Committee, which recommends who is elected senior partner and which operates in an analogous manner to the PCEC. I had the privilege of cochairing these various committees. The tradition when an evaluator leaves the committee is for him or her to be roasted by a colleague. When I finally did, I was given a set of bull horns as a symbol of my relentless quest to be "bullish" about candidates and to find the strengths and good in them, but to gore any candidates who had strong client records but fell short on the people side of the mission. Everyone knew my view: that a great client record can't overcome a lack of ability or interest in inspiring and developing colleagues. Any shortcomings in people management only get magnified in more senior positions and serve to drive real talent away from the firm. For me it was client *and* people, not *or*. Other senior leaders did not always agree with this viewpoint, and thus I had had plenty of opportunities to be vocal about it.

From Strategy to Leadership Development

Of course, I always had my own next step on the ladder to think about, as well. For a long time I set my sights on the leadership of McKinsey's Europe, Middle East, and Africa (EMEA) telecom practice, hoping to succeed Jurgen Schrader, a collaborative, values-driven client leader from Dusseldorf who had allowed me to lead the charge on emerging markets and on the knowledge agenda. When that job finally became available, however, I was passed over; it was given instead to Rolando Balsinde, an impressive and charismatic Cuban American senior partner from the Madrid office.

So it came as a big surprise when Ian Davis, the new McKinsey managing director who succeeded Rajat Gupta in 2003, called in 2004 and asked me to lead McKinsey's strategy practice. Ian, who is today the chairman of Rolls-Royce and a board member of storied institutions including Johnson & Johnson and British Petroleum, is a statesman and orator nonpareil; he is fashioned out of McKinsey-values cloth if ever a McKinsey leader was. After a nine-year Rajat Gupta reign characterized by global expansion, soaring revenues, and rising partner compensation, Ian Davis's leadership felt like a return of a strong, traditional hand on the tiller, steering us back toward a sense of noble purpose. Eschewing flashiness and trappings of success, Ian demonstrated humility and the importance of action, not boasting. He shared his philosophy with partners via maxims such as: "If you want someone to think you're funny, don't tell them you're funny. Tell them a joke."

In a management consulting firm, it is possible to organize people in any number of ways: into practices focused on industry sectors (such as the telecom sector I had specialized in, or consumer goods, or oil and gas); or focused on the various functions that all businesses share (such as marketing or finance); or focused on geographic regions (such as Europe or the Middle East and Africa). In a firm the size of McKinsey, all three kinds of organization coexist in a matrix structure. In the Gupta era, sector practices had taken strong precedence. When Ian Davis became managing director, one of his priorities was to rejuvenate the functional practices, including the strategy practice.

I could not have been more honored by his invitation. McKinsey has long been considered to be the preeminent strategy consulting firm in the world. But as someone who revered the strategic thinkers of McKinsey as legends and had never so much as attended a McKinsey strategy practice meeting, I was so stunned by his invitation that I asked: "Why do you think I would make a good leader of the strategy practice?" His answer made some sense. By doing strategic consulting within the telecom practice I had gained thorough knowledge of how the sector practices worked and could see how better to connect a functional practice to them. Still, I thought I was underqualified for what even Ian described as "one of the most difficult roles in the firm"—difficult because strategy is something about which almost all McKinsey partners are knowledgeable and have opinions. What sealed the deal was learning that I would be working again with my former partner mentor, Peter Bisson—the one who had supported Claire's and my move to Belgium. He had just been asked to lead the strategy practice in the Americas.

My fears of inadequacy were only intensified by the first interactions I had on my "listening tour," meeting with McKinsey's top strategists. Their most common question was: "What are the new and leading-edge ideas *you* have on strategy?" Who could blame them for asking? The strategy practice had always been led by great thinkers who had developed groundbreaking frameworks to help clients chart their futures. There was no question that I loved gaining knowledge, writing, and hatching new ideas, and was comfortable with devising strategy, particularly regulatory strategy, in the telecom world. But I was intimidated by any idea that I personally would dream up the next era-defining strategic concept.

The previous model of the strategy practice had been a bit like a brain trust, where the best brains carried out research, developed new frameworks, and shared them at sparsely attended internal strategy conferences after huge intellectual debate. However, the new-idea pipeline was starting to dry up. I soon came to the realization that not only was I not going to get the Nobel Prize for strategy, but that my colleagues also should probably be looking more to the huge amount of innovation in strategy taking place at the client face. Almost one-third of McKinsey's project work at the time was focused on helping enterprises chart future courses based on better knowledge of contexts and trends—yet few of the ideas developed in particular engagements were being circulated and considered for more general application. I viewed my role as not to be the smartest strategist but to enable the smartest ideas to come to the surface and be developed.

With a new leadership that trusted each other and banded together (both figuratively and literally: several of us were musicians and formed a strategy practice rock-and-roll group called McFloyd, ultimately performing in front of the full McKinsey senior partnership), the strategy practice was turned on its head in pursuit of important innovation. Strategy conferences that had been internal-only became conferences where perhaps a hundred clients, typically chief strategy officers and similarly forward-looking executives, also shared their ideas. Suddenly, partners who had been reluctant to attend saw a valuable opportunity to accompany their clients. Practice meetings also became knowledge-sharing events—and even competitions, as frameworks recently devised at the front line were presented by younger partners or consultants. Strategy roundtables focused on a hot topic for debate started being hosted in cities all over the world. We began partnering with clients and business schools in knowledge development, coproducing publications. A new generation of strategy leaders gained knowledge and networks, and client service soared.

For me, leading the strategy practice also offered the opportunity to return to the classroom. I was asked to lecture on regulatory strategy in Belgium by former MIT colleague Philippe Chevalier, who had become a professor at the Belgian business school IAG (Institut d'Administration et Gestion). Further, McKinsey started teaching internal courses every summer on the grounds of Cambridge University in the United Kingdom, having six-hundred-plus project managers from all over the globe descend upon that gorgeous campus to build core consulting skills and learn about current issues in various functional areas of business. I was on the strategy faculty and loved using the case method to teach my hundred or so project-leader students.

McKinsey undeniably "puts the client first" and has an almost cult-like admiration for CEOs—the most fashionable excuse for missing a commitment is "I was caught in a meeting with a CEO." Being so client-driven makes sense; after all, a consultant without a client is not a consultant. I saw plenty of evidence that my colleagues defined themselves by their client portfolios and thought the best answer to "How are you doing?" was to state how many studies they were doing. Yet, if you ask former McKinsey people what they value most about their time in the firm, they usually talk about how much they learned and were developed as leaders—through their work with amazing people, and through iconic programs such as the one in Cambridge; the introductory training programs now called EMBARK and LEAD; and, if they were among the many consultants who held advanced degrees other than MBAs, McKinsey's "mini-MBA" program. These were opportunities not only to gain valuable knowledge but to spend time with colleagues soaking up the firm's values and culture. Several partners have met their spouses at the mini-MBA program.

I remember my own first McKinsey program, the Introductory Training Program (ITP) at Lane End, England. It was led by Henry Langstaff, a retired brigadier general in the British army. Langstaff trained generations of consultants at McKinsey, inculcating its culture and values with case studies, long conversations, and debates—and, not least, the sheer force of his own integrity. Marvin Bower often came to the same programs, and the senior leaders of McKinsey participated as faculty, in the tradition of the parent-to-child or craftsman-to-apprentice model.

Cambridge University is not only one of the greatest hotbeds of intellectual activity in the world, home to countless scholars from Sir Isaac Newton to Stephen Hawking; it is also a place of great beauty, grandeur, and tradition. Most Americans will never see a dining hall as splendid as King's College's outside a Harry Potter film. Because, in the classic tradition, the university is a grouping of separate colleges, each McKinsey practice area holds its classes on a different campus. For inspiration, the strategy practice used Caius College, which since its founding in 1348 has seen twelve Nobel Prize winners emerge from its halls. Living in its dormitories and teaching on its hallowed ground, I was filled with a sense of honor and also a sense that time was warping. With every senior partner on the clock, and normally billed out at a rate of at least four figures per hour in any currency, it was a luxury to freeze time and spend even a couple of days focused on apprenticing the next generation.

King's College is one of the most elite and photographed colleges at Cambridge. Founded by King Henry VI, it has housed such brilliant minds as John Maynard Keynes and Alan Turing. Any visitor gazing over its manicured gardens and beautiful lawn encounters a prominent sign: "Please stay off the grass unless accompanied by a senior member of the college." McKinsey somehow obtains permission every year for that privilege: in a grand reception on the back lawn, senior partners serve the six-hundred-plus project leaders their champagne, personifying the concept of servant leadership. It was there on a glorious July evening in 2010 that I was approached by my friend and newly elected managing director Dominic Barton and Norwegian colleague Paal Weberg (with whom I had been an evaluator on many committees). Would I like to step away from the strategy practice, they asked, and become the leader of all McKinsey consultant learning programs worldwide, including Cambridge?

The truth is, on that summer night in 2010, I was torn. I had aspirations at McKinsey, and I had momentum. The strategy practice was very much on the right track, and while the 2008–10 financial crisis had hammered most companies and strained McKinsey's profitability in the process, my client platform in emerging markets telecom and broadband technology was booming. I yearned to be elected by my peers to McKinsey's equivalent of a board of directors, called the Sharcholders Council. I asked a few colleagues for their thoughts. Most warned that while Dominic and Paal were offering a prestigious role, it wasn't one that would position me to move higher in McKinsey. I asked for a few weeks to consider the decision.

To understand the importance I placed on the board of directors election, it helps to have an understanding of McKinsey's governance. The firm is the largest privately owned single partnership in the world; there is one global annual profit pool. Exact financial information is confidential, but public information estimates McKinsey to have north of $7 billion in revenue, about 1,500 partners, and more than 12,000 professionals spread over 110 offices in more than sixty countries. It is governed by a *primus inter pares* managing director, elected by the senior partners every three years, and the aforementioned Shareholders Council, also drawn from the partnership. (There are no outside board members.) I've noted that roughly one in fifteen or sixteen consultants makes it to senior partner. The odds are similarly low for any of the roughly five hundred senior partners to become one of the thirty selected to reach this board level; so roughly one in 225 who begin as a consultant at McKinsey make it to the board. This happens through a peer ballot where all senior partners are automatic candidates unless they withdraw their names, and each has one vote, regardless of the amount of equity each holds. Given a term length of three years, roughly a third, or ten, board slots are up for a vote each year. From the full set of senior partners, a first ballot reduces the candidates to perhaps fifteen to twenty finalists, and a final ballot selects the ten. Campaigning is not allowed, meaning that voting is fragmented and a global profile is needed to be elected.

Short of being elected managing director, election to the Shareholders Council is the greatest form of peer recognition and honor at McKinsey. I always admired those board members I knew, and aspired to be one of them. Under Ian Davis, I made the final slate four times—an honor unto itself—but went home a bridesmaid each time. When he called me each time to share the disappointing news, he encouraged me to keep being myself and to take solace in the many votes that had made me a finalist.

As I spent my two weeks considering what Dominic and Paal had offered, I kept hearing from the colleagues whose counsel I sought that a more client-centric role, such as leading an office or a sector, would be a much surer pathway to the board. In the previous few years I had been approached with and turned down a number of opportunities to lead offices in Asia and the Middle East. With three boys in high school in Brussels, I was not willing to turn their lives upside down. One day I happened to be in Silicon Valley working with a top client of the firm (a global Internet equipment provider) when I got a phone call from Rolando Balsinde—the partner who had beaten me out to become leader of the EMEA telecom practice—exhorting me to take the role of leading that practice in the Americas. He knew exactly what button to push: he said he knew how important it was for me to make the Shareholders Council, and assured me this was the golden ticket.

I had always wanted to be a telecom practice leader. Yet I declined. With my head saying yes, but my heart saying no, the heart won. Inspired for so long by people like Harry Langstaff and Marvin Bower, I found the allure of developing McKinsey's people too strong to resist. I accepted the role of leading all nonpartner leadership development programs, the huge university-like engine for building the capabilities of all future McKinsey partners.

Crisis Strikes

I might be creating the impression that life at McKinsey is a heady existence, and in many ways it is. But it does have its downsides. Most obvious of these are long hours and hard travel. I remember one particularly insane week during the time I was serving on partnership evaluation committees. In one evaluation cycle I was asked by Dominic Barton, by then chairman of McKinsey Asia, to be familiar with all the cases in Asia. In a matter of two weeks, I flew from Brussels to Tokyo, Hong Kong, Beijing, Shanghai, Singapore, Kuala Lumpur, Melbourne, Sydney, and back to Brussels via London. In this same time frame, another evaluator had a child diagnosed with a rare liver disease, so he stepped out. I provided the cover, writing up his Japanese cases at the last minute before flying to Washington, D.C., for the committee meeting.

Punishing schedules ultimately take a toll on health. Perhaps unsurprisingly, for the first time in my life, my body gave out in D.C., when a herniated cervical disk paralyzed my left arm. I presented my cases in extreme pain. Later, when a neurosurgeon told me I might never play tennis again if I didn't change my habits (including misusing my laptop computer by hunching over, sleeping upright in planes, and carrying heavy carry-on luggage), it was the beginning of an awakening inside me.

None of this was "family friendly." In October 1991, Claire and I had flown across the pond with nothing but our suitcases and student loans. As Brussels became home, we had the great fortune to have three healthy sons, Edouard, Philip, and Benjamin (born in 1992, 1994, and 1996). But because the committees always met over the same weekend in May, I had missed my youngest son Benjamin's birthday twelve years in a row. It was only when I realized he would soon be leaving home that I declined an invitation to continue my committee service. Still, for the most part, the demands of the job were manageable because the mission was uplifting. The work felt important.

Teaching at the global new partners orientation program at the Taj Mahal in 2014. McKinsey India colleagues convinced me to join them in sporting traditional regalia at the welcome ceremony. (Author's photo)

It was a terrible shock for me when scandalous news broke about our former managing director. In March 2011, McKinsey senior partners gathered for an annual conference in Washington, D.C. On the second day, we were stunned to learn that Rajat Gupta had been indicted for insider trading. It was bad enough that former McKinsey director Anil Kumar had channeled confidential information to billionaire Raj Rajaratnam to inform trades by the latter's Galleon hedge fund. (Kumar had pled guilty in 2009 to taking bribes for information about McKinsey clients' plans.) Now a wiretapped conversation between Rajaratnam and Rajat Gupta showed that Gupta, as managing director, had done the same. For any McKinsey person, it was painful to listen to Rajaratnam griping that Kumar wasn't appreciative enough of the millions he had been paid in "after taxes, offshore cash" for information—and excruciating to hear Rajat replying, "you're being very generous," and Anil "should sometimes say thank you."[6] Many, including me, had explained away the first crime as a one-off, chalking it up to Kumar's exceptional arrogance. But the former leader of the firm?

I personally couldn't believe what was happening. I had had immense regard for Rajat. I had first come to know him as a young principal around 1998, when the company Belgacom invited me to be its head of strategy and I was considering leaving McKinsey. I called Rajat to sound him out and found him to be very balanced and thoughtful; he exuded confidence and made me think that I had more to gain by staying. In 2000, when I participated in New Director's Orientation—a wonderful safari getaway to the South African game reserve Singita to reward consultants (and their spouses) for making senior partner—I found him as accessible as he was impressive. At partner conferences he read poetry. At the World Economic Forum at Davos, he seemed to know everyone. He gave me my first real role in shaping the future of the firm, appointing me to the personnel committee that elected partners. It had only been due to term limits that he was no longer managing director; as of 2003 he became director emeritus and moved into an active consulting role to the firm.

Now, however, as I searched my memory for explanation, I could recall moments when perhaps the signs were there that Rajat was blurring boundaries, and hubris was inching its way into his persona. Once I invited him to visit a telecom client in the Middle East, and later over an intimate three-person dinner at another senior partner's home, conversation turned to the external boards on which Rajat served. This was prior to the 2008–10 financial crisis, and he was on Goldman Sachs's compensation committee—a committee that would later come under public scrutiny when the pay package for Goldman's CEO, at $50 million-plus annually, caused real outrage in the world. In Rajat's opinion, as he blithely shared it with us, the CEO was, if anything, underpaid. The payout ratios to management versus shareholders could be higher. To me, the logic was absurd and the numbers worryingly high. I was also discomfited to learn from Rajat that he was approaching people he had met through me to invest in his private equity fund. He was retired by then and technically entitled to do so—but it was something an active partner couldn't and wouldn't do.

Back then, I had withheld judgment. Now, in Washington, D.C., I felt as if my own moral fiber and personal values had been compromised by the association. Like many McKinsey partners, I lived and breathed McKinsey values and felt that they somehow made me better. Different. But the currency by which I allowed myself to be somewhat defined had just been debased.

I did what I think always makes sense in a time of crisis: I focused on what I could control in the situation to help. On the spot, I went to Managing Director Dominic Barton and told him that I would do my part by doing a complete diagnostic on how McKinsey values were being taught in all of the learning programs, and finding ways to make them take hold more powerfully. Dominic was very supportive of the idea.

Not long thereafter, I was in Abu Dhabi for client work. After a long day of meetings, I was sitting by a hotel pool with my longtime friend and colleague John Tiefel when my telephone rang. Dominic was calling with the incredible news that I had been elected to the Shareholders Council. John and I toasted the occasion: I had finally achieved my aspiration and made it to the summit of McKinsey's Mount Olympus. At the same time, my feeling was not what I had long imagined it would be; in fact, John seemed to be happier for me than I was for myself. I don't know if it was because we had just been discussing Rajat, and some less-than-ideal dynamics between partners on our teams, but in that moment I felt more reflective than joyful. Would this stand as my life achievement, after which a denouement? Was it worth the price of more than a thousand nights on airplanes, away from my wife and three boys? What was next?

Fighting for Values

I genuinely feel that all of my senior colleagues on McKinsey's Shareholders Council had nothing but the best of intentions. I am very proud to know that I have been a peer to this amazingly talented group. They too were rocked by the Anil and Rajat incidents, and a lot of attention went to strengthening processes to ensure it could never happen again. Rules against insider trading were strengthened to become perhaps the most stringent in corporate America, effectively forbidding any member of a McKinsey employee's household to buy or sell stock in any McKinsey client of the previous five years. New efforts were made to communicate and ensure that whistleblowers would not suffer reprisals, and these led to real changes in concerns being communicated—and to real consequences.

For my part, I shared the result of my diagnostic study on the firm's values. The news I delivered was sobering. Consultants surveyed while participating in our learning and leadership development programs had witnessed many behaviors inconsistent with the firm's espoused values. My audit of the leadership development curriculum showed that the focus had gradually shifted to hard skills such as the use of valuable tools for problem solving; meanwhile, various modules traditionally used to impart "softer" strengths like values had quietly been dropped. I also discovered that many younger consultants had come through programs that featured no faculty contributions by active senior leaders. In a firm where each year's new hires constitute more than 20 percent of total professionals on staff, it only takes a few years for the transmission of values to fray.

I had always been viewed and valued as a "client animal" who was willing to fly to any corner of the globe to meet my clients' needs, but I felt strongly called to address these values issues and to fully deliver on the leadership development platform for McKinsey. In my view, even today, the only thing that could mortally wound McKinsey would be a perception by clients that it had succumbed to greed and its values and professional standards could no longer be trusted. Answering the Rajat/Anil crisis by developing a new generation of high-integrity, values-based McKinsey leaders was a purpose that drew me like magnetic north. Combined with an increased responsibility for all of leadership development at McKinsey, running programs for all partners and increasingly for clients, too (as what I liked to envision as "McKinsey University"), I felt it demanded at least half of my time. The only problem was that, as a senior leader on the board of directors, I was expected to spend 80 to 90 percent of my time rainmaking and otherwise making economic contributions at the client interface.

While my feeling was that values and people development were what the firm needed, many other senior leaders put less stock in soft stuff—particularly those in position to evaluate senior partners' accomplishments and determine compensation. In their own version of the old real-estate saw, there were three things that mattered to our restored growth: "client, client, and client." McKinsey was now a $7 billion enterprise, and many felt that harder commercial metrics were needed to measure partner productivity and billings and to increase the annual partner profit bonus pool known as "additional award" to ever-higher levels. The debate on moving McKinsey from a traditional mission-driven partnership to a more "corporate" culture was characterized by much the same hue and cry we see over the "corporatization" of public and higher education in America.

I was from the traditional school that resisted corporate-like short-term billings targets and felt that robust profits were a reliable outcome of pursuing our mission and living by our values fully. I had always been proud to be able to look a client in the eye and authentically say I had no billings target and was impact-driven; it was increasingly difficult to do that, and the increasing separation between the rhetoric and the reality of the firm profoundly bothered me. I believed that billings targets and metrics ran the risk of making a senior partner feel like just another high-paid salesperson. I wanted us to do more to build intrinsic motivation by inspiring people with a raison d'être of the sort Daniel Pink writes about in his book *Drive*. That, I thought, was the real key to unlocking more productivity in the partnership. And again, I felt the greatest risk to McKinsey's economic model and the partners' shares was a values breach; after all, it was exactly a values breach by a partner that had destroyed the venerable accounting firm Arthur Andersen.

From a time and energy standpoint, I felt I was being drawn and quartered. What was really happening was the classic (and still very present) tension in the McKinsey mission. It can never be just client, and it can never be just people (in many ways similar to the debate of being a great researcher or teacher in higher education—both matter). You do all you can to avoid compromising either, but giving your all in two directions can't be sustained over several years. For me, I realized, a moment of truth was at hand.

I vowed to reinstitute values from top to bottom in all McKinsey curriculum and to treat each value as a skill that needed to be learned and taught. I knew that McKinsey had a wonderful ability to be self-critical and to adapt. I also knew it was an institution where there is incredible latitude for senior partners to act independently according to what they think is right. At the end, the evaluation process renders a judgment as to whether those contributions had merit and how they should be valued monetarily. Just as partners are expected to make decisions for themselves, they are obliged to accept the judgment of their peers who ponder such questions as: "How do we value contributions to our values or people mission, versus client billings?"

I started a very time-consuming, largely under-the-radar process to revitalize McKinsey's approach to teaching its fifteen core values, while simultaneously overhauling the curriculum and increasing learning productivity with technology. Over the course of three years, my small team worked with

In front of the Rotunda at the University of Virginia with Dominic Barton, global managing partner at McKinsey & Company. (Photo by Andrew Shurtloff)

such experts as Dan Ariely (*The Honest Truth about Dishonesty*), a world authority on why otherwise good people cheat; Tal Ben-Shahar (*Being Happy: You Don't Need to Be Perfect to Lead a Richer, Happier Life*), a leading thinker on strengths-based leadership; and Mary Gentile (*Giving Voice to Values*), a Darden professor who teaches people how to speak up for what they know is right. We examined every program in light of which (if any) values it reinforced. We had teaching cases rewritten so that, even as they challenged students to apply their growing knowledge of management theory and tools, they would also raise issues of values—rather than leave those issues to be explored in other, stand-alone courses. The basic truth we wanted to honor is that values are tested and taught constantly in the course of everyday work and pervade everything that we are called upon to advise or decide about. When I was asked to note in my farewell memo what I was most proud of in my career, it was this values-oriented work.

Seeing beyond the Rabbit

Bob Buford, in his book *Finishing Well*, recounts the stories of many executives who chose to reshape their lives from success to significance by seeking some underlying noble purpose. In chapter 2, he draws an analogy between getting ahead in a corporate setting and being a greyhound in a race. The dogs chase mechanical "rabbits" around the track, which they never catch but which they also never doubt they should pursue with everything they have. One day at a real race, Buford reports, there was a malfunction and the machinery stopped. The greyhounds finally got a good look at and sniff of the prize they had been chasing, and the race ended with their utter bewilderment.[7]

When I accepted the responsibility for leadership development, my need to bring in more savvy instructors caused me to reconnect with some very smart folks who had retired from McKinsey. It was typical to find a former senior partner dabbling in a few boards or startups, but many seemed worried about becoming irrelevant and were happy to be asked back to teach. Yet most of these people were not what I would call old. At McKinsey, the mandatory retirement age is sixty, and many "retire" in their fifties; they still have plenty of energy to apply their enormous experience. I was getting my first real glimpse of life after McKinsey and perceiving that many had worked so hard while at the firm that they had spent little time considering what their post-McKinsey chapter would look like. It made me think. I had been on the McKinsey treadmill for almost twenty-five years, and, with my election to the Shareholders Council, I had accomplished the goal to which I had aspired. Had I, like them, finally caught the rabbit?

At this same time, Claire and I were getting close to our empty-nest phase. Our son Edouard had gone off to Beloit College, and in the fall of 2011 it was Philip's turn to visit campuses. Having spent their entire lives in Belgium, each of our sons had decided that by attending a liberal arts college in the United States, he could get a great education along with an immersion in his father's culture. As I did the obligatory tours, I plunged into research mode, parsing the rankings by *Fiske, Princeton, U.S. News & World Report,* the *Yale Guide,* and *Forbes,* and generally becoming a walking encyclopedia on the topic of American college and university admissions.

I'm sure I relished the tours more than my boys did. So many of my Beardsley relatives had studied liberal arts on campuses like these, with their lush landscaping and majestic trees. I loved the cultures of the schools—not only their traditions, teams, and histories but their missions based on the idea that education was central to the good life. I read and reread books such as Loren Pope's *Colleges That Change Lives,* a paean to liberal arts colleges. I had worked on strategy with the board of Husson University, in Bangor,

Maine, over several years. The insistence by these schools that a curious mind from any background could be filled with knowledge and equipped with the critical thinking skills to rise in any field, resonated deeply with me. My grandmother was an astrophysicist from Mount Holyoke and Smith College who worked for years using a Hartness equatorial mount telescope in Springfield, Vermont, invented by her husband's grandfather James Hartness (my great-great-grandfather); she was also a teacher. Inspired by her, growing up, I wanted to be an astrophysicist.

My own mother, Carol, was the first person in her hardworking dairy-farming family ever to go to college, the New England Baptist School of Nursing (part of the Lahey Clinic), and I knew firsthand the power of education to change lives. Both of my parents had worked at colleges when I was a child in Vermont and Maine—my mother as a teaching nurse at Champlain College in Burlington, Vermont, my father as a college basketball coach and public relations director at Champlain College and Maine Maritime Academy—before subsequently moving to Anchorage, Alaska, when I was eleven to both work in another university-related activity, a large hospital and health-care system. My brother, Andy, and sister, Katie, are educators, teaching English and French. My uncle Anthony W. Beardsley had taught in the Judge Advocate General (JAG) School at the University of Virginia Law School, uncle Benjamin Whitcomb had been on the faculty at the Yale School of Medicine, aunt Betsy Beardsley was a principal and gifted teacher for students with reading difficulties, uncle William H. Beardsley was president at Husson University, and another relative, John Perry, had served in the role of provost at Virginia Tech; I admired them, and all had their doctorates. My favorite undergraduate classes at Tufts University were liberal arts courses such as Yiddish literature, German expressionism, astrophysics, and alpine geology. I enrolled at Tufts in the College of Arts and Sciences, yet I became an electrical engineer in my second semester after winning a near-full scholarship from Eastman Kodak that required me to pursue engineering. I loved playing on the varsity tennis team, singing Bach's Magnificat in the choir, tutoring physics, speaking French, and being part of a fraternity. I was proud but also jealous of my own children who would get to enjoy all this.

Somehow my interest in colleges' workings persisted even after Philip made his choice of Emory. It was during an Internet search trying to learn more for some friends' children that in 2012 I stumbled over the news that Dartmouth College was looking for a new president. Ignore for a moment

My grandmother Margaret Whitcomb Beardsley carrying out her astrophysics research on the Hartness equatorial mount telescope in Springfield, Vermont. Growing up I wanted to be an astrophysicist. (Author's photo)

the obvious fact that Dartmouth would never have considered someone with my lack of credentials for that role—even so, my excitement in reading through that presidential search announcement revealed something I hadn't recognized about myself. I had been getting progressively more restless for change and was undeniably captivated by the world of higher education. Even in my current career, I had felt a calling to help outstanding people achieve their full potential. Now, finally, I saw clearly what I had to do next.

It is probably best that I did not suspect how difficult and time-consuming the transition would be. That very week, full knowing it was a long shot, I pulled together a CV and a cover letter for the Dartmouth job and got my first inkling of why nontraditional candidates struggle in academic leadership searches: confident as I was in my capability, I found it very hard to make a succinct and compelling case that my past career made me a good fit for the position, despite the fact that there was a relevant personal narrative: my grandfather had attended Dartmouth, and all of his children, including my father, were born on the Dartmouth campus.

I was delighted when I was asked to Boston for a first-round interview with the search consultant, Isaacson, Miller. John Muckle of that firm made no secret that he was fascinated to hear why a board member of McKinsey would be applying for the Dartmouth presidency. He personally could see what I might bring to the table—being himself a professional-services firm executive and also an MBA from the Sloan School—and in an extraordinarily useful meeting he helped me understand many things about the college president–recruiting process. But he flatly named two major liabilities. One was big—"you don't have a doctorate"—but at least it was obvious how to overcome it. The other—"you are a nontraditional"—was a lot more ambiguous. It was the first I had heard the term, much less had myself summed up by it, and I was intrigued. Muckle suggested I meet the founder of his firm, John Isaacson, at some point. A few weeks later it was reinforced for me that the vague label I had jotted in my notes really mattered. The polite turndown letter I received noted that Dartmouth was focusing on more traditional candidates. What exactly was the distinction?

This time, when my old streak of perseverance kicked in, I had my McKinsey-honed skills to help me. I started gathering facts and analyzing the problem. As I began consulting my network, it wasn't long until the term was applied to me again. McKinsey was a good client of the executive search firm Spencer Stuart, and I sought the advice of Jennifer Bol there, who is well connected in the world of higher education. She generously gave me an hour of her time and reviewed my CV, but she warned me that, as a "nontraditional candidate," I had little chance for a good presidency. She advised me, too, not to waste my time working to earn an advanced degree that ultimately wouldn't make enough difference. I appreciated her brutal honesty—which was underscored later when Spencer Stuart conducted a search (for the Yale presidency) and my application didn't even get a reply— but my pursuit of what I now recognized as a calling went on.

I then met with John Isaacson, who spent almost two hours with me. John is known as the kingmaker of higher education, having placed more college presidents than probably anyone else. He focused on questions about character and who had shaped my life, tapping out notes on his laptop as I spoke. I remember he counseled me that my initial foothold in higher education would most likely take one of three forms: (1) as a dean of a strong business school; (2) as a chief operating officer or executive vice president of administration in a top school; or (3) as a president of either a less famous liberal arts college or a larger complex institution with an average ranking or in need of change or a turnaround. Regarding the pursuit of a doctorate, he was very encouraging.

By then I knew that, whether or not a doctorate would open doors, I was aching to learn. I am a voracious learner with insatiable curiosity and always wanted a doctorate. At work, it had been a decade since I had been part of a formal learning program; I was faculty. After some weeks of unproductive browsing on the Internet, looking for part-time options in Europe to fit my crazy McKinsey life, one day I clicked on the University of Pennsylvania's Executive Doctorate for Higher Education Management program. This unique two-year doctoral program had a cohort of twenty-four students and insisted on a master's degree as a prerequisite; it could also boast dozens of nontraditional college and university presidents as alumni. It required just two days away from work per month in the first year, and one day a month in the second. It might seem absurd that the most practical option for a part-time student was to commute to school on another continent, but I had constant needs to travel to the United States, anyway. It would be tough, but surely no program could make it more possible for me.

The Curtain Rises on a Second Act

In February 2013, I crossed a personal Rubicon and applied. Rationally, I knew that completing a doctorate while maintaining a very high level of performance on the McKinsey board of directors was almost "mission impossible" when viewed throught the lens of pure client billings, but I was rated highly enough that I felt I could afford the hit to my productivity while I invested in the pursuit of my calling. (McKinsey has many performance categories that allow for differentiated compensation among senior partners.) Perhaps most importantly as a professional, I knew I would learn things that I could apply immediately in my role leading "McKinsey University" to help advance the firm's people mission and address what I believed to be McKinsey's greatest vulnerability. Nevertheless, in no way was this billable, short-term client service. I put my friend Dominic Barton (still McKinsey managing director) in a bit of a tough spot by asking him to write my recommendation to U Penn. He graciously did, telling me he admired my choice but to keep it to myself—which I did. In April 2013, while I was in Tokyo for a senior partners' conference, my cell phone rang one night at 3:00 a.m. It was U Penn calling. I was in.

In the meantime, I started to be contacted by various search firms as my name got out there. I got to know a few executives, and they gave me advice on my CV. Many told me that getting a doctorate was a great idea and were highly complimentary of the Penn program. I got involved in one presidency search for a prestigious east coast liberal arts college where Storbeck/Pimentel was the lead search firm. I made it to the "airport interview," by which point a hundred-plus applicants had been narrowed down to ten or so. I was told I was the token "nontraditional" candidate. That term again. Of course, in a broad sense I knew what they meant, but at an analytical level it was frustrating. Without a more precise understanding of the category I was being placed in, it was hard to know how to tell my story or improve my prospects.

At that airport interview, I was fascinated by the questions I received. One board member asked, "Do you know that this role pays much less than your current role?," to which I replied, "Yes. My motivation is not monetary." In another setting, I was asked, "Do you think our institution is prestigious and big enough for you after an international career like you've had?" For the first time, I became very aware that, even given the purest intentions, a businessperson like me would be treated with great suspicion. My sense of calling, so clear to me, was not obvious or necessarily believable to others.

In the summer of 2013, our son Philip was diagnosed with a dangerous tumor in his abdomen. On his gap year in Bolivia he had taken ill, and doctors recommended he have it removed in a delicate surgery. A fellow McKinsey board member, Bill Huyett, was extraordinarily helpful and made arrangements for him to be admitted to the Columbia Cancer Center in New York, just two days before my first class was to begin. Arriving in Philadelphia just after that anxiety-filled time, I met my twenty-three cohort mates. All lived in the United States and had high-level positions in higher education. Two were already college presidents of liberal arts colleges: Michael Sorrell, a Duke lawyer who led HBCU Paul Quinn College in Dallas, Texas, and Michael Schneider, of McPherson College in Kansas, and incidentally the youngest college president in the United States at the time. Others had various associate or assistant dean roles at places such as Dickinson, Princeton, University of Chicago, Southern New Hampshire University, Colby College, and Fordham, and ranged in age from thirty-five to sixty-five. I was the only student from industry. However, none of us had our doctorate, and by most definitions we had something else in common: we were all nontraditional.

In the first class on the first day, we settled in to a lecture by one of higher education's thought leaders and the founder of the Penn program, Robert Zemsky. Not one to suffer fools, he immediately put us in our places and showed us that we had a lot to learn. Partway through that first class, I received a text message from Philip, who had just been released from the hospital. My wife, Claire, and the three boys were on their way from the Columbia Cancer Center to visit Franklin & Marshall, of interest to our third son, Benji, who was a rising senior in high school (and is now at the University of Virginia). The message said: "We have been hit by a semi." My heart dropped. It turned out that no one was badly hurt, but it was an inauspicious start. My classmates rallied to support me, and very quickly I made a new group of friends.

In the meantime, at McKinsey, I went into overdrive innovating in the leadership development space. In some part of my mind I still believed I could pursue my calling inside the firm. I helped to launch McKinsey Academy, an online executive education offering, and also helped drive a new client offering called McKinsey Leadership Development, providing offsite programs for C-suite-level managers. If McKinsey could become preeminent in the space of executive education, I might become a higher education leader without going anywhere.

I came to Penn with a few things resolved. First, I was determined to enjoy the opportunity to spend time just learning. In my earlier pursuits of academic degrees I had been exceedingly focused on GPA; now my only goal was to soak up knowledge, and I vowed not even to look at my grades until after graduation (a vow I kept). I committed to participating fully in the experience, investing the time to get to know my classmates and participate in the life of the program. Second, I resolved to learn the language of higher education. Third, I decided that my dissertation research should produce new knowledge about the incidence of nontraditional leaders in American higher education (using a data set focused on liberal arts college presidents)—and draw on a previously untapped source of knowledge in the executive search firms so embroiled in presidential selections. By then I had spent two years exploring opportunities but feeling as though I had "NT" stitched in scarlet on my jacket—and largely getting nowhere. I also saw that I wasn't alone in this. I didn't know exactly what I had in common with other nontraditional candidates, or how any of us could turn our different backgrounds to our advantage. But I was determined to find out.

1 | The Rise of the "Nontraditional" President

A KIND OF REVOLUTION has been taking place in the ranks of higher education leaders—the presidents, deans, and administrators of American colleges and universities. These leaders, once almost invariably the products of the same scholarly, tenure-track career pathway, are rapidly becoming a group with much more varied skills and backgrounds.

Take, for example, Patrick Gamble, appointed in 2010 as president of the University of Alaska. Prior to his arrival on campus, he was a four-star general in the United States Air Force, then chief executive of the Alaska Railroad Corporation. Or John Fry, who before taking the top job at Franklin & Marshall College held an executive position at the University of Pennsylvania—not on the academic but on the operations side. Or Bruce Harreld, the former IBM senior executive named president of the University of Iowa in the fall of 2015. Backgrounds like these used to be anomalies. They were the exceptions that proved the rule—the rule that dictated any journey to the president's office should begin in the tenure-track professorial ranks, advance through department chair and provost positions, and almost never detour off campus.

Today, such exceptions are frequent enough that they constitute a substantial threat to the status quo, and their collective challenge has sparked a hot debate. A label has been attached to the presidents and candidates who don't fit the old mold—they are "nontraditionals"—and the question has been framed: Are they better or worse for the job than the traditional types?

For those engaging in it, this debate is not, shall we say, academic. In any given year, hundreds of schools find themselves in need of new leadership and must set parameters for the search. However, in this book I'll argue that "Should we go the nontraditional route?" is the wrong debate to have. Indeed, it might be an impossible one to have productively. The "nontraditional" category may be too expansive, encompassing as it does every possibility outside the narrow bounds of convention, to display any meaningful patterns of behavior or achievement. Just as vast is the range of challenges leaders face in different colleges and universities. A different and better debate would focus on context and take place at the level of the individual institution. It would ask: *What set of strengths do we need in a leader given who we are and what we need to accomplish now?* This theme will be explored at length in the chapters to come. Interestingly, no one disputes that the need for great leadership and leaders in higher education today is acute.

At the outset, one thing is certain: No constructive debate is possible without accurate data—an objective basis of facts. Providing that is the task of this first chapter. To put the finest point on things, we'll look at the realm of higher education in which trends can be most reliably studied: liberal arts colleges in the United States. As we'll see, the rise over recent decades in the proportion of their leaders who are "nontraditional" has been dramatic. A label that might have applied to only a few percent of them thirty or forty years ago now describes fully a third of liberal arts college presidents.

To be sure, the "traditional" president coming up from the ranks of tenure-track faculty is still the norm, and by a two-to-one margin. Yet at the rate change is occurring, the continuation of the established trend line could turn nontraditional presidents into the majority of standing liberal arts college presidents within another decade or so. It is important to stress, moreover, that this is not a change limited to liberal arts (or to the top office of the president or chancellor). If anything, it would seem to be even more common in higher education settings overall and clearly extends also to deans. As Matthew Hartley of the University of Pennsylvania's Graduate School of Education writes: "Liberal arts colleges are invaluable to educational researchers because they have historically been bellwethers of change. They are the 'indicator species' of American higher education, signaling the health or fragility of the overall system."[1] For that matter, the trend toward nontraditional leadership extends even beyond the world of higher education. In many sectors, both nonprofit and for-profit, the need and willingness to expand pools of candidates and conceptions of qualified leaders is evidently growing.

With facts in hand, it will be more possible to have insightful discussions about the questions they raise. Why, for example, is the rise in nontraditional leadership occurring? Have conditions changed so much for U.S. colleges and universities as to require different skill sets—or have the main changes been to the processes by which good candidates are found? Are there patterns to be found in where nontraditionals are appointed, and in where they have most positive impact? Such questions will be taken up in the chapters to come. For now, however, it is important to understand the details of the trend, and the definitional issues that have, up to now, made it difficult to track.

Defining the Liberal Arts College

There is a reason that there has never been a quantitative analysis of nontraditional presidents in the liberal arts context. To be able to track their rise and success, consensus definitions of both what constitutes a "liberal arts college" and who counts as "nontraditional" must be established and remain stable over time. The easier part of this, you might think, would be to define the liberal arts, and which institutions should be called liberal arts colleges. After all, they date back centuries, to the time when the term *liberal arts* referred simply to the education provided to free people—*liber* being the Latin for "free." Some 1,500 years ago, in the fifth-century medieval Western university, those arts were divided neatly into seven disciplinary areas within two major realms: the Trivium—grammar, logic, and rhetoric; and the Quadrivium—arithmetic, geometry, music, and astronomy.

For a more modern take on liberal arts, we might look to the *Merriam-Webster's Collegiate Dictionary*, which defines them as "college or university studies (as language, philosophy, literature, abstract science) intended to provide chiefly general knowledge and to develop general intellectual capacities (as reason and judgment) as opposed to professional or vocational skills."[2] Or we might refer to more eloquent descriptions, to capture more of the ethos of such studies. Thomas Cronin, a college president himself and author of *Leadership and the Liberal Arts*, returns to that "free" etymology and declares the liberal arts to be "the liberating arts—freeing us from prejudice, dogmatism, and parochialism, from complacency, sentimentality, and hypocrisy, from sloppy reasoning and careless writing."[3]

In whatever way the liberal arts themselves are defined, there is also the matter of which institutions can claim them as their focus. Over time, the designation "liberal arts college" has come to stand for not only what subjects are studied, but by whom and in what setting. At a 1995 roundtable hosted by Pew Charitable Trust, for example, liberal arts colleges were characterized as "residential, devoted to instruction in a broad curriculum of the arts and sciences, designed as a place of growth and experimentation for the young—that remains the mind's shorthand for an undergraduate education at its best. Architecturally and philosophically, the liberal arts college embodies the ideal of learning as an act of community, in which students and faculty come together to explore and extend the foundations of knowledge."[4]

The Pew group's emphasis on community is echoed by Daniel Weiss, who believes "the distinguishing characteristic of most liberal arts colleges is their capacity to create learning environments that integrate the curricular, extracurricular, and co-curricular experiences for all students." He applauds their emphasis on "the development of critical thinking, a civic perspective, and service to the world as critical components in building intentional communities that can serve as incubators for linking knowledge, freedom, and democracy."[5] Similarly, the Annapolis Group, a nonprofit alliance of more than 130 liberal arts colleges, provides this description: "Liberal arts colleges develop intimate learning environments where extensive interaction between faculty, students, and staff fosters a community of serious discourse."[6]

Others have named additional features as typical of liberal arts colleges, such as faculties focused on teaching rather than research and publication, curricula that stop short of vocational training, and student bodies of fewer than 2,500 students. The University of Virginia's Dean Emeritus David Breneman, who has devoted a long career to studying liberal arts colleges, characterizes them as "single-purpose institutions, with no rationale for existence beyond their capacity to educate undergraduate students"—a rationale that distinguishes liberal arts colleges from community colleges and research universities.[7] Yet to further complicate matters, thousands of universities and colleges do offer courses and majors in the liberal arts, without being stand-alone liberal arts colleges.

With so many criteria being proposed and with the colleges themselves evolving in various ways, membership in the liberal arts group is fluid. But nailing down just which institutions fit the category is essential to doing research on the overall landscape of liberal arts colleges—to find out, for example, how they range across further segmentation dimensions such as religious affiliation, graduation rate, public or private, size, selectivity, financial situation, ranking, and geography. The first major effort to create a categorization system came from the Carnegie Foundation for the Advancement of Teaching, beginning in 1970. In creating its Carnegie Classification system, this independent, nonprofit organization provided a basis for decades of educational research and policy studies. For example, Breneman used it in the early 1990s to conduct his highly influential study for the Brookings Institution of 212 colleges with a combined enrollment of 260,000 students.

By the time I began the research for my own dissertation, building on Breneman's trend data was unworkable; the Carnegie classifications have been revised several times since his work, so that today's statistics are not strictly comparable with those published in the past. An alternative for me might have been to limit my study to the members of the Annapolis Group, all of which applied to join and were accepted into an alliance of "leading national liberal arts colleges across the United States."[8] Instead, I opted for the categorization system developed by the magazine publisher *U.S. News & World Report* (USNWR) for the purpose of producing its popular rankings. This system allowed USNWR to identify 251 stand-alone liberal arts colleges as of 2013 (when I undertook my analysis), categorized as such because they emphasize undergraduate education and award at least half of their degrees in the arts and sciences (a category that includes such disciplines as English, the biological sciences, physics, chemistry, history, political science, foreign languages, and the visual and performing arts, and excludes professional disciplines such as business, education, and nursing). Among these, there were 223 private and 27 public liberal arts colleges; one was for-profit. (Note that my analysis reports on 248 of these, since by 2014, three had gone off the list.)

By using this set, my hope was to conduct research on which others could continue to build. With a clear definition applied consistently across years, we can track trends not only in the total size of the liberal arts colleges group but also, within the group, in how they compare along institutional characteristics such as geography, religious affiliation, graduation rates, selectivity, size, and ranking. It is the USNWR-defined group for which I have also tracked financial characteristics such as endowments, tuition prices, and expenses. Government databases make the data on these characteristics available—and other examinations of these parameters (especially comparing them before and after the 2008–10 financial crisis) have amply revealed a liberal arts college context that is rapidly changing, and undeniably challenging. Before my research, however, no one had analyzed the data in light of the question of traditional versus nontraditional leadership. This was one major contribution my dissertation made: the construction of a fact-based database that would allow any correlations to be discovered between such readily measured parametric characteristics in liberal arts colleges and the backgrounds of their presidents.

Defining the "Nontraditional" Leader

If it is hard for people to reach consensus on exactly what constitutes a "liberal arts college," it is doubly hard to say with authority what makes a higher education leader "nontraditional." Again, however, if we are to measure the prevalence of such leaders and how their numbers change over time, a clear definition must be established.

Today, whether you find yourself in the company of presidents or search professionals, talk of traditional versus nontraditional higher education leaders, whether they be presidents or deans, is commonplace. Yet it quickly becomes clear there are no uniform definitions behind the references. The fact that people are picturing different kinds of backgrounds or leadership styles as they invoke the terms is perhaps acceptable in everyday conversation, but when it comes time to conduct quantitative research, these nuances matter. At the simplest level, defining "traditional president" more narrowly automatically increases the number of nontraditional presidents.

An early study by Michael Cohen and James March did exactly that. When they published their book *Leadership and Ambiguity* in 1986, they defined a traditional president as someone who had come up through the tenured faculty ranks along a standard, six-rung ladder: (1) student or teacher (or in a college with strong religious affiliation, minister), (2) professor, (3) department chair, (4) dean, (5) provost or academic vice president, and (6) president.[9] They further concluded that virtually all presidents came up through this path and that the rare individual who did not—such as Gen. Dwight D. Eisenhower, who led Columbia University after World War II—was a nontraditional president. Cohen and March's tight definition of a traditional president has served as the de facto standard for decades among education scholars and is still accepted even by some whose job it is to identify presidential candidates. Comments to me by Sue May—partner at the executive search firm Storbeck/Pimentel—hinted that this narrow definition was an expression of her clients' preference. "For a small liberal arts college," she says, "the traditional candidate is someone who's come up through academic affairs, has served as the vice president of academic affairs or provost . . . at a very similar institution. That's the highest comfort level you'll see at an institution."[10]

Steadily, however, working definitions are changing. Jackie Zavitch, for example, works in the education practice of the executive search firm Heidrick & Struggles (and, when interviewed, worked at Korn Ferry). When I spoke with her, she shared her "really narrow" definition of a traditional candidate: "Someone who has come up through the ranks of faculty, has established his or her research agenda and publication record, and has credibility with peers in his or her own discipline." Anyone who hasn't "grown up through academia" she considers nontraditional. Yet this definition is much less narrow than the one provided by Cohen and March since it doesn't require a president to have been a department chair or provost.

Today, all of us would certainly agree that a president who has been a full-time faculty member and come up through the academic ranks to be a provost or chief academic officer is traditional. But we might also broaden those parameters slightly—such as by including people who had *at one time* been tenured faculty members (whether or not they subsequently pursued other careers) or who had only been tenure *track* faculty (whether or not they were granted tenure). Likewise, we would all agree that a president who had never previously worked in the education sector—such as John Thrasher, the Florida State University president appointed in 2014 after a distinguished career in state politics   is nontraditional. In the strictest sense, as Sue May puts it, "a nontraditional would be someone who comes from outside academia, [lacks] a PhD, and has not spent time in academia at all." Yet we might also put Marty Meehan, the University of Massachusetts president who for most of his career represented his state in the U.S. Congress, in the same category, despite the seven years he spent as chancellor of UMass Lowell prior to winning the top job in the UMass system.

Robert Birnbaum and Paul Umbach, back in 2001, subdivided both the traditional and nontraditional categories in a way that some consider useful. Traditional presidents, in their system, include both the *scholars* that March and Cohen described and also *stewards,* defined as presidents who were not faculty but whose two previous jobs were in higher education. As for nontraditional presidents, they divided them into *spanners,* whose pathways to the office alternated between higher education and contributions to other professions (and who may or may not have been faculty but had one of their past two jobs in higher education), as well as outright *strangers* who have never been faculty and whose reputations were made not in higher education but in business, politics, the military, the clergy, or leadership of other nonprofit organizations.[11]

Birnbaum and Umbach's addition of a "stewards" category clearly allows for many more presidents to be called "traditional" because it explicitly takes a group that was historically considered nontraditional—those who rose through an administrative pathway on campus—and places them in the traditional camp. Thus, adopting this system would mask, to some degree, any trend toward more nontraditional leadership. At the same time, however, it allows some individuals who would otherwise appear quite traditional to be called nontraditional, if they happen to have held one of their *last two jobs* outside higher education. (Imagine, for example, a tenured faculty member who became department chair and then provost, but then spent a number of years working in multiple business or government roles before being considered for a presidency. That person would be considered a nontraditional "spanner.") Whether for these methodological quirks or other reasons, Birnbaum and Umbach's framework has not seen much uptake in practice. In the course of my in-depth interviews with twelve presidents and search firm executives, and countless more casual conversations, I never heard a reference to it; nor have there been any subsequent longitudinal studies updating Birnbaum and Umbach's data set. In practice, there seems to be agreement only at the ends of the spectrum, with the former provost or department chair as traditional, and the total stranger to higher education as a nontraditional, and nothing but a muddle between them.

Another framework for categorizing presidents comes from the American Council on Education (ACE) *On the Pathway to the Presidency* study, which offers the great value of having captured longitudinal data over almost a twenty-year period. It sorts first-time college and university presidents simply according to the positions they held immediately prior to being appointed to their roles, allowing for six possibilities: Previous President, Chief Academic Officer, Other Academic Officers, Non-Academic Officers, Chair/Faculty, and Outside of Higher Education. The ACE survey does not use the terms traditional and nontraditional, but its "outside higher education" could reasonably be used as a proxy for the nontraditional camp. Still, its focus on only one prior position probably means that some presidents the bulk of whose careers have been nontraditional are placed in traditional categories—and vice versa.

All the debate and discussion about traditional and nontraditional presidents would lead one to believe that there is a common understanding about their definitions, and that search committees and executive search firms consistently apply these definitions in their identification and assessment of candidates. But evidently that is not the case. It is an irony, really, to note that a scholarly community usually so concerned with research methodology would allow the debate over traditional versus nontraditional presidents to rage on without demanding more definitional clarity. On the other hand, the lack of such clarity is undoubtedly a large part of why the debate is not progressing more quickly toward answers.

To allow for more progress, my own research therefore established baseline definitions that reflect the modern spectrum of presidents and focus on their most salient differences. According to this "Beardsley definition," *a traditional president is someone who—at some point in his or her career—has come through the full-time tenured-faculty track, whether or not he or she attained tenure as a full professor.* Any president who does not fit that description is considered to be nontraditional.

Thus, by the Beardsley definition, David Greene of Colby College in Maine counts as nontraditional, despite the fact he has always worked in an academic environment. Indeed, he could claim to be born to the trade, with a professor father who went on to become a college president. No stranger to the scholarly life, Greene earned doctoral degrees in education and social policy from Harvard, on top of master's degrees in those fields and in human development and psychology. Yet by my definition he counts as a nontraditional president because he was never a tenure-track professor. His jobs at Smith, Brown, and the University of Chicago were all on the administration side. Likewise, Michael McRobbie at Indiana University (IU), despite serving as provost before ascending to the presidency, was the product of an administrative career. He was first hired by IU as vice president for information technology, ten years earlier. Another nontraditional would be John Rudley, who became president of Texas Southern University in 2008. He came to office via a series of academic finance positions, after a first career in public accounting.

And conversely, by the Beardsley definition, a president such as Shirley Ann Jackson of Rensselaer Polytechnic Institute (RPI) counts as traditional, despite the fact that her career prior to that appointment featured much more time in senior leadership positions in government, industry, and research than in higher education. For fifteen years after becoming the first African American woman to earn her PhD in Physics at MIT, she worked at AT&T's Bell Labs—and in the four years prior to joining RPI, she served as chair of the U.S. Nuclear Regulatory Commission, by President Clinton's appointment. But from 1991 to 1995, she was on the tenure track as a professor of physics at Rutgers University, teaching, conducting research, and supervising PhD candidates. Thus she gets the Beardsley definition's "traditional" stamp.

Similarly, by the Beardsley definition, a president such as Francisco Cigarroa, who spent five years as chancellor of the University of Texas (UT) System, counts as traditional—despite his remark to the *New York Times* that "I would say that I've been one of the most nontraditional choices ever for chancellor." In the twenty-five years leading up to his 2009 appointment, he spent far more time in surgery theaters than in lecture theaters. But from 1995 to 2000, he was on the tenure track as an assistant professor in the UT Health Science Center at San Antonio.[12]

Why should the simple presence or absence of a tenure-track faculty position on a president's CV be the litmus test? Because, in the most straightforward and measurable way, it goes directly to the essence of the "tradition" being upheld or challenged. The greatest tradition in higher education leadership is not that presidents are steeped in the workings of the institution (as Birnbaum and Umbach's administrative stewards are) but that they are steeped in scholarship. Faculties have traditionally chosen to be led by one of their own because they want the pursuit of knowledge to be the primary objective guiding decisions on policy. Thus the Beardsley definition is an insistence that any definition of a "traditional" president that does not acknowledge the tradition of leaders rising from the tenure-track faculty ranks does not in fact respect tradition.

At the same time, my definition does not insist that the tenure-track faculty member must have actually gained tenure to be called a traditional candidate. This marks a difference from the view of, for example, John Isaacson, founder of the executive search firm Isaacson, Miller. His firm focuses on university and college leadership placements; higher education is by far its largest and most comprehensive practice. In his assignments, Isaacson told me, he considers a faculty member who had "a tenure-track job and didn't get tenure . . . to be a nontraditional."

When William Bowen, former president of Princeton University and an authority on higher education, responded to my question about definition, his answer sounded right to me: "A nontraditional candidate is one who hasn't come through the faculty ranks." My definition honors that straightforward test while putting a slightly finer point on it to make it measurable. To explore some of its implications a bit further, it would mean that the ranks of traditional presidents could include someone who had been a tenured or tenure-track (assistant or associate) professor but then chose to step away from academia for a while rather than take the next steps on the academic ladder to become department chair or provost. But they could not include an adjunct or non–tenure track professor (e.g., general faculty or professor of practice) who, despite working for years in higher education, was never on a tenure track. This represents a definition that allows current research to build on past work—because some comparability can be established with both the ACE and the Birnbaum and Umbach definitions—but also makes it possible for a firmer foundation to be laid for future studies. (See the appendix for more details on research methodology.)

A Long-Term Trend toward Nontraditional

With sound definitions established of "liberal arts" and "nontraditional" we can track trends in college presidencies with much greater confidence. First, we can clearly see—perhaps not surprisingly, given the general perception of their rise—that nontraditional liberal arts presidents are now commonplace. Applying the Beardsley definition, fully a third of the 2014 generation of presidents at stand-alone liberal arts colleges are nontraditional. This represents a slight dip in their numbers from the last generation (meaning the set of all of their predecessors, regardless of when the transitions took place), when 38 percent counted as nontraditional. Considered over the long term, however, the weighted average across these past two cohorts of 35 percent nontraditional presidents represents a dramatic rise from what would have been a very low single-digit base three to four decades ago. (See table 1.1 and figure 1.1, below, for recent cohort tallies.)

The rise of nontraditional presidents is not limited to the liberal arts context but common to higher education settings overall. Recall the ACE survey, for example, and its periodic snapshot of the recruiting sources for first-time presidents across all U.S. colleges and universities. Its 2013 edition reports a rise in the proportion of first-time presidents recruited from "outside higher education" to 23 percent—more than double the percentage it reported in 2001 (and more than five times the portion cited in Cohen and March's 1974 research).

The ACE *On the Pathway to the Presidency* 2013 report says: "According to the American College President 2012, 20 percent of ALL presidents (whether first-time or not) came directly from a position outside academe. Another 20 percent came to their current presidency after leading another institution and 4 percent moved directly from a faculty or department chair position."[13] Let's compare this with my own analysis of the 2014 cohort of liberal arts college presidents. It finds the percentage of presidents

TABLE 1.1. Number of traditional and nontraditional presidents, 2014 and previous cohort

	2014 current liberal arts presidents	Previous cohort liberal arts presidents	Past two cohorts liberal arts presidents
Traditional	165	113	277
Nontraditional	83	68	153
Total	248	181	430

Sources: Data from Internet searches and analysis; USNWR Compass 2014 data.

Note: The time frame of the previous cohort varies since the transition of various presidencies takes place in different years.

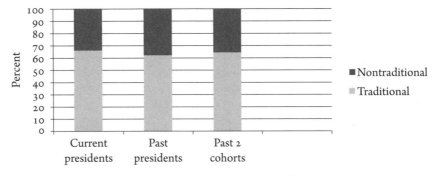

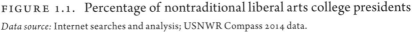

FIGURE 1.1. Percentage of nontraditional liberal arts college presidents

Data source: Internet searches and analysis; USNWR Compass 2014 data.

coming directly from *a faculty or department chair* background to be the same, at 4 percent. However, liberal arts presidents from the 2014 cohort are recruited directly from *another presidency* 20 percent less than the typical university or college president. Further, the typical college president in the ACE 2013 survey (using 2012 data) is 43 percent more likely than a liberal arts president in the 2014 cohort to have been recruited directly from *outside higher education.* Thus, the typical liberal arts college president in 2014 is more likely to be directly recruited from a nonfaculty, nonpresidential senior leadership position within higher education than the typical college or university president.

To understand the difference more precisely, I took the extra step of adopting the ACE 2013 *Pathway to the Presidency* methodology to look spe-

TABLE 1.2. Recruiting source and previous job for first-time presidents

Role immediately before becoming president	Previous liberal arts college president cohort (%; *n* = 148)	2014 liberal arts college president cohort (%; *n* = 190)	ACE 2012 first-time president data (%)
Provost or chief academic officer	19	24	44
Other academic officer	27	29	13
Nonacademic officer	20	25	16
Chair or faculty	8	5	4
Outside higher education	26	17	23

Sources: Data from ACE 2013; Internet searches and analysis; USNWR Compass 2014 data.

Note: The *n* of 148 is smaller as a sample than today's cohort because complete data were available for only 148 of the predecessor presidents' backgrounds. For an incumbent who has been in office for, say, more than fifteen years, granular data on the predecessor are often not accessible.

cifically at liberal arts college presidents. The results show that pathways to the presidency for first-time presidents in the liberal arts context diverge substantially from the experience of U.S. college and university presidents overall. Those in the liberal arts are much more likely to be recruited from other academic officer or nonacademic officer positions, such as a dean, and much less likely to be recruited from a provost or chief academic officer position, than the national average of all presidents. (See table 1.2 for the comparative data.)

In fact, first-time presidents in the liberal arts were more than twice as likely to be selected from an "other academic officer" position such as a dean of arts and sciences position than the average first-time university president, and for the 2014 cohort, 56 percent more likely to be recruited from a nonacademic officer position such as an executive vice president of administration or dean of students. Conversely, they were 45 percent less likely than the average president to be recruited from the provost or chief academic officer ranks.

The number of *first-time* liberal arts presidents recruited from outside higher education is in a comparable range, at 17 percent of the 2014 cohort and 26 percent of the previous cohort (weighted average of the two cohorts of 22 percent), compared to 23 percent of the overall university president profile. Overall, the first-time university presidents of the 2013 ACE study were directly recruited from nonacademic positions (nonacademic officers and outside higher education) less frequently than the liberal arts college presidents in the 2014 and predecessor cohorts, by as many as six percentage points.

The decrease in the percentage directly recruited from outside higher education between the previous first-time liberal arts president cohort and the current cohort is notable, but the research cannot determine if this is a definite trend. Part of this variation could be due to differences in sample size (148 versus 190) or to missing data. For instance, only 120 schools have ACE data for both cohorts.

More Strangers Come to Liberal Arts

It is also instructive to replicate Robert Birnbaum and Paul Umbach's method, and apply it specifically to the liberal arts context, to determine how things might have changed since his study was conducted. As a reminder, Birnbaum and Umbach, recognizing that pathways were increasingly segmented, created a different definition of a traditional president as including *scholars* (similar to traditionals as defined by March and Cohen) and *stewards,* who were presidents but were never faculty and whose two previous jobs were in higher education. Nontraditional presidents are defined by Birnbaum and Umbach as including *spanners,* who may or may not have been faculty but had one of their past two jobs in higher education, and *strangers,* who have never been faculty and never worked in higher education. (Note, too, that this definition makes it easiest for a leader to be classified as "traditional.")

Birnbaum and Umbach's study was published in 2001 but uses 1995 data for a cross-section of U.S. colleges and universities. For purposes of comparison to the liberal arts in focus here, the most relevant part of their data is the subset they created of "baccalaureate colleges" (although it includes many colleges other than the liberal arts colleges on which my analysis focuses). Table 1.3 below presents their 1995 data for the subset as well as their whole set, alongside new data created by sorting the 2014 liberal arts president cohort into their four categories. What jumps out from the table is the substantial growth in percentages of nontraditional presidents over the past two decades.

It is important to be cautious in reading these percentages; especially within the categories of strangers and spanners, they reflect small bases. (Even in 2014, these nontraditional categories as Birnbaum and Umbach defined them combine to account for just 21 percent of liberal arts college presidents.) Yet there is no mistaking the leap in the number of "strangers" now occupying presidencies in liberal arts colleges: they are almost twice

TABLE 1.3. Comparison of 2014 traditional and nontraditional liberal arts presidents versus the Birnbaum and Umbach study

Birnbaum/Umbach category	Birnbaum/Umbach: Baccalaureate colleges (% from 1995 data)	Birnbaum/ Umbach: All colleges and universities (% from 1995 data)	2014 liberal arts college president cohort (%; n = 236)
Scholar	62.4	66.3	59.3
Steward	23.3	22.4	19.5
Traditional total	85.7	88.7	78.8
Spanner	10.3	7.4	13.6
Stranger	4.1	3.9	7.6
Nontraditional total	14.4	11.3	21.2

Sources: Data from Robert Birnbaum and Paul D. Umbach, "Scholar, Steward, Spanner, Stranger: The Four Career Paths of College Presidents," *Review of Higher Education* 24, no. 3 (Spring 2001): 203–17; Internet analysis; USNWR Compass 2014 data.

as prevalent as they were in Birnbaum and Umbach's survey of 1995 data. The jump in the percentage of "spanners" in liberal arts is striking, as well.

Birnbaum and Umbach's data reveal that baccalaureate colleges were more likely even in 1995 to appoint nontraditional presidents. Thus the contrast between today's liberal arts presidents and baccalaureate college presidents of 1995 is more muted. Still, the percentage of nontraditional liberal arts presidents in 2014 is 47 percent higher than at the baccalaureate colleges two decades previously.

To be sure, most liberal arts college presidents continue to hail from the traditional tenure-track faculty ranks. (And there has been little change in the proportional mix of these traditional types.) We can see the continued dominance of the traditional higher education path in the data. Whether defined as ACE or as Birnbaum and Umbach define it, that path is still more than three times as common as any alternative path. Birnbaum and Umbach concluded, using 1995 data, that among all college and university presidents, fully 89 percent (66.3 percent scholars and 22.4 percent stewards) of presidents took the traditional route (by their definition), while only 11 percent (7.4 percent spanners and 3.9 percent strangers) had nontraditional backgrounds.[14] Among baccalaureate colleges, many of which are liberal arts colleges, Birnbaum and Umbach's analysis revealed 14 percent were nontraditional, slightly higher than the overall population. Using somewhat different definitions, and eighteen years later than Birnbaum and Umbach, ACE reports that the greatest source of first-time college presidents is still the traditional provost or chief academic officer. Its five categories stack up as follows: Provost or Chief Academic Officer (44 percent); Other Academic Officers (13 percent); Non-Academic Officers (16 percent); Chair/Faculty (4 percent); and Outside of Higher Education (23 percent).[15] The ACE 2012 president profile study reports that 70 percent of presidents still come from full-time faculty positions.[16]

But just as surely, tenured faculty experience is no longer an obligatory step along the pathway to a liberal arts college presidency. For that matter, if the long-term trend continues at the rate already established, nontraditional presidents could come to represent the majority of standing liberal arts college presidents within another decade or so.

And again, what is being depicted here is a conservative version of the trend. As noted earlier, the effect of my "Beardsley definition" of the traditional president, versus the Cohen and March definition, is to make it more difficult for someone to be classified as nontraditional. If I had applied the definition proposed by Cohen and March and favored by most of the search executives I interviewed, many presidents who had not achieved tenure as faculty or been promoted to provost would need to be reclassified as "nontraditional." Thus, the number of traditional presidents would be smaller, and the number of nontraditional presidents even greater. (In fact, by the Cohen and March definition, more than 50 percent of today's first-time presidents would be considered nontraditional; see the second and third columns in table 1.2.)

Thus, stepping back from the fray, what we see is the following: no matter what the definition, the number of nontraditionals has grown substantially, from a base of almost zero in the 1980s to a significant proportion today by any standard. Using my methodology, the number of liberal arts college presidents who have come from outside the tenure-track tradition is one-third. But depending on which definition they use (Birnbaum and Umbach, ACE, Cohen and March, or Beardsley), others could find a percentage of nontraditional presidents today as low as 21 percent, or as high as over 50 percent. No wonder there is so much confusion and intrigue.

The Traditional Leader Personified

Scholarly data points aside, it may be useful to have a model in mind of what "traditional" looks like in the flesh. (And for models of nontraditional leadership, see the sidebar "Three Nontraditional Pathways to the President's Office.") As an ideal, it would be difficult to find better than the late Bill Bowen, the longtime leader of Princeton University. Bowen himself was a product of liberal arts education, graduating in 1955 from Denison University in Ohio. From there he went on to graduate studies in economics at Princeton and, after earning his PhD in 1958, immediately joined the faculty. By 1967, he had become the university's provost, and five years later, at just thirty-eight years of age, Bowen was installed as president. Not only did Bowen spend the next two decades at the helm of a renowned and growing university, he drew on that experience and on continued, rigorous research to publish frequently on issues and trends in higher education. After retiring from Princeton, he advanced such studies for another two decades as president of the Mellon Foundation. In recognition of his contributions, he was awarded the National Humanities Medal in 2015 by President Barack Obama.

Another good example would be David Oxtoby, who served many years, starting in 2003, as president of Pomona College in Claremont, California. He began his academic career as a Harvard-trained theoretical chemist and spent the next three decades moving up the ranks at the University of Chicago, holding both faculty and administrative titles. By the time he became director of its James Franck Institute, he had authored or coauthored more than 150 scientific articles. His last position before leaving Chicago was as dean of the Division of Physical Sciences. At Pomona College, he continues to keep a hand in as a professor, teaching an annual environmental chemistry course. Commenting at the time of his appointment, Stewart R. Smith, chairman of the Pomona College Board of Trustees, had this to say: "In David Oxtoby we have found a person who is, first of all, brilliant of mind and staggering in his scholarly credentials. In the best tradition of a liberal arts education, he is also something of a Renaissance man — accomplished in French, German and Italian, knowledgeable about classical music and architecture, active in theater and athletics. Most importantly, he is a leader of intelligence, integrity and vision. He deeply understands, and eloquently articulates, the essential role for liberal arts colleges in this new century."[17]

Slightly less typical, only because of her gender, would be Georgia Nugent, who spent more than a decade at the helm of Kenyon College. She arrived there having spent the previous ten years advancing through academic officer roles at Princeton University, holding titles from assistant to the president, to associate provost, to dean. Before that, she spent thirteen years as faculty, teaching classics at Princeton and at Brown University.

Three Nontraditional Pathways to the President's Office

Just as no two liberal arts colleges are exactly alike, the same goes for the pathways of nontraditional presidents. In these pages I will make repeated reference to three nontraditional presidents I got to know over the course of in-depth interviews and correspondence. Here are brief introductions to them, focusing on their backgrounds.

JOHN FRY is one of that small percentage of university presidents who do not hold degrees past the master's level. Having earned a liberal arts undergraduate degree in American civilization from Lafayette College, and an MBA from New York University's Stern School of Business, Fry pursued a successful career in management consulting at KPMG Peat Marwick and Coopers & Lybrand. He made his transition to higher education in 1995 by joining Judith Rodin's new presidential team at the University of Pennsylvania as executive vice president of finance, having previously served Penn as a client. Seven years later, he was recruited directly to serve as president of Franklin & Marshall College in Lancaster, Pennsylvania, in 2002. He is currently the president of Drexel University, a position he has held since 2010.

DAVID GREENE is a classic example of what Robert Birnbaum and Paul Umbach (2001) would categorize as a "steward" president, meaning his background was in higher education, but in administrative, not academic, leadership positions. Having graduated from Hamilton College with a liberal arts degree, Greene went on to earn master's and doctoral degrees at Harvard University in the fields of psychology and education. His career took him through various roles at, first, Hartnell College, then Wells College, Smith College, and Brown University, where he led organizations and initiatives related to planning and the educational environment. Prior to his appointment at Colby College in Waterville, Maine, in 2014, Greene was executive vice president at the University of Chicago, where he oversaw a very large budget and several departments. Although he has never been on a tenure track and is thus considered nontraditional, he has conducted research and taught courses.

LAWRENCE SCHALL started his career as a lawyer in Philadelphia, specializing in civil rights litigation, after obtaining his JD from the University of Pennsylvania. After a dozen years as a trial attorney, he shifted his career to higher education, returning to his alma mater—Swarthmore College—to serve as its vice president for administration. While at Swarthmore, Schall decided he would like to become a university president, and he completed his doctorate in higher education management at the University of Pennsylvania, where he also became an adjunct faculty member. Soon after earning his doctorate, Schall left Swarthmore to join Oglethorpe University in Atlanta as its sixteenth president.

It should be noted that two of these nontraditional presidents are not convinced that the nontraditional label should be applied to them. Greene told me it might be a misnomer, given that he has "done research and writing and teaching, and been at the best universities in the world in senior leadership and academic administrative positions." Schall pointed out that times have changed: "Ten years ago I was a nontraditional president. Today I'm not. . . . There are so many presidents who haven't done [the traditional provost route] that I think the use of traditional and nontraditional is probably not the right terminology."

There are clearly common threads woven through these traditional presidents' backgrounds. All were first accomplished scholars. All saw an orderly progression from teaching as tenure-track professors to leading their colleagues as department chairs and deans. Academic officer roles followed, increasing in their scope of responsibility and potential impact on the institution. Such a traditional CV offers much-needed assurance to the boards of trustees and search committees tasked with assessing candidates that they have what it takes to ascend to the top office. They have developed the sensibilities and strengths to lead often fractious faculties. They are comfortable with and properly respectful of the academic culture. They have had the opportunity to observe, over long careers serving under other presidents, what works and does not work.

At the same time, there are valuable threads that are often missing from these backgrounds—strengths that are not selected for or naturally developed at those earlier rungs of the traditional career ladder. If the presidency is conceived as primarily an academic role, leaders are chosen for the internal-facing impact they could have on, for example, updating the curriculum, developing the faculty, and raising student achievement. Today, however, presidents in higher education are also increasingly responsible for external-facing tasks—chief among them, fund-raising. As the face of the institution, they quickly find themselves embroiled in legislative affairs and community relations, as well as managing alumni and donor relations—all responsibilities that put the emphasis on their abilities to deal with stakeholder groups beyond the faculty.

Most painfully, for at least some traditional candidates, the new demands also call for deep skills in business management. Donald K. Hess headed the search committee at Franklin & Marshall College that selected nontraditional president John Fry in 2002. "You have that mass of activity that a true academic doesn't want to get his hands dirty with," Hess told the *New York Times*. "Colleges and universities are major enterprises, and they deserve the attention that I think many of them don't get, in terms of the management."[18]

Nontraditional is the term applied to everyone who departs from the long-established norms of career background. But often these differences in background are exactly why they have been able to cultivate certain strengths colleges desperately need today.

Challenging the Leadership Comfort Zone

For the boards of trustees and search committees evaluating candidates for presidencies, there is still clearly a comfort zone that is difficult to move beyond. It would appear that any nontraditional features in these candidates still need to be tempered with reassuring traditional ones; candidates who differ on too many dimensions from the classic image tend to wash out of the process.

It is interesting to ask, therefore: Is this at least part of the reason that the women chosen to lead liberal arts colleges are less likely to have nontraditional backgrounds than their male counterparts? My analysis of the gender composition of traditional versus nontraditional presidents reveals that women are substantially more prevalent among the traditional group than among the nontraditionals.

This is particularly interesting to note because, if we ignore the question of traditional versus nontraditional backgrounds, we find that the gender diversity in the ranks of liberal arts college presidents mirrors that of university presidents overall. The overall data capture a problem many have observed without having to cite precise percentages: that gender diversity in leadership positions remains a challenge in higher education. Previous studies, such as the 2013 ACE *On the Pathway to the Presidency* report, using data from 2007 and 2012, have documented that there have been small in-

TABLE 1.4. Gender diversity among liberal arts college presidents and comparison versus the university president population overall

Gender	Previous cohort of liberal arts presidents (%; n = 206)	ACE 2007 overall president study (%)	2014 cohort of liberal arts presidents (%; n = 248)	ACE 2012 overall president study (%)
Male	80	77	74	74
Female	20	23	26	26

Sources: Data from ACE 2012, 2013; Internet searches; USNWR Compass 2014 data.

creases in the percentages of women during the past five years—but women still constitute only about one-fourth of college and university presidents.

In my research, I first went a step further than these studies to break down the percentage of female presidents in *liberal arts* colleges. Gender diversity for the past two liberal arts college president cohorts is shown in table 1.4.

As of the summer of 2014, 26 percent of liberal arts college presidents were female, identical to the percentage observed in the ACE 2012 data of the total college and university president population. Compared to the previous cohort of liberal arts presidents, this represents an increase of six percentage points, mirroring the smaller increase noted in the ACE studies. Gender inequality clearly persists, and there remains a long path before gender equality will be achieved in the presidential ranks. However, a change in the male-to-female ratio from 4:1 to 3:1 in just one generation of presidents counts as progress.

The analysis becomes still more interesting with a second step, looking at how many of these women are also nontraditional. My data show that women liberal arts presidents are substantially less likely to be nontraditional than their male counterparts (see table 1.5). Indeed, men are 63 percent more likely to fall in the nontraditional category than women are. Put another way, the ratio of traditional to nontraditional presidents is 4.6:1 for women, versus 2.4:1 for men.

To sum up the data, then, it is first clear that, despite undisputed progress in recent decades, the number of male presidents still dwarfs the absolute number of women presidents. Second, the chance that a woman will be in the president's office is substantially greater if that woman comes from a traditional versus nontraditional background. In the light of this context, I am especially proud of two of my U Penn doctoral classmates. While complet-

TABLE 1.5. Gender diversity of 2014 liberal arts presidents for traditional versus nontraditional

Gender ($n = 248$)	Nontraditional (%)	Traditional (%)
Female	17.9	82.1
Male	29.2	70.8

Sources: Data from Internet searches and analysis; USNWR Compass 2014 data.

ing their studies, Stacy Sweeney and Colette Pierce Burnette were named presidents of Bay State College in Boston and Huston-Tillotson University in Austin, respectively. Both were nontraditional candidates, but having seen their incredible abilities in action firsthand, I was in no way surprised to learn of their selections.

The Effect of Longer Tenures

One more set of data belongs in this chapter, because it adds to the story of why the numbers of nontraditional presidents are rising. My research shows that, in the liberal arts context at least, nontraditional presidents are proving to have longer tenures than traditional presidents.

We know from available data that the average tenure for a liberal arts college president in 2014 is lower than the average for all college and university presidents was in 2012. However, my question had to do with a subset of the liberal arts college presidents: Do the ones with nontraditional backgrounds tend to have longer or shorter tenures than their traditional peers? The answer is shown in table 1.6. The data indicate that the average tenure of nontraditional presidents (whether measured as mean or median) is substantially longer than that of traditional presidents.

As of 2014, nontraditional presidents' mean tenure was 8.3 years, and median tenure 6.9 years—three or more years longer than the traditional presidents. The research does not determine the root cause of these meaningful differences; it is possible, albeit unlikely, that these tenure numbers could converge over time as a large number of low-tenure presidents continue their careers. Should this pattern of difference persist, however, simple math dictates that over time, the number and percentage of nontraditional presidents would mechanically and substantially increase, even if the percentage recruited each year were to stay constant, given the higher attrition of traditional presidents.

TABLE 1.6. Tenure of 2014 traditional versus nontraditional liberal arts college presidents

	All 2014 liberal arts presidents (years; $n = 248$)	2014 traditional liberal arts presidents (years; $n = 164$)	2014 nontraditional liberal arts presidents (years; $n = 84$)
Mean	6.2	5.2	8.3
Median	4.6	3.9	6.9
Range	0 to 45.9	0 to 39	0 to 45.9

Sources: Data from Internet analysis; USNWR Compass 2014 data.

Will the Trend Continue?

With a foundation of data now established to describe the rise over time of the nontraditional president, we can now move to the interesting discussion and debate it inspires. Among the biggest and most contentious of the questions is the obvious one: Will that rise continue?

The coming chapters will build the case that the trend is bound to continue, thanks to the combined force of several factors. Changes in the context of liberal arts colleges over recent decades (as detailed in chapter 2) are unlikely to be reversed, and these changes will increasingly demand leadership strengths that are difficult to develop in the course of the traditional academic career. Most likely, the coming decade will bring even more challenging contextual change, calling for still more capabilities that fall outside today's favored leadership model. Meanwhile, these changes will increasingly be recognized in reforms of colleges' search and selection processes—and shifts in the gatekeepers, influencers, and decision makers who play a role in them.

As we'll see, the sheer problem of numbers (that is, a projected shortage of candidates in the traditional mode) also suggests that in the future more liberal arts colleges will turn to nontraditional leaders. And liberal arts colleges will not be alone. Searches for deans or university presidents face much the same set of challenges. Combined with the changing requirements of the higher education leadership, the rising number of searches being conducted every year will expand the number of candidates who come under consideration—and among them will be many more whose reputations and capabilities were formed outside of the tenure track of higher education.

2 | A Transformed Context

WHEN REBECCA CHOPP stepped down from the presidency of prestigious, highly ranked Swarthmore in 2014 after five years in office (and announced simultaneously her appointment as chancellor at the University of Denver), many in the education community were shocked. Of all the implications of Title IX—the landmark legislation that prohibits gender discrimination in any federally funded education activity—no one would have expected that it might have played a role in the departure of a self-described feminist and pioneering female college leader. But under Chopp's watch, Swarthmore had landed on a list of schools to be investigated for inadequate handling of students' sexual violence complaints. There was nothing new about the college's practices and nor were they unique to Swarthmore; more than fifty other schools were listed at the same time by the U.S. Department of Education's Office for Civil Rights. But the time had come, the government decided, to do some naming and shaming. To be clear, no one I know is privy to the real reasons for her departure, and Chopp herself has emphasized her family roots in Colorado as the positive draw to Denver.[1] Still, many speculate that the investigation contributed to her exit and Swarthmore's inability to retain her.

Here, in other words, was a situation where the institution was traditional: Swarthmore was a classic, outstanding liberal arts college that had pursued its mission for more than 150 years. Its leader was also traditional: Having begun her academic career as a professor of religion, Chopp rose to become provost at Emory University, then dean at Yale Divinity School, before becoming president of Colgate University, her last job before Swarthmore. But the challenges to both institution and leader were far from traditional (and certainly rendered the job less pleasant). The context had changed.

There is a truth about leadership that is hardly limited to the higher education sector: When the context of an enterprise shifts, the kinds of leaders who seek to be part of it and who thrive in it also change. We saw another striking example of this in late 2015, when both the president and the chancellor of the University of Missouri stepped down at the demand of African

American students and their supporters. Who would have predicted when those two leaders were chosen for their roles that the main thing they would have to manage deftly would be racial tensions?

In this chapter, we'll map the context change for higher education in its many forms. New powers wielded by student activists and rising social justice concerns represent only two of its underlying trends. At least as dramatic have been the changes in the competitive environment for colleges and universities. With choices proliferating and costs escalating, many now face a mortal threat in the very economics of their operations. As we'll see, liberal arts colleges offer some of the most vivid cases of the crying need for new business models. David Breneman called them the "standard bearers" of higher education who "at their best . . . provide the finest undergraduate education in the country"—but some are now perilously close to raising white flags. Among the challenges they all face: unfavorable demographic shifts; the lingering effects of a punishing recession; aggressive competition from public universities offering look-alike honors colleges at subsidized prices; price cutting by the richest universities to attract top students forcing more tuition discounting by others; greater emphasis by students on vocational instruction; and rising affordability concerns. Most of these issues are in fact faced by all colleges and universities and their business, law, medical, and other schools.

Context change in higher education is inherently interesting to study, but I will also acknowledge that, for me, this is personal. I owe my own job to such fast-changing times—and even more, to an institution that recognized them. I remember a meeting with a group of faculty at the University of Virginia's Darden School of Business that took place late in their consideration of my candidacy. (Interestingly, with seventy-two tenured professors, an endowment of about $450 million, and just over a thousand students including executive education, Darden is roughly similar in size and scope to some elite liberal arts colleges.) At a certain point, it occurred to me to turn the tables on my interviewers and ask, "What about you—what have you learned about the needs of the school in this process?" The responses—indicating an openness to stepped-up innovation, more global orientation, smart use of technology, increased agility, and augmented resources, and a belief that all this could go hand in hand with building traditional strengths in teaching and educational experience—not only aligned with my thinking but struck me as a set of priorities that would not have been present and allowed me to have been named dean just five years earlier.

Context change is a sprawling topic that is appropriately studied at the "macro" level of high-level trends and statistics. Its implications are just as large-scale. But it's vital to remember the very down-to-earth reasons that make it so important to understand. The current reality of an enterprise and predictable trajectory of its change dictate what is needed in a leader. So whether you are that aspiring leader or part of the community that will select new leadership, your knowledge of context will have profound impact—on the career of the leader, the success of the school, and the education of the student.

Competition from All Sides

In some ways, liberal arts colleges seem able to defy the ravages of time. Visits by alumni to their liberal arts campuses reliably bring them back to their youth, with the same towering trees and classic buildings dominating grounds now sprinkled with a few new structures. Indeed, many of the same faculty members are still there delivering the same cherished classroom experience. But just like a placid lake, a college, university, or business school can present a surface that is calm while a lot of movement and change goes on beneath.

Looking across their whole histories, the biggest story of change for liberal arts institutions is the move from essentially no competition to intense competition. Today, higher education in the United States has become big business, a giant industry in its own right. According to the National Center for Education Statistics (NCES), in academic year 2013–14, expenditures by postsecondary institutions in the United States reached $517 billion (of which $324 billion was spent at public institutions, $173 billion at private nonprofit institutions, and $21 billion at private for-profit institutions).[2] But when higher education began in the United States, the liberal arts college was the only game in town. These colleges were the country's first type of higher education institution, beginning with Harvard's founding in 1636, and they dominated the landscape for more than two centuries. That changed with the rise of the university structure in the second half of the nineteenth century. As Victor Ferrall points out in *Liberal Arts at the Brink*, "It was not until after Yale College became the first US institution to grant a Ph.D. degree, in 1861, and passage of the first land-grant bill, the Morrill Act of 1862, launched the state universities, that undergraduate education outside the liberal arts began its ascent toward the preeminence it now enjoys."[3]

It isn't only the colleges that specialize in liberal arts that are under competitive pressure; the liberal arts degree itself has gradually been displaced as a favorite course of study. Vocational and professional degrees, designed to prepare students more specifically for well-paying jobs after graduation, have steadily risen in popularity. Sarah Turner and William Bowen noted in a 1990 study that the share of degrees awarded in the arts and sciences, core liberal arts territory, had dropped from 47 percent in 1968 to just 26 percent in 1986.[4]

Even to the extent that liberal arts degrees are still sought, however, the classic stand-alone colleges no longer hold a monopoly on them. As the authors of the Pew Roundtable report note, "When larger institutions wish to design special undergraduate environments that would provide a quality experience in residential learning and mentorship, they build small subcommunities that replicate the model of the liberal arts college."[5] When I spoke with Lawrence Schall, president of Oglethorpe University in Atlanta, he confirmed that these much larger universities with their diverse sources of revenue put real pressure on liberal arts colleges. "Our competitors are the big, public universities . . . [such as] University of Georgia, Georgia Tech, Georgia Southern, University of Florida, the University of Tennessee," he said. "Families are making the choice between an inexpensive, in-state, big, public institution that's probably created some kind of Honors College to make it look like a liberal arts college, but it's also got all the football, basketball, big life around it." Adding to the competition from public universities, the rise of elite, private universities has provided attractive alternatives for students at the high end. These include the Ivy League as well as big research universities such as the University of Virginia, the University of Michigan, and the University of California at Berkeley.

No wonder, then, that David Greene, president of Colby College, told me that for his school, "the competition comes from all sides—above and below and side-to-side." He isn't alone, and as a result, the "market share" of liberal arts colleges continues to shrink. In 1999, Michael McPherson and Morton Schapiro estimated that, of the 14 million students enrolled in higher education each year, no more than a quarter of a million were attending liberal arts colleges, and fewer than one hundred thousand were enrolled in that subset of schools "where the majority of students major in the liberal arts and live on campus, and where admission is moderately selective (turning down, say, more than a third of those who apply)."[6] Robert Zemsky, in his *Checklist for Change: Making American Higher Education a Sustainable En-*

terprise, makes clear that, a decade on, "that diminishing continues. Liberal arts colleges account for substantially less than 2 percent of all undergraduate enrollments."[7]

It is perhaps no surprise, given this decline in share, that the number of liberal arts colleges has also fallen in recent decades, both as a proportion of all higher education institutions and by simple raw count. When David Breneman was conducting the research that went into his 1994 Brookings Institution report, he found that "in 1955 liberal arts colleges still accounted for nearly 40 percent of all institutions—732 private colleges . . . enrolled only 7.6 percent of all students. By 1987, the Carnegie Foundation identified 540 out of 3,389 institutions (16 percent) as private liberal arts colleges, with only 4.4 percent of total enrollments."[8]

The amazing thing to note, in light of these numbers, is the extent to which liberal arts colleges retain their influential stature—or, as one leader I interviewed put it, "still punch above their weight." Undoubtedly it is because they still provide a form of education recognized to be outstanding. Unfortunately, they have also retained their very high fixed-cost structures (that is, the inflexible costs of their buildings, tenured professors, and staff)—and a habit of hiking tuition rates beyond the rate of inflation. Some speculate that there will come a "tipping point" in the market's willingness to pay, after which what has been a slow decline will turn into a much faster one. (To borrow Hemingway's phrasing, some colleges could go bankrupt two ways: gradually, then suddenly.) "In broad terms, there will just be a market reaction," John Fry believes. He told me the point would come when students and their parents would say: "Enough is enough. Penn State is good enough, and we're moving to other models because, in the end, the most important thing is to get that degree."

The scale and scope of any such market reaction is impossible to gauge, but given the fixed-cost structure of these institutions, any further constriction of revenues will be painful. For now, many anxious administrators are watching for higher-education enrollments to begin climbing overall, after several consecutive years of decline (the natural result of a recovering economy's greater job creation). The U.S. Education Department issued a report in 2014 projecting that, over the decade of 2012–22, undergraduate enrollment will rise by 13.3 percent, even as the U.S. population in the age range of eighteen to twenty-four declines. Even if that proves true, however, it is hardly assured that a rising tide will lift all boats.

A Sorry Measure of Who Wins

As we've seen, new forms and levels of competition have created problems for traditional institutions. They have also created confusion for prospective students and their families. How does one choose among options as different as apples and oranges? If the whole point of getting a college education is, for many, to raise one's employment prospects, how do different institutions measure up?

My interviews with college presidents revealed that the pressure on them to show outcomes is rising. Families and students wondering why they should pay far more for the privilege of a liberal arts education look for answers in terms of "return on investment." It should be no surprise that people would become more attuned to this as the cost of a liberal arts degree in constant dollars keeps rising. But measuring the payback on education dollars invested has never been a straightforward exercise, and this is especially true for a kind of education designed for the long-term payoffs of teaching students how to think and succeed as lifelong learners rather than for the short-term payoff of teaching them the specific knowledge and skills required in a first job out of college.

Given so many choices and so little information about relative strengths, students and their parents are hungry for guidance and tools to help narrow down the options. As a result, and to most colleges' and universities' dismay, a kind of service industry has grown up to meet the need: the business of college rankings.

Rankings are inherently troubling because, in a world of easy information access, they help to drive winner-take-all effects. The best students flock to the "best" schools, and the gap between those schools and the rest of the pack grows. Rankings become more troubling when you realize how subjective the definition is of what constitutes better or worse performance. In order to produce their lists, ranking organizations must decide what matters most in an education, what factors drive or can be used as proxies for those outcomes, and over what time frame relative outcomes should be expected to materialize. For mission-driven organizations such as colleges, rankings also attempt to define the objective function of a higher education enterprise externally, in ways that may conflict with the institution's mission.

U.S. News & World Report, as the leading source of such rankings in the United States, prides itself on the comprehensiveness and objectivity of its survey and therefore sticks to factors that can be readily compiled from data all schools collect. Its algorithm combines numbers relating to endowments, graduation rates, levels of selectivity, and more to determine ranking. Others place different relative weights on the same factors or look at other variables.

Few are the students who haven't consulted these rankings and their accompanying data, such as average SAT scores (or GMATs for business schools, or LSATs for law schools) and GPAs of accepted students, as they compile their lists of "reaches" and "safeties" to apply to. They are more likely to apply to institutions labeled with words such as "elite" or "little Ivys" or "medallion." But few, too, are the applicants who have looked very hard at how raters arrive at the scores and labels, and thought carefully about whether their own priorities were the same. Commenting on such rankings as a global phenomenon, Bahram Bekhradnia, president of Britain's Higher Education Policy Institute, recently told the *Economist:* "They're worse than useless. They're positively dangerous. I've heard presidents say this all over the world: I'll do anything to increase my ranking, and nothing to harm it."[9]

In a less competitive era, rankings and outcome measurements weren't prominent concerns for liberal arts colleges. Now, they are—and for the large majority of schools that are not top-ranked, the fuzzy connection between the instruction they offer and career success is a particular problem. President Schall made a wry reference to the kind of elite college that is still in a position to "host a symposium on the value of the liberal arts, and tell all sorts of people to come talk—and pretty much do pure liberal arts in the same way they always have because everyone there is going off to graduate school afterwards." Most schools today, he emphasized, need to be able to craft a better story about the pathway from liberal arts to life success. Saying "get a good education and you'll be fine," he told me, unfortunately doesn't sell.

Changing Economics for All

Understand the dramatic rise of competition they face, the new power of rankings to send schools into spirals (some upward, most downward), and the need to deal with increasing issues related to cybersecurity and regulatory compliance, and you begin to appreciate why so many liberal arts colleges are finding themselves economically challenged. To be sure, most liberal arts colleges are nonprofit organizations, designed not to be oriented toward making money. Yet they all have budgets and must generate revenues (including philanthropy) at least equal to their costs. Their leaders are all responsible for making them succeed on financial terms and must sometimes make very tough decisions. That fact jumped into the public consciousness in the spring of 2015 when Sweet Briar College, a women's college in southern Virginia that had maintained a high standard of education for more than a century, announced abruptly that it would be closing its doors following the end of that very school year. The flood of alumni donations that has since kept it afloat only amplifies the message that many schools like this do not have a sustainable business model.

It isn't only for liberal arts colleges that times are tough. Public universities certainly have their own financial woes, including the escalating costs of compliance demands, crippling pension liabilities, rising health-care costs, and reductions in state-funding levels. According to a 2016 report by the American Academy of Arts and Sciences' "Lincoln Project," state spending per full-time-equivalent (FTE) student is 30 percent lower in real terms than it was in 2000, while spending on Medicaid, by contrast, has gone up by 52 percent. Increased spending on Medicaid, K–12 education, and corrections has driven state spending on higher education to historic lows. At the extreme, Colorado spends only $220 per FTE student.[10] To make up for falling state appropriations, universities increasingly turn to other sources of revenue. Many are admitting more out-of-state and international students who can by law be charged higher tuitions—and raising out-of-state tuition rates as they do it. Naturally, allocating fewer seats to in-state applicants raises the admissions bar for them and fuels the common complaint that we are seeing a "privatization of the public universities."[11] Many schools are charging in-state students more, as well. William Bowen's observation on the current scene is that the most significant tuition hikes are being made by "the mid-level public universities," and he expects the changes to spill over to liberal arts colleges. It could be that by raising their tuitions, public universities will decrease their attractiveness relative to liberal arts colleges, although the complexity of considering all the merit scholarships and tuition discounts being offered on both sides makes it difficult to assess the true price gap between liberal arts colleges and public universities. Depending on the comparators used, the answer to how large that gap is can vary quite a bit.

It is unwise to generalize too much in any discussion of liberal arts colleges and their changing fortunes. Yet even when we look across a range of schools who have staked out very different "competitive positions" and have very different resources at their command, we can see a broad pattern of financial pressure. In the cases of three colleges I analyzed in depth—Vassar College, Wheaton College (Massachusetts), and Whittier College—there is no question that problems vary from place to place in both their type and their intensity but that all are feeling a need to change. The brief case studies below reflect my "outside-in" analysis, relying purely on publicly available data.

CASE STUDY 1: VASSAR COLLEGE

By any measure, Vassar College of Poughkeepsie, New York, counts as an elite liberal arts college. One of the oldest siblings among the famed "seven sisters" (all founded as private women's colleges in the nineteenth century), Vassar is now co-ed. During the 2014 time frame I used in my analysis, it enjoyed a robust endowment of $861 million and high demand for its roughly 2,500 places. That year, it accepted 22.8 percent of applicants. Yet even a cursory review of financial data across a five-year period (from 2008 to 2013—see table 2.1) reveals trends putting obvious strains on the school's financial model.

Note in particular that, in spite of a list-price tuition hike of more than 21 percent, Vassar's tuition and fee revenues fell, both overall and on a per-student basis, by more than 10 percent. Given that inflation during this same period was about 10 percent, this represents a reduction in real terms of about 20 percent in revenue—a dramatic reduction that translates directly to the bottom line.

How did that happen? In part because 5 percent of Vassar's students moved from paying full tuition and fees to receiving large financial-aid packages. During the five-year period, Vassar increased the average amount of grant aid per student by more than 40 percent, from $27,635 to $38,739, while increasing the mix of those receiving aid from 55 to 60 percent. In other words, 60 percent of Vassar's students received, on average, a tuition and fees scholarship offer (that is, a tuition discount) of 83.7 percent to attend Vassar in 2013. This is a lesson in how sensitive a college's economics are to shifts in the number of full-paying students. That five-percentage-point shift cost Vassar $4.8 million, essentially in profit.

Perhaps believing that level of tuition revenue to be the "new normal," Vassar clearly made a deliberate adjustment to its cost structure during this time frame by reducing the number of staff by 6.7 percent. Without

TABLE 2.1. Overview of five-year financial parameters at Vassar College

Institutional financial dimension	2007–8	2012–13	Absolute five-year change	Five-year percentage change
Out-of-state tuition and fees ($)	38,115	46,270	8,155	21.4
Revenue from tuition and fees per FTE enrolled ($)	26,866	24,134	−2,732	−10.2
Total revenues from tuition and fees ($)	66,028,651	59,083,322	6,945,329	−10.5
Endowment assets at year-end per FTE enrollment	344,489	351,860	7,371	2.1
Core expenses	136,490,699	147,002,997	10,512,298	7.7
No. of FTE staff full-time instructors	1,057 (293)	986 (279)	−71 (−14)	−6.7 (−4.8)
% of full-time, first-time under-graduates receiving institutional grant aid	55	60	5	9.1
Average amount of institutional grant aid received by full-time, first-time undergrads ($)	27,635	38,739	11,104	40.2

Sources: Data from IPEDS.

being privy to the deliberations, we can only speculate as to whether these changes were explicitly desired or not. A charitable interpretation would be that Vassar decided to provide more scholarship grants (perhaps in light of the recession following the 2008–10 global financial crisis) and voluntarily reduced its revenue from tuition and fees, even turning down very qualified students who could pay full price who would have been accepted in 2008. A different interpretation would be that the market for top students is becoming more competitive, and Vassar felt compelled to spend more money to sustain the same quality of class.

CASE STUDY 2: WHEATON COLLEGE

As clear as the challenges are to Vassar's financial model, its substantial endowment provides a strong cushion against crisis. It's useful, then, to look at a college that lacks that level of cushioning and is far more tuition-dependent in its financial model. Wheaton College of Norton, Massachusetts, is a "brand-name" college that has been producing liberal arts graduates for

TABLE 2.2. Overview of five-year financial parameters at Wheaton College

Institutional financial dimension	2007–8	2012–13	Absolute five-year change	Five-year percentage change
Out-of-state tuition + fees ($)	36,690	43,774	7,084	19.3
No. of FTE students enrolled	1,663	1,763	100	6
Acceptance rate (%)	40.5	60.2	19.7	48.6
% of full-time, first-time under-graduates receiving institu-tional grant aid year-end per FTE enrollment	68	91	23	33.8
Avg. amount of institutional grant aid received by full-time first-time undergrads ($)	18,466	23,259	4,793	26
Total revenue from tuition and fees ($)	40,838,696	38,743,342	−2,095,354	−5.1
Core expenses	57,958,109	59,712,000	1,753,891	3
No. of staff FTE	527	478	−49	9.3
Endowment assets year-end per FTE enrollment ($)	112,012	107,486	−4,526	−4

Sources: Data from IPEDS.

more than 180 years; its graduation rate of 76 percent helped it attain a 2013 USNWR ranking of 65. But at $176 million in 2013, Wheaton's endowment is only about a fifth the size of Vassar's. Table 2.2 summarizes the financial changes it experienced over the same five-year period.

During this five-year period, Wheaton increased its annual list-price tuition and fees by 19.3 percent, presumably following price increases made by higher-ranked schools. At the same time, it increased enrollment by 6 percent. Yet revenue from tuition and fees declined by 5.1 percent, because Wheaton saw its proportion of full-paying students drop from 32 percent to 9 percent. Its financial aid packages, which had extended tuition discounts through grant aid to 68 percent of students, averaging $18,466, shot up to discounts for 92 percent of students, averaging $23,259. Meanwhile, perhaps because its list-price increase produced sticker shock or perhaps due to other factors, applications fell. Wheaton, despite having reduced the actual costs to students, found itself having to become less selective in admissions. Its acceptance rate jumped from 40.5 to 60.2 percent.

Wheaton's endowment didn't cut it any slack; in fact, over the same period, assets per student declined by 4 percent. Given the change in financial in-flows, it wasn't terribly surprising when administration announced a staff cut of 9.3 percent.

Wheaton is still not a college that should be described as being in imminent danger, and again, we don't know the extent to which Wheaton felt forced by dismal economics to make the changes it did. It could be that in response to the crisis and the financial plight of many families and students, it chose altruistically to give more aid to more students, and by increasing its acceptance rate and class size it offered opportunities to greater numbers of qualified students. An alternative hypothesis is that Wheaton hoped for higher revenues from its higher list-price tuition fees and thought it could maintain its selectivity with more limited use of discounting to keep up yield rates—but that the strategy simply did not work.

CASE STUDY 3: WHITTIER COLLEGE

Stacked up against "medallion" Vassar College and "name-brand" Wheaton, southern California's Whittier College rates as a "good buy." (The terminology comes courtesy of Robert Zemsky and colleagues.)[12] Known for being, among other things, Richard Nixon's alma mater, the school has a pragmatic, self-made quality about it. Its endowment is relatively modest ($88.3 million at year-end 2013) so that it must generate tuition and fees to cover almost all its core expenses. For the academic year 2012–13, the U.S. Department of Education's Integrated Postsecondary Education Data System (IPEDS) reported that Whittier's tuition and fees covered 96 percent of its core expenses. Based on my analysis, I would hold it up as an example of a liberal arts college that has managed to move forward, grow, and improve its financial model with some deft, forward-thinking moves.

Like Vassar and Wheaton, across this five-year period, Whittier increased annual list-price tuition and fees substantially (by 28.1 percent) and deepened its discount rate (from 27.8 to 47 percent). But as table 2.3 details, the change translated very differently to the bottom line. Net tuition and fees per student increased by 16.7 percent—and because Whittier also increased its number of full-time enrolled students by 43 percent, its total revenue from tuition and fees rose an impressive 49 percent.

Whittier was able to do this without much change in its selections standards (its acceptance rate rose from 61.1 to 63.6 percent) because it managed to increase applications to the school by 70 percent. At the same time,

TABLE 2.3. Overview of five-year financial parameters at Whittier College

Institutional financial dimension	2007–8	2012–13	Absolute five-year change	Five-year percentage change
Out-of-state tuition + fees ($)	30,160	38,640	8,480	28.1
Average tuition discount rate (%)	27.8	47	19.2	69.1
No. of FTE students	1,186	1,695	509	43
Revenue and fees per student FTE	21,469	25,047	3,578	16.7
Total revenue from tuition and fees ($)	38,819,824	57,828,918	19,009,094	49
Core expenses ($)	49,522,173	60,438,599	10,916,426	22
No. of FTE staff	373	456	83	23.3
Endowment assets year-end per FTE enrolled ($)	42,578	38,487	−4,091	−9.6

Sources: Data from IPEDS.

Whittier increased its endowment from $77.1 to $88.8 million, although its enrollment of more than five hundred additional students meant its endowment per student dropped by almost 10 percent. Rather than having to cut core expenses and staff levels, Whittier was able to increase both by more than 20 percent and still substantially increase its operating margin.

While this quick review of public data doesn't tell us how Whittier achieved these results, it is unlikely that it simply got lucky and benefited from demographic shifts or an increasing desire to study the liberal arts in California. More probable is that it explicitly pursued a growth strategy involving new investments in marketing to reach well-targeted applicant pools, and perhaps larger admissions budgets to allow for new people, tools, and training. What is clear is that Whittier College has proven that it is possible to grow revenues, increase margins, increase applicants, and hold the line on selectivity at a liberal arts college during a sharp economic crisis.

THE THEMES THAT weave through these three institutions' finances— expenses rising above the rate of inflation; tuition prices rising well above the rate of inflation; rampant tuition discounting; endowment dependency and volatility challenges at the wealthy schools; tuition dependency at others—surfaced over and over again in my interviews with college presidents.

They are equally true for many business schools, law schools, and public and private universities. John Fry worried that among liberal arts colleges, "the only business model that works is the Williams model, which is: you have a gigantic endowment." He was referring, of course, to Williams College, whose 2014 endowment of $2,253,330 puts it at or near the top of the most richly endowed liberal arts schools. Fry added the caveat, however: "The only problem with that is if you have a 2008"—that is, a stock market crash that materially damages the endowment with investment losses and leaves the college short of operating income.

Lawrence Schall succinctly declared that, for most liberal arts college presidents, their current business model simply "doesn't work—it's brutal." His school, he admitted, was "in the merit scholarship game hugely, as is everyone else," and he knew of others resorting to greater than 50 percent discount rates. That tuition-discounting model not only "has its limits," in William Bowen's understated phrase, for the colleges individually. It rolls up to a broader problem, because "the fraction of institutional aid that goes to merit aid rather than need-based aid is very high and very worrying . . . a huge mistake nationally."

Fears of Mission Drift

Economic pressures often force direct changes that, in turn, bring about indirect, and usually unintended, knock-on effects. Nowhere is this more clear than in the plummeting percentages of tenured faculty on college teaching staffs. William Bowen and Eugene Tobin, in their recent book *Locus of Authority*, document the shift, pointing out that "in 1969, tenured and tenure-track faculty accounted for over three-quarters of all faculty (78.3 percent); in 2009, tenured and tenure-track faculty accounted for just over one-third of all faculty (33.5 percent)."[13] This trend is only expected to continue, as Bowen and Tobin's analysis makes clear. While my own quantitative review of liberal arts colleges did not focus on trends within the faculty, it did document that the total number of instructional teaching staff across the 248 USNWR liberal arts colleges remained relatively stable in the five years examined.

The topic came up repeatedly in my interviews with presidents, who agreed the composition of faculty is evolving from a largely tenured group to a more diversified cadre. At the same time, administration staffs have ballooned. This was a focus of Benjamin Ginsberg's research for *The Fall of the Faculty: The Rise of the All-Administrative University and Why It Matters.* In a 2011 article in *Washington Monthly,* he notes that, from 1975 to 2005, the faculty-to-student ratio in American higher educational institutions held steady, at about fifteen or sixteen students per instructor. However, he notes: "One thing that has changed, dramatically, is the administrator-per-student ratio. In 1975, colleges employed one administrator for every eighty-four students and one professional staffer—admissions officers, information technology specialists, and the like—for every fifty students. By 2005, the administrator-to-student ratio had dropped to one administrator for every sixty-eight students while the ratio of professional staffers had dropped to one for every twenty-one students."[14] Such changes in the composition of an institution's staff do not only affect its payroll costs, of course. Much more profoundly, they change the character of the place. For one thing, the shared-governance model that has been central to so many institutions' decision making and cultures now involves only a minority of professionals on campus. Increasingly, rising administrative staff are demanding their say.

Quite separately, but also dramatically, the intensifying competition for students has set off what is known as "the amenities war." In a segment on NPR's *Marketplace* radio show, a reporter begins her story with lighthearted references to the Tempur-Pedic mattresses and granite countertops now gracing University of Kentucky dorms. Her interview with the university's Penny Cox, however, makes it clear this is not just fun and games. "If you visit places like Ohio State, Michigan, Alabama," Cox told her, "and you compare what we had with what they have available to offer, we were very far behind."[15] The same amenities race is occurring in the liberal arts colleges that compete with their larger university brethren, and it is also under way at many elite business schools. Dining halls, meanwhile, have come a long, long way from the days when they dished up mystery meat. Again, the effect of these direct responses to rising competition is, indirectly, to change the tone of the enterprise. Traditional colleges and universities did not trouble themselves to be so "customer centric" in their response to what students wished for, versus what professors thought was good, and good enough, for them.

Within the liberal arts sector, the biggest worry is that, in their quest for revenues and their eagerness to respond to student priorities, colleges are falling prey to "mission drift." As recently as the 1990s, this did not seem to be a problem. Breneman in 1994 argued that one of the more admirable and interesting aspects of liberal arts colleges "is their commitment to their central educational missions . . . and [refusal] to shift curricula toward more immediately marketable technological or vocational subjects." He foresaw, however, that they would come under increasing pressure to add more career-oriented majors and programs.[16]

Two decades later, there is no question Breneman was right. Robert Zemsky observes that "liberal arts colleges, . . . in substantial numbers, have survived by becoming something else: comprehensive master's degree institutions with a growing array of professional programs requiring advanced study and specialization."[17] Victor Ferrall offers data documenting the shift: "In 1986–87, more than half of the 225 liberal arts colleges had more than 90 percent liberal arts completions. . . . In 2007–2008, the number of colleges with more than 90 percent liberal arts completions had dropped by half (to less than 25 percent). Over the same period, the number of colleges with 30 percent or more vocational completions increased from 33 to 118."[18] This mission drift is important as it strikes at the heart of a college's value proposition and what it means to various constituents. As Matthew Hartley points out in his research on three liberal arts colleges' mission changes over time, "mission matters to members," and by extension to all stakeholders of an institution.[19]

Everyone seems to agree that the classic liberal arts college mission is still vital. For centuries, studying the liberal arts has changed the lives of countless students. In these cloistered environments, they discover their passions for learning in general and for new subjects in particular. They learn how to learn, mastering critical-thinking techniques. They mature socially and intellectually through an intense but intimate residential experience, guided by committed faculty who care and know their students' names. As John Fry, former president of liberal arts college Franklin & Marshall (and current president of Drexel University), put it to me, "the gift that is given in these places is amazing."

Keeping colleges focused on that mission not only benefits individual learners; it also would appear to be a boon to society. As Victor Ferrall notes, even though liberal arts students "represent no more than 1 or 2 percent of total US higher education enrollment, for two centuries tiny liberal arts colleges have produced a . . . large percentage of leaders. Their graduates have been and continue to be at the forefront in every field."[20] Loren Pope agrees, writing that liberal arts colleges "have been on the cutting edge for decades. . . . They have outperformed most of the Ivies and their clones in the percentages of graduates who become America's scientists and scholars."[21]

New, Nonfinancial Pressures

After so much time spent in this chapter exploring how the context has changed for colleges and universities in competitive market and financial terms, it might seem abrupt to return to the kinds of shifting sands referenced at the beginning of this chapter—the changing societal expectations that rattled Swarthmore and the potent activism that toppled the leadership of the University of Missouri.

Such changes are harder to quantify and therefore to research in a comparative fashion, but of course they are no less challenging for institutions and their presidents. When the author of the American Council on Education's seventh annual (2012) report in the American College President Study series summed up the biggest problems confronting today's leaders, he not only cited "ballooning enrollments, escalating fiscal pressures, [and] the change engines of technological advances." He also pointed to the difficulty of dealing with "a wide array of constituents, and a tumultuous political climate"—which "make it more important than ever for college and university presidents to understand and be responsive to their communities and the contexts in which higher education takes place."[22]

Recent events at Trinity College, in Hartford, Connecticut, show how difficult that can be. In 2012, the liberal arts college's then president, James F. Jones Jr., decided that the right response to growing social disgust with fraternities—long blamed for increasing levels of alcohol abuse and sexual violence, as well as being inherently gender-discriminatory—was to force Trinity's Greek houses, both male and female, to go co-ed. There is a reason Jones is the former president (and the chairman of the board of trustees, Paul Raether, who agreed with him, stepped down as well); the change created a furor not only among powerful alumni but across fraternity and sorority networks nationally. Jones's successor, Joanne Berger-Sweeney, promptly reversed the decision as one of her first official acts after taking office in 2015.

Or consider the situation that played out in 2015–16 at Hope College in Michigan. Here, the controversy brewed over how tolerant this religiously affiliated school should be of people whose views on sex and marriage don't align with conservative Christian belief. The push by Hope's president since 2013, John Knapp, for greater tolerance put him at odds with some powerful, fundamentalist board members. It was no secret that his job was in jeopardy as a result. On the bright side, he had the very rare pleasure of seeing a quad full of students and professors chanting for him to stay. Ultimately, the board chair resigned in May 2016. One wonders if President Knapp's early career training as a crisis management consultant to corporations is part of what enabled him to weather the storm.

Perhaps it is not the case that the expectations of a college's various stakeholders are so different than they have been in the past. What has surely changed is a leader's ability to fall short of those expectations in any way and have that shortfall go unnoticed and unremarked. Over the past decade especially, there has been a dramatic change in the transparency of institutions' activities, decision-making processes, and impacts. Unprecedented access to information allows every misstep to come to light, and social networking sites, the proliferation of devices connected to the Internet, and the Freedom of Information Act (or FOIA) for public institutions (which allows virtually all e-mails of any university leader to be examined by virtually anyone at any time upon demand) ensure it will be magnified 24/7/365 at the speed of a few clicks.

This forced transparency in turn fuels expectations of ever-greater, voluntary transparency by institutions. In 2016, for example, at the University of Iowa (UI), a full-scale rebellion emerged over the hiring of a very nontraditional president, the former IBM and Boston Market executive Bruce Harreld. Faculty members have said many disparaging things about Harreld and his lack of academic experience, but their greatest statements of outrage involve accusations of backroom deals. A faculty organization (the UI chapter of the American Association of University Professors) issued a statement deploring what it called the Iowa Board of Regents' "preconceived determination" to hire Harreld, flouting its shared-governance tradition. "In retrospect," it said, "it is clear that the assurances of fairness and transparency in the hiring process given to us by the regents, the chair of the search committee, the search firm, and the Faculty Senate leadership were untrue."[23] In the full report the AAUP issued on Harreld's hire, it claimed that "the search was structured and engineered by the regents' leadership from the outset to identify a figure from the business world congenial to its image of 'transformative leadership.' Once such a person was identified, the rest of what followed was only an illusion of an open, honest search."[24]

I caught a glimpse for myself of how extreme the nonfinancial pressures on a higher education leader can be, during my application process at the

University of Virginia. In my final interview round in December 2014, I found myself in UVA president Teresa Sullivan's office at the moment when the news arrived that *Rolling Stone* magazine would retract its sensational story on campus rape, which centered on an alleged incident at UVA. Having navigated through camera crews camped outside Madison Hall, I encountered armed police officers ominously standing guard outside the president's wood-paneled office door. The ringing of telephones was incessant. I am grateful President Sullivan found any time to spend with me, as it appeared to me that this issue that had captured the interest of the nation had hit like a hurricane, amassing huge energy and demanding intense attention. Her grace and integrity under pressure impressed me, and also impressed upon me just how rapidly a leadership context can morph due to events totally beyond a president's control. "We don't get to choose our adversity," Sullivan would later tell a journalist from *Fortune*.[25] And that goes for schools in general, whether they are led by traditional or nontraditional presidents. (President Sullivan is a traditional president, formerly provost at the University of Michigan.)

Challenged by the Change

Depending on the time scale selected, trends take on a different hue. Given their resiliency as iconic institutions of higher education for centuries, many liberal arts colleges have enjoyed long-term stability that would make a normal business flush with envy. But change has been dramatic over the long term.

To be sure, it is hard to generalize. Treating liberal arts colleges as a group masks important variations that exist among institutions. Liberal arts institutions are far from homogeneous. When liberal arts colleges are comparatively analyzed by examination of institutional characteristics such as geography, religious affiliation, graduation rates, selectivity, size, ranking, and financial characteristics such as endowment, price, or expenses, it becomes clear that there is no such thing as the typical liberal arts college and that there are wide variations on each variable. Using 2008 data, Victor Ferrall explored several of these dimensions and clearly portrayed many of the variations.[26] In some ways each institution can be looked at as a segment of one.

Yet, while today's 248 stand-alone liberal arts colleges vary dramatically in their particulars, as an overall group they are similarly challenged. The context changes described in this chapter create new and pressing problems for traditional institutions—and for the people responsible for leading them. The contextual perceptions and experiences of the liberal arts college presidents I interviewed are nuanced, but all agree the job of the president has become more difficult. In the coming chapters, we'll look at how that increasing difficulty relates to the increasing numbers of nontraditional presidents over the past few decades.

3 | New Pressures and Pathways

R AISE THE TOPIC of "headhunters" in any gathering of college or university leaders, and the name John Isaacson is sure to come up. Founder of the 170-person executive search firm Isaacson, Miller, he has helped hundreds of them over the years connect with the institutions they lead. He is also a delight to meet—not least because, in person, he doesn't cut the buttoned-down, pin-striped figure you might expect. More likely, he's wearing a Harris Tweed. Definitely, he's sporting an impressive gray beard—which, combined with his pronounced Maine accent, gives him a gruff, grandfatherly affect. Isaacson has never had to conform to any slick image already set for higher-ed executive recruiters. As one of the pioneers of his field, he's an original.

In his evaluations of candidates, too, he makes a lasting impression. When I met him, we weren't too far into our conversation before I found myself telling him about my grandmother. He must have asked; it's a good way of getting a sense of a person's values and who they are when they're just being themselves. Inquire into Isaacson's own family history and you get a sense of why a Dartmouth-educated Rhodes Scholar, with all the options in the world, would choose the profession he did. His father, as a soldier from Maine in the Second World War, helped to liberate a concentration camp—and among the people interned there was the woman he would marry, Isaacson's mother. The boy grew up hearing how they both came to be in that awful place, and learning how much it matters who makes their way into leadership positions. Isaacson has dedicated his life to ensuring great leadership in the institutions that educate our society.

Today, Isaacson himself is part of a small army—one that also includes David Bellshaw, Anne Coyle, Ken Kring, Ellen Landers, Sue May, Shelly Storbeck, Jackie Zavitch (all of whom I interviewed in my research), and many, many others. Collectively, the firms they represent now conduct a substantial portion of college and university presidential searches. This marks a sea change over just a few decades. Until the 1980s, candidates almost all emerged from the same well-recognized, narrow pathway; few boards felt they needed professional assistance to find them. We have moved from an era when there were virtually no search firms used, to an era when practically no searches are done without them.

As we move into a chapter exploring the new pathways to the presidency in higher education, we should of course be clear that headhunters aren't the only new feature on the landscape. Candidacies are being reshaped much more generally by rising job demands, thinning talent pipelines, shifting board priorities, and other factors. Yet it makes sense to start with the rise of executive search firms. Their increasing role not only reflects these contextual changes—it also helps to drive them.

For anyone interested in studying nontraditional presidents, search firm professionals are also a great, previously untapped source of insight. Early in my research I was surprised to find no attempts by previous scholars to capture their collective knowledge. It is hard to imagine a group with a better vantage point for observing both the process by which presidents are hired and what happens to them after they take up their roles. To do their jobs well, these intermediaries must also understand the changing context of higher education and how it affects particular schools' priorities, since these will guide their drafting of presidential job descriptions. While each search executive's perspective is shaped by his or her own experience, the veterans among them have by now been involved in more than enough searches to observe true patterns in them.

The Rise of the Headhunters

In chapter 1, I recalled Cohen and March's description of the traditional pathway to the college presidency as a clear set of rungs. Originally that ascent from tenure-track faculty to department chair to provost to president tended to occur within the context of one institution. Even as trustees began looking beyond their own campuses, they relied on their members to suggest candidates, all of them still internal to what we might call the guild.

That started to change in the 1970s, as boards of trustees began seeking the assistance of two not-for-profit organizations—the Presidential Search Consultation Service and the Academy for Educational Development. Soon, as Judith McLaughlin and David Riesman document, the executive search firms that had already been established to serve corporate needs (such as Heidrick & Struggles, Korn Ferry, Russell Reynolds, and Spencer Stuart & Associates) noticed the opportunity and started serving higher education clients, as well. Indeed, McLaughlin and Riesman note, search firms flourished in at least five forms: "not-for-profit search firms, corporate search firms with sidelines, not-for-profit work, small specialty firms, and individuals who regularly or occasionally take on search consulting."[1] The emergence of these go-betweens coincided well with the increasing complexity boards were experiencing in the process of choosing new presidents. Marcus Lingenfelter notes three trends in particular that were complicating boards' work at the time: affirmative action, the need for more representative participation in the search process brought on by shared governance, and the difficulty of maintaining confidentiality given open-meeting laws and new technologies.[2]

The involvement of search consultants has grown steadily since. By 2001, the American Council on Education (ACE) study on the academic presidency was reporting their use in half of all searches by four-year colleges and universities. A decade later, the same organization reported: "The share of searches between 2007 and 2011 that used a search consultant was 80 percent."[3]

Over the decades, search firms also expanded the range of services they provided to their clients. When the Association of Governing Boards (AGB) recently compiled an "overview for board members" on presidential searches, it detailed that a search firm could help organize the search process and the search committee, help develop a position profile, assist in developing a communications plan, manage nominations and applications, provide counsel to applicants, interview references, perform due diligence checks, organize candidate interviews, and advise the search committee on developing its final recommendations to the board.[4] Ted Marchese of AGB Search sums things up when he writes, "At their best, consultants and firms lend speed, expertise, confidentiality and objectivity to a search process."[5] They got the opportunity to do all that because, from the start, they solved some basic problems.

First, they ensured that a larger slate of strong candidates came under consideration. As Sue May, of executive search firm Storbeck/Pimentel, puts it, search committees started "recognizing that you're not going to find a great president in the want ads." Neither are they confident of finding that on the premises. Susan Resnick Pierce, herself a president emerita and now an adviser to boards and presidents, notes that when a board hires a search consultant, that is most fundamentally an indication that it recognizes it needs to look outside. Beyond the board's obvious interest in "hiring the very best in the nation," it might particularly want candidates who are more diverse, offer new ideas, are not invested in the status quo, or simply don't carry the baggage of having held senior administrative positions in which they "will inevitably have made decisions that not everyone supports."[6] A 2007 survey revealed that only 28 percent of presidents had been promoted from within (and among liberal arts colleges, just 21 percent).[7]

Second, external consultants' involvement takes pressure off boards by helping to ensure that searches are consistent with "best practice" across the industry. The typical succession process has many constituents anxious to see that it is thorough and inclusive, and boards who are accustomed to exercising collegial judgment behind closed doors can be shocked by demands for transparency and rigor. Rita Bornstein has written thoughtfully about what she terms "legitimacy in the academic presidency"; she notes that a search firm "can protect a board's independence and shield it from criticism."[8] More important, she believes the president's own ability to lead is affected by how his or her recruitment to the post is perceived; a good process helps legitimize a candidate.

Hiring search consultants, however, can also raise some hackles—and seems to do so increasingly as their influence grows. In a vivid example of this, veteran recruiter R. William (Bill) Funk was recently hit with a vote of no confidence by the Florida State faculty senate. The *Chronicle of Higher Education* called it "just one indication of professors' growing skepticism about a private industry that plays an outsize role in selecting academic leaders."[9] At the 2016 annual conference of the American Association of University Professors, James Finkelstein, a public policy professor at George Mason University, presented new research on the use of recruiters in presidential searches. In case there was any doubt about his feelings, he called the presentation "Executive Search Firms and the Disempowerment of Faculty."[10] McLaughlin and Riesman were early in warning of the tensions that can result from the fact that many search consultants' backgrounds are not from the academy. "Faculty members," they note, "often view corporate search firms as belonging to the trustees' world rather than to their own."[11]

A Thinning Pipeline

With such broad knowledge of the higher education leadership context and such deep access to boards' deliberations, you might think some executive search professionals themselves would find their way to presidential roles. In the course of one research interview, I put the question directly to a top search firm executive: "Would you personally want to be a college president?" The answer came back instantly: "No way!"

That adamant lack of interest speaks to a big reason that search firms have become so integral to the process—because it isn't only consultants who shy away from today's presidencies. For many faculty, too, the presidency has lost some of its magnetic pull. Back in 1990, McLaughlin and Riesman noted this happening in more research-oriented universities. Many professors, they observed, "soon realize that it is often more satisfying and even more lucrative to be a professor than to take on the responsibilities and headaches of administration."[12] As the office becomes more demanding and far more risky for its occupants, fewer qualified candidates put themselves in the running—and colleges and universities find themselves in intense competition for top talent. "The best search committees recognize that they are both buyers and sellers," they write. "From the very outset of the process, these search committees realize the need to court candidates."[13]

There are problems of sheer numbers within the traditional talent pipeline that exacerbate the shortage. To begin with, recall the reduction in tenured faculty described earlier. Bill Bowen has compiled statistics showing colleges' and universities' ever-increasing reliance on untenured faculty to teach courses. As he put it to me in an interview, "Between two-thirds and three-quarters of faculty today are non-tenured faculty, whereas twenty-five years ago, it was the reverse." In his opinion, one of the biggest factors affecting the number of traditional candidates at the top is that far fewer professors make it onto that first rung.

Then there's the fact that the occupants of those traditional gateway roles to the presidency, the provosts and chief academic officers, are on average older than they used to be. The 2013 ACE *On the Pathway to the Presidency* survey finds an average age of fifty-seven for chief academic officers, with more than a third (34 percent) of them over sixty-one. That sixty-one-plus category constituted just 23 percent as recently as 2008.[14] Whether people are taking longer to attain these roles or choosing to linger in them longer, they're left with little time for bold new career moves.

Unfortunately, no research has quantified just how attractive the top jobs in higher education are, let alone on a longitudinal basis. We know that, in many ways, a college presidency remains a plum post; it offers the noble purpose and mission of educating the next generation, a vibrant intellectual environment and life of the mind, often the ability to live in beautiful surroundings, and the sheer prestige of leading a revered institution. Yet we know that when the American Council on Education surveyed 1,715 chief academic officers (CAOs) in 2008, only 30 percent of them said they aspired to become presidents. Authors of the report speculated: "This may be due to a lack of desire given the demands CAOs perceive as inherent in a president's job. Personal considerations are also a factor for many. However, given that the responsibilities of CAOs and presidents often do not overlap, many CAOs may feel ill-prepared for a presidential position."[15]

Search executives confirmed to me that a major trend in their work over the past decade has been a fundamental underlying decrease in the attractiveness of the presidential position. Sue May expressed the sentiment of many when she said, "It's hard to find good candidates, and there just isn't a great pipeline." Ken Kring of Korn Ferry (the search firm that attracted me to the University of Virginia) agreed: "The talent pool of traditional candidates is really not sufficient on a macro level to get the job done." Commenting on the sustainability of the traditional candidate pools, he likened the situation to "reverse musical chairs. Every time the music stops, there aren't enough [candidates] to sit in the seats." Anne Coyle of Storbeck/Pimentel agreed with this sentiment, observing, "The traditional candidate pool is . . . in decline."

Lack of time and lack of interest probably combine to keep many of those professionals parked on the doorstep of the presidency. And we might add that their current jobs undoubtedly offer more than enough challenge to keep them engaged. The ACE survey of chief academic officers revealed that they are overwhelmingly satisfied with their jobs. Many of the trends in higher education explored in previous chapters affect their work just as deeply as the president's and make constant calls on their creativity and judgment. As provosts and chief academic officers, they may be living in the best of all possible worlds: occupying jobs that are stimulating yet secure, and for which their backgrounds thoroughly prepared them. That is more than we can say for the transformed presidency.

No Longer a Sinecure

Not so long ago, the presidency was essentially a sinecure—a position that gave its holder handsome benefits in a comfortable environment. It was often a way of letting an accomplished scholar take a victory lap, and sometimes a political thank-you. In an era when higher education institutions, and especially liberal arts colleges, had strong, stable faculties and underwent only gradual change, the relative qualities of presidents had less impact. As search executive Jackie Zavitch told me, "For a long-time . . . schools just needed a caretaker at the top."

A look at a recent position description shows how much has changed. Here are the six-hundred-plus words Trinity College in Connecticut used to describe its ideal president in 2013:

THE NEW PRESIDENT WILL HAVE THE OPPORTUNITY
TO FOCUS ON THE FOLLOWING PRIORITIES:

Stewarding and raising the institutional profile and visibility of the College

Provide the intellectual leadership and integrity to inspire and achieve the College's ambitions; Strengthen Trinity's reputation as a leading liberal arts college and help define the value of a Trinity education with national and international audiences; Articulate the College's distinctive characteristics, accomplishments, and aspirations to internal and external constituencies to convey the strong value of a Trinity education; Continue the great momentum of strengthening the academic stature of the faculty and support its continued development; Expand data-driven decision making by utilizing institutional research, marketing, and communications capabilities to determine creative strategies for raising Trinity's profile; and Creatively and strategically leverage the College's resources to continue enrolling the high-quality student body for which Trinity is known.

Increasing the financial capacity and resources of the College

Strengthen relationships with alumni and diverse constituents to grow the endowment in support of Trinity's ambitious goals; Continue the tradition of attracting and closing transformative gifts for the College; Invest in advancement to enhance fundraising capabilities; and Manage resources in a fiscally responsible manner toward the College's long-term, strategic interests.

Envisioning and articulating an innovative long-range plan that builds on Trinity's rich history and traditions and affirms Trinity's distinctive location in a capital city

Build on the solid foundation already in place, consulting widely to make wise, bold, and visionary decisions for Trinity's future; Think strategically and guide and support concrete steps to achieve clearly articulated goals; Weave together the campus and community for the enrichment of both liberal education and public life; Embrace the Hartford community and participate actively in its economic development and community efforts and conversations; and Link classroom learning to the community.

QUALIFICATIONS

Trinity seeks an individual with deep enthusiasm for the College and a distinctive set of qualifications and attributes, with particular attention to the following:

Innovative, creative, and energetic leadership

Ability to bring the community together around a powerful vision of what Trinity can be, while leading the campus in celebrating its many successes; Innovative, entrepreneurial thinking, with an openness to strategic change and new possibilities, with a record for leading in new directions and spearheading groundbreaking initiatives; and Collaborative leadership style with the ability to encourage and facilitate campus-wide collaboration among diverse constituencies.

Relationship building and community engagement

Ability to engage with a passionate, global alumni body; Effective communication skills across a diverse range of constituents with the ability to build mutual respect, trust, and confidence among faculty, staff, students, alumni, trustees, and the community; Reputation for cultivating faculty as partners in shared governance and institutional decision making; and Appreciation of Trinity's urban location, enthusiasm to connect with the surrounding community in mutually beneficial ways, and understanding of the politics surrounding an urban environment.

Management, marketing, and business acumen

Readiness to lead the overall administrative and educational operation with an ability to delegate responsibility; Ability to collapse silos and facilitate a campus culture in which all members think globally about the impacts of their work on the greater institution; and Technical, fiscal, and budgetary agility.

Passionate and effective fundraising

Record of inspiring and persuading individual donors, and corporations and foundations, to financially support the College; and Enthusiasm around broadening the base of philanthropic support from a variety of constituencies and reengaging with alumni around new initiatives, visions, and aspirations.

Student-centered champion for academic excellence and rigor

Expectations of the highest level student academic performance and social behavior; and Appreciation for the values of an educational experience in a liberal arts setting.[16]

Based on this description, the ideal president would appear to be a kind of superhuman, combining the traits of distinctive visionary, CEO, politician, innovator, academic, fund raiser, and advanced-analytics marketing expert all in one package. One is reminded of the quip made to Richard Kaplowitz by a senior colleague serving on a search committee. "In the old days, it was easy," the fellow said. "We always invited our old friends to the campus. Those who were able to walk across the campus pond were interviewed."[17]

Often, the kind of glossy recruiting brochure Trinity produced betrays an unwillingness to prioritize among many diverse constituencies' hopes and expectations. (Trinity College ultimately selected Dr. Joanne Berger-Sweeney, former dean of the School of Arts and Sciences at Tufts University, for the role.) Yet its laundry list of capabilities does convey the new reality of a multifaceted job requiring a multitalented leader. And, if we were to compare it to equivalent position descriptions from a decade ago, the biggest additions would be the capabilities least likely to be cultivated in an academic career.

Start with the newly dominant focus on finding fresh sources of revenue. For a scholar whose career has been driven by research, publication, and teaching excellence, it can be a shock to discover that, at its heart, the higher education institution is just as fundamentally a business to be run; larger universities have multi-billion-dollar budgets, thousands of employees, a hospital system, and are as or more complex than many Fortune 500 companies. Recently, I talked to a president appointed to his role, at a large private university in Pennsylvania, in late 2014. (We had struck up an acquaintance when he was provost of another school.) When he asked a high-placed trustee to name the three things on which they wanted him to focus most, the answer, he said, amounted to: "fund-raising, fund-raising, and fund-raising." Not long after, I talked to the head of a prestigious European business school and asked him to name his biggest strategic priority. "Revenue growth," he replied, "by far." Whether via philanthropy, new degree formats, executive education, or online programs and certificates, finding new forms of revenue is a priority for any top business school dean or university president, including at the University of Virginia, as net tuition revenue increases from hiking tuition stagnate. Across many conversations, this has been the consistent theme, and it echoes what the American Council on Education found in the 2012 edition of its American College President Study series: "fundraising was the area presidents stated they were least prepared to address when they began their presidency."[18]

David Bellshaw of Isaacson, Miller told me that new college presidents often have their eyes opened to problems they didn't realize institutions struggled with. He recalled Mike Peters, the president of St. John's College in Santa Fe, saying, "I did not understand how much I'd have to focus on enrollment management." Questions like, "What's my discount rate? Do I have the candidates? Do I have the class and diversity? Do I have the retention rates?" are matters with which they never had to concern themselves in the past.

A new president emerging from the traditional academic pathway might also be surprised at how many stakeholders beyond the faculty he or she must regularly acknowledge and address. Ann Die Hasselmo, president of the American Academic Leadership Institute, notes that the president's job "is hard; it's complicated; and it's very political—there are so many constituencies who have an interest in the institutions."[19] Many search executives share her sense that the sheer complexity of the job has increased, pointing to Title IX regulations, compliance issues and lawsuits dealing with federal regulators, and increased needs to communicate with diverse stakeholders. Between the fund-raising imperative and the need to balance these competing and conflicting demands, the presidency has transformed into a role that is more outside- than inside-facing. Listen, for example, to how one newspaper described Rebecca Chopp's first year as chancellor at the University of Denver, the role she moved to from Swarthmore: "Chopp's first year at the university included a meet-and-greet process on a massive scale as she racked up 18,000 frequent-flier miles talking to alumni, met scores of civic leaders, became a fixture at galas and visited faculty, staff members and student groups to bond with the school and the city."[20]

Reading that passage was, for me, like a glance in the mirror. By the end of my own first year as a dean, I had interviewed all seventy-plus faculty members of the Darden School in one-on-one meetings that ranged from one to four hours each. I racked up more than one hundred thousand frequent-flier miles; made seventy-five formal speeches; attended dozens of alumni, admissions, press, alliance and fund-raising events all over the country and in Asia, Europe, Latin America, and Africa; had half my school's students to my home; led a multiplicity of board meetings; led faculty meetings and made tenure decisions; delivered multiple guest lectures with students and created three courses I taught in my second year; wrote this book; participated on a doctoral dissertation committee; crafted a facilities master plan and strategic plan; met federal and state stakeholders; and attended university-wide functions and panels with the president and provost in the United States and abroad. The good news is, I enjoyed it. My sense is that this level of intensity is nothing out of the ordinary for a higher education leader.

More than anything, today's presidents are confronted with the need to reinvent whole business models. Imagine, for example, if you had Dennis Hanno's job as the new president of Wheaton College. Recall the case study from chapter 2 that showed Wheaton's financial position trending in an unfavorable direction. Given the staff reductions that have just taken place, further expense reductions may be difficult, meaning the financial challenge for Wheaton's new president is likely to involve substantial fund-raising—as well as improvement of the admission marketing model, among other changes to curriculum, programs, and facilities. Perhaps that is why his experience as Babson's business school dean appealed to Wheaton.

Search firm consultants see clearly how the traditional institution is being stressed by financial trends: expenses rising above costs, list-price tuitions rising well above inflation, unsustainable discount rates, endowments under pressure, stagnating or shrinking net revenues for many, and challenging demographics leading to flattening student demand. Jackie Zavitch bluntly summed things up: "The financial model just doesn't work. Escalating costs, the research burden, the cost of producing research that doesn't make any money, is a hard job for schools. They bring in tuition, discount it a lot . . . the whole thing is spiraling upward in a really scary way."

That would be daunting enough, but the situation becomes even less appealing to would-be presidents when they realize that enacting any fundamental change will require them to go to trustees and say difficult things. They might, for example, need to advocate for lower-cost alternatives to traditional classroom teaching, or propose giving no raises for faculty. Few people relish being in roles that make them bearers of such bad news.

Finally, for someone hoping for a comfortable life as a "caretaker," it may be a rude awakening to realize the loss of privacy that comes with the top job—and how easily a misstep caught on a cell phone video can come back to haunt a leader. David Bellshaw explained, "Presidencies are becoming more and more detrimental to one's reputation given the advent of the Internet, the blogs, the democratization of knowledge and communication." In particular, he said, if "the faculty go rogue on you, it is amazing how they can undermine you in a heartbeat." Some presidents feel they live their life under a microscope. Shelly Storbeck recounted a conversation with one leader acutely aware of the scrutiny that comes with her on-campus residence. "I don't know how *you* dress to go get the mail at the end of your driveway," the woman remarked, "but let me tell you how I dress: I put on my pumps and my pearls every time."

Although I can assure you that I don't put on pumps and pearls, life as a dean also involves being under the microscope in ways I never suspected. One Saturday morning early in my tenure I went incognito, which is to say very casually dressed, to the incomparable Marie Bette, a new French patisserie in Charlottesville. I ordered a kouign-amann pastry—a buttery, calorie-laden Breton delicacy rare to find outside of Brittany, except at prestigious Parisian bakers such as Ladurée on the Champs-Élysées. When I showed up on the Darden Grounds the next week, several people asked about my experience at Marie Bette; I was amazed that this was noteworthy.

One weekend in August I disappeared to Maine to write several speeches I needed to make. It was stifling hot in Charlottesville, I wanted to get out of the limelight, and I felt the Maine sea breeze would inspire me to write prolifically—which it did. To take a small break I went to the Blue Hill Country Club—a tiny club not far from Acadia National Park with three clay courts—to play tennis with my son Benjamin, who was preparing to compete for a slot as a freshman on the Trinity College tennis team. The club was practically empty, as most members sail on breezy, blue-sky afternoons. However, when I walked out on the tennis court someone yelled, "Dean Beardsley!" Of all places, two different University of Virginia alumni, one from Darden, happened to be there and had recognized me. Whether it is the type of car I drive, my choice to wear a tie or not, where I buy my coffee, or to whom I talk, it is clear that my actions are being noted, and this seemed even more the case in the search process. I don't and didn't really mind, however, since from the beginning I have vowed just to be myself—and luckily I am fairly extroverted, truly enjoy the intellectual environment and faculty, and love talking to students and passionate alumni. Higher education leaders perform their roles in an environment much like the one Thomas Jefferson imagined for his "Academical Village": interaction is intense, degrees of separation are tiny (everyone you meet always knows someone you know), the gossip grapevine is highly efficient, and secrets are hard to keep. It's just life in a small town.

Churn, Churn, Churn

Add another major factor to the mix, and the problem of filling presidential positions starts to look like a perfect storm. Not only has it become a more demanding job with a thinner pipeline of traditional talent (shrinking not only the pool of people who can do it but the number who are interested), it is also a job category that now has more openings to fill. This is not due to an increase in the number of institutions; it is because, as Sue May puts it, "there's more turnover and presidencies are shorter."

In the same way that the tenure of CEOs in the corporate world has declined during the past two decades, it appears that higher volatility and shorter terms have come to academe. Some of this is due to involuntary departures, as rising job requirements lead to more executives falling short. When Trachtenberg, Kauvar, and Bogue studied turnover among college, university, and system presidents during 2009 and 2010, they found that fifty of them "resigned, retired prematurely, or were fired."[21] Much of the term-shortening, however, comes down to demographics. Whereas, at the beginning of the twentieth century, the mean age of a president was thirty-eight years old, the presidency has aged substantially since.[22] As the ACE 2012 American College President Study report explains: "Two decades ago, the average age of college and university presidents was 52. Today, it is 61. In fact, in 1986 just 13 percent of presidents were over the age of 60. In 2011, 58 percent of presidents are over 60."[23] The ACE report authors go on to speculate that this aging of the office might be a result of postsecondary institution's becoming more complex organizations to lead. "As colleges and universities face a growing number of internal and external challenges, governing boards and search committees are likely looking for more experienced lead-

TABLE 3.1. Distribution of tenure in office of 2014 liberal arts college presidents

N = 248	Tenure (years)
Mean	6.2
Median	4.6
Range	0 to 46

Sources: Data from author database compiled from Internet searches; USNWR Compass 2014 data.

ers," they write. Whatever the reason, the effect of presidents' appointments at more advanced age is that they have less time to spend there. ACE also found in 2011 that, over the course of the past five years, the average tenure of presidents had decreased by over 20 percent—dropping from 8.5 to 7 years.

My own data set finds this phenomenon playing out even more dramatically within liberal arts colleges. Given the difficult context facing many liberal arts college presidents, I had hypothesized that their tenure might be shorter than the average college or university president. This turns out to be the case. As shown in table 3.1, the average tenure of a 2014 liberal arts college president is just 6.2 years.

To be sure, there is quite some variation in the distribution. While forty-nine presidents, or about one-fifth of the group, had been in office only a year or less as of June 2014, there were also many who had been in office for more than a decade. At the extreme, Norman Francis of Xavier University in Louisiana was marking his forty-sixth year as president (he since announced his retirement). But the majority of 2014 liberal arts presidents had been in office 4.6 years or less.

The fact that the baby boom generation has now entered its retirement years also does not bode well for the demographics of presidential successions. With roughly ten thousand boomers retiring daily from 2010 through 2029, and a substantially smaller cohort coming up behind them, it is hard to imagine that colleges and universities will find a new generation of leaders as plentiful as the last one, or have less need for executive search firms.

The rise of search firms is a result, to some extent, of this greater churn in presidential ranks. But conversely, it is also undoubtedly a contributor to it. As highly networked intermediaries, search firms increase the mobility of professionals and the efficiency of talent markets. Experienced search consultants know the leaders who are succeeding in their roles, many of whom they have met, if not placed, in past search assignments. They regularly persuade people with good jobs to leave for even better jobs—thereby creating new holes to fill. Meanwhile, because they can be relied upon to assemble a field of strong candidates, they effectively make it easier for boards to oust sitting presidents whom they perceive to be falling short. Search professionals frequently bemoan the fact that the demand for excellent presidential candidates exceeds the supply, but of course that is the situation that justifies their involvement. They have helped to create it—and by increasingly expanding their searches beyond the traditional pipeline, they are helping to solve it.

Paving the Way for Nontraditionals

For nontraditional candidates, the pipeline problem we've been exploring represents an opportunity—a door cracking open to the possibility of their being seriously considered. Jan Greenwood, founder of the search firm Greenwood/Asher & Associates, told *Inside Higher Ed*, "Because demand exceeds the supply of traditional candidates, we see search committees rethinking what is 'acceptable' and what is best for their own institutions."[24]

It is not a coincidence that the clear trend toward greater search firm involvement since the 1980s coincides with the rise in nontraditional presidents, no matter how they are defined, over the same period. Another key way that search firms have contributed to trends in higher education leadership is by making it more possible for nontraditionals to be considered, and to be selected.

To be clear, search firms have no general bias in favor of nontraditional candidates. If anything, they must have the opposite, since their goal is to fill positions as quickly as possible with leaders who will be embraced by their clients—and those clients are, more often than not, biased toward the traditional model. Nontraditionals represent a harder sell, and a longer one, as well as posing more risk that, if the hire turns out to be a bad one, the consultant's judgment will be questioned. They are beholden to the search committees that hire them, and the search committees generally represent a rainbow of stakeholder groups from administration, to faculty, to students, to alumni and trustees. Among these, it is often easier for nontraditional candidates to connect with trustees, and a major hurdle to win over the faculty. This was the case with my candidacy, albeit for a dean search.

At the same time, however, search firms are expected to assemble lineups of hopefuls who represent different kinds of options. Thus, especially in the early stages of a recruiting process, a consultant is likely to include a nontraditional candidate in the field, if only as a dark horse. Jean Robillard, who chaired the most recent search committee at the University of Iowa, told *Inside Higher Ed* that, from the onset of the search, regents were interested in interviewing nontraditional candidates as well as academics. Regents asked the search committee to "present them a group of candidates that are different" from one another, he said. They wanted to hear different approaches to the "challenges of higher education today," such as tuition and student accessibility. "It was very clear that was the mandate we got," he said. "They want a choice and they want a different group of people and that's what happened."[25] In this respect, nontraditional candidates are a form of diversity, a fact I pointed out to the mild surprise of the dean's diversity advisory council interviewing me, despite my being a WASP.

In the case of some consultants, that inclusion might be accompanied by some valuable advice to the nontraditional candidate, or even coaching. That was certainly my experience, particularly when I would ask for help or perspective. For instance, I asked Sue May for feedback on my CV after a failed search, suspecting I was struggling to convey my experience in terms most relevant to academe. She urged me to remember that while McKinsey valued client impact and productivity, higher education valued shared-governance experience, knowledge, and an understanding of the classroom and higher education trends. She encouraged me to rework my CV into different sections such as Knowledge; Shared governance and board experience; Fund-raising/securing financial resources; and Learning/executive education. She also urged me to highlight more the higher education pro bono work I had carried out for Husson University, and the "faculty" roles I had played in McKinsey's leadership development program. It was exceptionally helpful, constructive feedback that I fully implemented.

Search firms might also persuade the client institution to be open-minded about the possibility of a nontraditional leader. A consultant might, for example, make a point of mentioning where nontraditionals have succeeded elsewhere. (In my case, Korn Ferry's Ken Kring, who did my search, had previously placed a colleague, Bernie Ferrari, as dean at the Johns Hopkins Carrey School of Business, an experience that gave him familiarity with a profile like mine.) Search firms, as mentioned earlier, are well positioned to see the challenges faced by many colleges and universities and to think objectively about the leadership qualities those situations call for. Many see the logic for choosing a nontraditional president, and in particular—given that many schools have budgets and endowments in the tens and hundreds of millions of dollars (or, in the case of public universities, billions)—one with proven skills at running a business unit or corporation.

Anne Coyle is one such consultant. "Functional areas have become more professionalized," she noted, and that calls for "a president who is much more like a CEO of a company, running a business, than a dean of faculty or the leader of academics." The top job has become much more focused on money-raising and marketing conundrums such as how to attract more "whole tuition paying" students, she observed. Like it or not, she added pointedly: "I think the old days, when the college president could just be an uber-academic and Mr. Chips figure, are gone."

A New Generation Joins the Board

Sometimes, a board of trustees is willing to take a nontraditional candidate more seriously because its own composition has changed.

In a contributed chapter to *Remaking College: Innovation and the Liberal Arts,* search consultants Susan Frost and Shelly Storbeck explore trends in higher education governance catalyzed by the recession of 2008, technological discontinuities, and geo-demographic changes resulting in budget deficits, aid cuts, and rising competition for students and philanthropy. Among these trends, they point to a "growing culture clash" on higher education boards as a new generation begins to arrive on the scene. Many of the newest members have attained success at a young age by being successful entrepreneurs and venture investors. Frost and Storbeck note: "Although many of these young leaders have only a few years of experience governing a college or university, they feel strongly about how institutions should change and how that change should be managed. For the most part, they do not favor the collaborative, incremental approaches that are a hallmark of the academy, but they prefer to move quickly to apply strategies that worked in their business ventures."[26] They go on to say that business types like these younger board members are also making their way into the presidential ranks, bringing more commercial practices with them and "often clashing head-on with more traditional faculty decision-making practices."

One thing that goes unstated here, but seems implied, is that this new generation is also made up of "digital natives," who believe in the power of technology to transform how work is done and have come to expect "disruption" of every kind of incumbent institution. In the nontraditional candidate, a technology-savvy board member might see a greater chance of such a threat being countered.

In my own conversation with David Greene, the nontraditional candidate Colby College chose to be its president in 2014, I heard real enthusiasm for greater reliance on technology. "If you can't charge a $50,000 per year price tag," he stressed, "then you're going to have to have larger classes, you're going to have to use technology to deliver education . . . [to] drive costs down." But productivity wasn't the only benefit he saw. He also pointed to the promise of big data, which he could envision making it possible to assess the true impacts of liberal arts educations. Using publicly available information from LinkedIn or Facebook, for example, to track alumni careers longitudinally could prove to be "game-shifting in the way that places are understood."

Thinking like this is bound to be more valued by a board more attuned to the transformational power of digital technologies—and perhaps less likely to be found in presidents whose entire careers have been spent in scholarly work relatively untouched by technology. Thus nontraditionals may owe some of their rise to the changing membership of boards, and to an ivory tower that, as *Trusteeship Magazine* put it, "has been wired, wi-fied, and moved to the cloud."[27]

More or Less Powerful

For the many reasons already discussed in this chapter, it is becoming more difficult for higher education institutions to identify and hire the talent called for in the president's office. That might not be such a problem if presidents were mainly figureheads and lacked the opportunity to make much difference to their institutions. It is a problem, however, in an era when the actions of the president are pivotal.

There has long been disagreement as to whether the role of president is very important. Michael Cohen and James March (in *Leadership and Ambiguity*) argue that presidents are more symbolic than significant. On campuses dominated by faculty, they "occupy a minor part in the lives of a small number of people" and "have some power, but little magic."[28] Presidential power, they point out, is held in check by the natural constraints of shared governance and loose organizational structures bordering on anarchy. When Robert Birnbaum took a whole-systems (or cybernetic) view of "how colleges work" in 1988, he came to the same conclusion: "Leaders in higher education are subject to internal and external constraints that limit their effectiveness and may make their roles highly symbolic rather than instrumental."[29]

At the other end of the spectrum we would find, for example, James L. Fisher, author of the 1984 book *Power of the Presidency.* In it, and its 1996 follow-up *Presidential Leadership,* coauthored with James Koch, can be found an emphatic case for leaders who are (in the language of leadership theory) *transformational* and not simply *transactional.* The latter types operate purely by consensus and are generally able to avoid crises under their watch. "Their institutions, however, acquire inertia and slowly, incrementally garner the reputation of being dead in the water," write Fisher and Koch. By contrast, as they demonstrate with ample empirical evidence, presidents with vision, entrepreneurial courage, and the charisma to engage others "make a difference, and are capable of transforming their institutions."[30]

McLaughlin and Riesman, while giving both of these camps their due, come out in support of the notion that a college president can make a difference. "There are a significant number of presidents who do change the course of colleges or universities they head," they conclude.[31] Indeed, when Matthew Hartley did the case research that became the core of his book *Call to Purpose: Mission-Centered Change at Three Liberal Arts Colleges,* there was no mistaking the impact of the schools' leaders, good and bad. Especially in times of turmoil when colleges needed to reconcile their core values with changing circumstances, some presidents were more able than others to present a compelling vision or create the venue for its development. The strongest individual presidents managed to raise their institutions to positions of truly national prominence.

Some see the power of the president growing as the number of tenured faculty declines and their power in the shared-governance model erodes. If it's true, this only raises the stakes on the selection of a president being a good one. The more difference a president makes, the more damage can come from a bad choice. Stephen Joel Trachtenberg and his coauthors begin their book *Presidencies Derailed* on this cautionary note: "A derailed presidency can undermine an institution's image, destroy campus morale, and cost millions of dollars."[32] Even quiet failures are expensive, given the high cost of what should have been an unnecessary search. One researcher, James Turpin, found presidential searches ringing up expenses in excess of $1 million.[33]

Managing to Succeed

Presidential searches among the more than 5,200 Title IV degree-granting higher educational institutions in the United States now exceed four hundred per year, with no indication that the steady rise in that number will stop; add to that dean and provost searches, which often compete for some of the same candidates, and the number of annual searches for senior leaders must be approaching a thousand. Each of these situations is unique, but across hundreds of them, common themes can be noted. The work of the leader is growing more complex, and more consequential. Candidates must bring a combination of "hard" and "soft" skills to the task of reconciling urgent economic imperatives for change with powerful faculties' habits of deliberation and passion for tradition. Traditional talent pools are evaporating, as the ranks of tenured faculty are reduced and high-ranking academic officers display less appetite for the top job. And the costs of poor presidential selections have risen, as leaders are increasingly pulled into the public spotlight and scrutinized as the embodiment of their institutions.

Little wonder that colleges and universities increasingly call on professional help to fill these positions. And perhaps it is inevitable that those searches will increasingly bring nontraditional candidates into consideration, and that the number of presidents with nontraditional backgrounds will continue to rise.

It also seems safe to say, however, that nontraditional candidates would not be making the inroads they are if they were broadly perceived to be failing. Sometimes it can appear that way. Traditional biases often reassert themselves when a presidency does go off the rails. If that ousted president came into office via a nonacademic pathway, observers are quick to conclude that must have been the problem—that the president lacked the cultural sensitivity or respect for mission to lead effectively. When was the last time an article profiling a failed presidency concluded it was the result of the president's "traditional" pedigree? Yet by raw numbers, most failed presidencies involve leaders who did climb the traditional rungs—and no such broad-brush statements are made about their shortcomings.

Can we say that nontraditionals are enjoying greater success than traditional leaders? We cannot. But neither can it be said they are doing worse. The signals in the data are mixed. My research shows nontraditional leaders enjoying longer tenures on average than their traditional counterparts, which suggests that they are performing to their boards' satisfaction—but perhaps also indicates that they are not being recruited out of their positions as eagerly. Further, nontraditional candidates are unambiguously gaining market share as a percentage of presidents, up from almost zero a few decades ago. Perhaps most tellingly, however, we can look at successions after nontraditional presidents do leave their posts. If they were generally falling short of expectations, we would expect to see a wave of reversions to the traditional model. That has not been the case. In some cases, the next president is more from the academic mold, but just as often he or she is followed by another nontraditional (see chapter 5 and, specifically, table 5.7). In the next chapter, we'll look at the attributes that many of these nontraditional presidents bring to the office, and in chapter 5, at where they are most often being given a chance to succeed.

4 | A New Breed

TO EXPLAIN THE rise of nontraditional leaders in higher education, we might well ask: What exactly do colleges and universities believe they will get from such individuals? What benefit is there to be gained from looking beyond the beaten path to the top? Talk to people in generalities and it quickly becomes clear that a set of associations tends to go along with the label "nontraditional." When people hear it, they tend to picture a managerial, corporate type—someone who was brought up through a bureaucracy that rewarded skills in cost-cutting, delegating, hiring, and firing—more likely than not in a for-profit industry. They assume an ethos grounded in market logic, inclined to define success in terms of beating competitors and enriching the bottom line. They imagine a kind of *dirigiste*, making decisions and plans on high and expecting lower layers of the organization to execute them. In other words, they summon up a caricature of a corporate CEO.

Listen, for example, to Richard Ekman, president of the Council of Independent Colleges since 2000. In a 2010 commentary for the *Chronicle of Higher Education* entitled "The Imminent Crisis in College Leadership," he expresses real concern with the growing number of colleges "being led by people who have never had direct experience in the heart of the enterprise as faculty members, department chairs, deans, or provosts":

> If the number continues to increase, the risk is that higher education will become an industry that is led by people who do not truly understand it, who view it as a commodity to be traded, a production problem to be solved efficiently, or a brand to be marketed. What makes colleges distinctive may be ignored—their role as sources of new ideas and as places where judgments about the quality of intellectual achievement are made routinely. The responsibility of higher education to prepare engaged citizens may come to be measured in only the short run, for example by how much money has been raised

in a year or how many students were recruited or graduated in a given time period.[1]

But, as we saw in chapter 1, the nontraditional category is actually a very big tent. It includes former politicians like Glenn McConnell, who served as South Carolina's lieutenant governor prior to becoming the College of Charleston's president in 2014, and public servants such as John E. Moore Jr., whose exemplary twenty-two-year leadership of Drury University followed a stint as assistant commissioner of education for the State of Missouri. In the tent is Michael Sorrell, whose experience practicing law and working at the White House evidently gave him the skills he needed to revive Paul Quinn College, and William H. Beardsley (my uncle), a former businessman who served as president of Husson University in Maine for twenty-two successful years and was acting commissioner of higher education for the State of Maine until the end of 2016. Within it, too, are managers who learned to lead in philanthropic, nonprofit, or servant leadership settings, including men and women of the cloth, like the Reverend Dr. Robert Michael Franklin Jr., past president of Morehouse College. More than anything, it includes people who have spent long careers in higher education, but not as tenure-track scholars. They might have led successful development, finance, or student affairs functions.

Indeed, the number of people entering the ranks of higher education leaders from industry is quite small. The American Council on Education survey found presidents coming directly from private business to constitute under 2 percent of all presidents in 2011, and that nontraditional presidents were far more likely to have public service or non-governmental organization (NGO) leadership backgrounds. Ellen Landers of Heidrick & Struggles was right when she told me, "The most *extreme* definition of a nontraditional president would be someone who has no university or college experience and really only comes from the corporate world." Yet this extreme is somehow the stereotype.

I've noted before how undescriptive the term "nontraditional" turns out to be. It's as if the ice-cream-loving public had collectively decided that frozen treats really come in only two flavors: vanilla and nonvanilla. Walking into a Baskin-Robbins, it would certainly be possible to assert that—but doing so wouldn't change the reality that there are actually thirty-one very different choices. The one thing the label does bring into focus is what the candidate lacks. If you're using the Cohen and March definition, that means he or she lacks a prior job as provost. By my definition, he or she lacks experience as a tenure-track professor. Either way, the term is meaningful only as a negative construction. Little wonder, perhaps, that when nontraditional presidents stumble in dealing with some challenge of the office, the mistake is immediately chalked up to their insufficient backgrounds. (The same is almost never said of traditional presidents, though they also make their share of missteps.) From the beginning, people might be expecting a failure—they have been primed to think of these leaders as lacking.

More vital than the matter of what nontraditionals lack, however, is the positive question: Is there something valuable that they tend to have? Are there traits or attributes that institutions seeking leaders find in general to be more present in nontraditional candidates than in traditional ones? In this chapter we'll look at the answers to that question offered by presidents, search executives, and scholars—and suggested by the activities and accomplishments of nontraditionals succeeding in the job.

The point this chapter will make is that, in selecting nontraditional candidates, many schools are making positive choices to prioritize certain needs, in line with the evolving challenges they face. Their nontraditional choices need not be read as signs that their institutions are being forced to settle in a fierce war for scarce talent for presidents who are less than perfectly qualified. Sometimes, where the need is for a change agent or a strategist, or where the most critical activity of the foreseeable future is better enterprise management, fund-raising, or external relations, the very best candidate for the job could very well turn out to be a product of a different path.

Many Flavors of Different

In chapter 1, we explored the widely disparate ways that scholars define "nontraditional." In common parlance by executive search firm consultants, members of the media, and leaders themselves, there are even more shades of gray, even when they are talking only about career paths. Shelly Storbeck, cofounder of the search firm Storbeck/Pimentel, told me, "I define a nontraditional candidate as someone who is in a nonacademic environment currently." Her colleague Sue May, however, expanded that to "someone who comes from outside academia, may not have a PhD, and has not spent time in academia at all." For example, by these definitions I would now be considered a traditional leader, yet quite recently I was squarely a "nontraditional." The confusion over what constitutes a nontraditional president only increases when we try to pin down what attributes they bring to the office.

It can be hard to imagine what common traits might exist across a set of people that ranges from Gwendolyn Boyd, who became president of Alabama State University after three decades working as an engineer at the Applied Physics Laboratories of Johns Hopkins University, to former White House chief of staff Andrew Card, now president of Franklin Pierce, to Lee Todd Jr., president of the University of Kentucky since 2001, and previously a senior vice president of IBM's Lotus Development Corp.

Looking for patterns, I went first to the most objectively measurable of attributes, including presidents' previous institutional ties, genders, terminal degree attainments, and college affiliations. For purposes of statistical analyses, I captured variables and markers including whether a doctorate had been earned, whether the president was an alumnus/a, whether he or she previously worked for the college or was a trustee, and whether the president had been a professor in a non-tenure-track role. (All might indicate more of an "insider" status in the academic guild than job history would betray.) I also looked at whether their immediate predecessors had been traditional or nontraditional, and at how long they had been in office. All these data are interesting to track. More important similarities, however, might well be along lines not so readily measured and compared.

For example, it might be fair to assume that nontraditional presidential candidates are more likely to have a certain intestinal fortitude as leaders, allowing them to venture more boldly into frightening territory. The evidence is in their own career moves, which have them making sorties outside their comfort zones and subjecting themselves to sometimes harsh rebuffs. Recall chapter 3's mention of the new reality of a social-media-filled world, in which presidents must live their days in a fishbowl—and David Bellshaw's comment that "presidencies are becoming more and more detrimental to one's reputation." Some search executives feel this trend benefits nontraditional candidates. Anne Coyle told me the story of a traditional president at a top liberal arts college who didn't last long after activists concerned with Title IX compliance and other nonacademic issues put the school in their cross hairs: "This leader couldn't stand the heat and had to get out." In such situations, Coyle believes, "a tough, tough nontraditional manager such as Clayton Spencer [of Bates College] rather than a pure academic could make more sense."

By the same token, nontraditional candidates might typically be more comfortable in roles that are more external-facing, having been part of the world outside academe and having cultivated networks wide enough to connect them with unconventional (for them) opportunities. This would be consistent with what Holly Madsen discovered when she observed four former lawyers turned liberal arts college presidents. In them, she found a pattern of specific skills and capabilities such as fund-raising acumen, international contacts, and an ability to raise the standing and stature of the institution. (It helped, she also noted, that legal partnerships also operate with a shared-governance model similar to the academy.)[2]

Being, by definition, not of the tenured faculty, nontraditional candidates might fairly be assumed to be more aware of and receptive to the desires of an institution's other "stakeholders." In the caricature painted by their detractors, they would be far more responsive to the financial imperatives coming from the board of trustees and the budget increase requests of administrative functions. But equally, they might be inclined to give more consideration to students and their parents, potential employers of graduates, alumni, government agencies, and civic leaders.

Finally, it seems obvious that another strength nontraditional candidates would commonly offer would be fresh perspective—and by extension, the ability to strategically question things that people raised within a scholarly tradition might take for granted. This was my perception of John Fry, for example, when he shared his thoughts on the conventional four-year undergraduate degree. Colleges are under enormous pressure to decrease students' "cost to degree," he noted, yet few are acting on what he sees as an obvious solution: "Give someone the opportunity to graduate in three years." Why send students home every summer, he asks, when they "don't want stupid summer jobs" and would rather spend those months "with their friends in the [college] community"? The fact that colleges are "following an agrarian schedule in America in 2014" goes unquestioned by most people in academic settings, but to Fry, it is nothing short of "insane."

Jackie Zavitch sees this kind of thinking as the real strength of nontraditionals. She told me: "The best candidates I've seen in the nontraditional realm are those that can challenge schools [by saying] . . . have you thought about XYZ? Here are two things I see coming, and these are ways you might address it, understanding you have all these constraints." She noted that it is difficult for any candidate to come across as "smarter than the institution" about its challenges. However, knowing what questions to ask and having a different perspective on those challenges, or knowledge of how analogous issues were faced in other realms, can be an advantage.

Strategic Skills Come to the Fore

Perhaps more alike than nontraditional candidates themselves are the reasons that boards of trustees choose to consider them as an option. Search executives agree it has become the norm in succession processes to include at least one nontraditional candidate on the slate as a form of diversity. What are they expecting to see in those hopefuls?

Of course, all depends on context, and no two searches are alike. Yet we can note that some attributes are commonly sought today that were not as salient in the past. For a quick summation of them, we might begin by quoting Bruce Rastetter, president of the Board of Regents that chose Bruce Harreld at the University of Iowa. At a press conference after the selection, he said: "What we ended up with is someone who has spent his life providing leadership in organizations that he has been a part of, in terms of collaboration, in terms of team building, in terms of reaching out to disparate groups and involving them, and developing a strategic plan on how you can get better."[3]

The *transformational* ability called for by that last phrase is surely a common need in colleges and universities facing the unprecedented challenges laid out in chapter 3. Search executives I interviewed made it clear that the institutions they see hiring nontraditional presidents are those with a greater desire for change and transformation—and the higher propensity for risk taking that implies. It may be true that traditional candidates are just as capable of it as nontraditional ones. As Richard Ekman goes on to urge in his "Imminent Crisis" piece: "Boards of trustees should resist the assumption, however instinctive, that a person who has had mainly academic experience is incapable of solving the college's problems, especially financial problems."[4] In many specific cases, leaders from a traditional background have successfully led large-scale change and are eminently qualified, capable, and the best fit for the job at hand. Yet it is also true that it is possible to rise in an academic system without ever challenging its status quo.

Lawrence Schall started his career as a lawyer specializing in civil rights litigation after obtaining his JD from the University of Pennsylvania. After a dozen years as an attorney, he shifted his career to higher education, returning to his alma mater—Swarthmore College—where he was vice president for administration. While at Swarthmore, Schall decided he would like to become a university president and completed his doctorate in higher education management at the University of Pennsylvania, where he also became an adjunct faculty member. Soon after his doctorate was completed, Schall left Swarthmore to join Oglethorpe University, a private, liberal arts college in Brookhaven, Georgia (an inner suburb of Atlanta), as its sixteenth president.

When Schall came to Oglethorpe, the institution was in such dire financial straits that its accreditation by the Southern Association of Colleges and Schools was at risk. According to the *Atlanta Journal-Constitution*, Oglethorpe was running several-million-dollar deficits on its $20 million annual budget. A mere four years later, the newspaper was reporting: "Annual applications have more than quadrupled, from about 1,000 to 4,600. The freshman class has increased from 200 to nearly 300, even as average SAT scores escalated by 50 points. Revenue has grown by 40 percent, while expenses stayed flat. Annual fund-raising more than doubled, from $2 million to about $5 million."[5]

For a liberal arts college with a modest endowment that is already dependent on tuition, finding a way to grow revenue represents a form of salvation. When I asked Schall about Oglethorpe's success in doing this, he pointed to initiatives to tap alternative sources of revenue. "We have moved into the study abroad business," he said, featuring "Oglethorpe faculty, Oglethorpe courses, Oglethorpe credit—but with a partner doing on-the-ground logistics." At the same time, the school established an English-language institute on its campus with capacity to serve 260 international students. It also leveraged some of its Atlanta real estate into a $60 million property-development project. Schall firmly believes that boards are becoming open to nontraditional presidential candidates because they want to see more strategic thinking about alternative revenue streams like these. As John Isaacson put it: "They have economic model problems they can't escape, and their faculty's power is greatly reduced. So they're going to be open to people who say we have to have different product lines."

Some search firm executives especially stress marketing acumen's becoming more relevant in presidential searches. At a high level, marketing is about defining a value proposition and positioning an offering as distinct from others in a crowded marketplace. Schall tells the story of meeting with the Oglethorpe selection committee after having heard many people in the process describe the school as "Atlanta's best-kept secret." He put the question to the group, "What's the secret?" and stressed the need to articulate just what Oglethorpe had to offer. "Unless we can be clear that there's a market," he said, "we will continue to flounder." On a more tactical level, marketing is about getting pricing right and getting the word out to prospective students. Observing that liberal arts colleges are "struggling with enrollment management every year," David Bellshaw, for example, said presidents must know to ask and answer questions like: "What's my discount rate? Do I have the candidates? Do I have the class and diversity? Do I have the retention rates?"

As more institutions run up against the limits of their traditional "business model," many too will need to find innovative ways to reduce costs. Consider the phenomenon that has come to be known as "Bowen's Law" or "Baumol's cost disease," after scholars William Bowen and William Baumol. Their work, as Bowen would later describe it, showed the "inexorable tendency for institutional cost per student ... to rise faster than costs in general over the long term." He elaborates: "The basic idea is simple: in labor-intensive industries such as the performing arts and education, there is less opportunity than in other sectors to increase productivity by, for example, substituting capital for labor. Yet, over time, markets dictate that wages for comparably qualified individuals have to increase at roughly the same rate in all industries. As a result, unit labor costs must be expected to rise relatively faster in the performing arts and education than in the economy overall."[6] Thus, for example, if a class size today is the same as in 1990, there is little if any increase in productivity, but faculty wages have risen, often above the rate of inflation.

If the current course and trajectory of tuition price increases goes unaltered, then running the clock forward to, say, 2030 results in tuition bills twice as large as they are today—in other words, easily topping $100,000 per year at many liberal arts colleges or for public universities' out-of-state tuition. One of the University of Virginia's more quotable economists, the late Herbert Stein, once made a pronouncement that later became known as Stein's Law: "If something cannot go on forever, it will stop."[7] This would seem to be one of those situations: it is simply not possible that higher education will indefinitely be able to raise fees so far above the rate of inflation. Instead, innovative leaders will make more use of blended learning (combining online and in-person instruction), shared infrastructure, pooled procurement, and other savings strategies. In line with John Fry's thinking, some schools will go to three-year degrees, much like European business schools have adopted a one-year MBA.

To state the need in broadest terms, schools must have leaders who can look at the big picture of unfolding trends and formulate a vision of the future. Here is how Bowdoin trustee John Studzinski described what that

school saw in Barry Mills, the nontraditional president (and alumnus) it selected in 2001: "When Barry returned to this small school in New England
fourteen years ago, he brought a new breadth of outlook with him as he
sought to redefine a liberal arts education for the twenty-first century. This
vision grew not just from his professional experience as a lawyer in the business world, but also from his awareness that, in this digital, globalized age,
Bowdoin needed to take a more cosmopolitan view."[8] This kind of strategic
need, says Dr. Judith McLaughlin of Harvard's Graduate School of Education, is at the heart of the growing interest in looking beyond the classic leadership pipeline. "Universities hiring nontraditional presidents are looking
for someone who will take the institution beyond its immediate context."[9]

More Strengths in Nontraditionals

If having a vision of change is important in a leader, knowing how to translate that vision into reality is at least as important to ultimate success.
Change-management skills are required to the extent that strategies have implications for institutional structures, processes, and roles. While clearly a
traditional president who has navigated change as a dean or president may
have strong experience, it may be that such skills are more prevalent in nontraditionals. While change has become a constant for all kinds of enterprises
in today's world, it may prove especially challenging to colleges that have
especially prided themselves on continuity and tradition.

Anne Coyle of Storbeck/Pimentel shared an observation about the professors on search committees she has dealt with: "Faculty in general are
change-resistant types." While she was talking about the kind of candidates they tend to support, the same might be said about them *as* potential
leaders. By contrast, the institutions that hire nontraditional presidents, her
colleague Shelly Storbeck said, "have to be risk takers." Storbeck notes that
for search committees and trustees attuned to the need to adapt, "It can't
just be about 'polishing the stone.' Those that have hunger for change and
transformation, that's the kind of institution that will very eagerly embrace
a nontraditional."

Institutions might also embrace nontraditionals for their operational
abilities to pull together highly competent cabinets and oversee the kind of
sprawling organization that now features many operational functions. This
is why Patrick Gamble, the four-star general and former Alaska Railroad
CEO appointed in 2010 to be president of the University of Alaska Statewide

System says he was hired. "I'm not an academician by trade," Gamble told *Public Purpose* magazine: "What I bring mainly is the ability to organize and run a large organization. Because not only do we have students and faculty and the education that goes on between the two, but surrounding that is the whole operating entity—with 16 campuses and three major universities—and all the mundane stuff that goes on within those small cities. I bring those kind of talents, and then a recognition and respect of the specific talents of our faculty with regard to what they can do with our specific programs."[10]

Many have noted that the job of the college president is increasingly similar to running a business unit or corporation. After all, most schools now have budgets and endowments in the tens and hundreds of millions of dollars; for many universities, the number is in the billions, with thousands of employees and a hospital system on top. As they have grown, Anne Coyle explained, "function areas have become more professionalized . . . requiring a president who is much more like a CEO of a company running a business than a dean of faculty or the leader of academics." It is hard to imagine in larger, complex university environments that business experience should be considered to be a weakness or undesirable, or that the converse, little to no business experience is deemed to be a strength or prerequisite to be a university president.

Many, too, speculate that in this context evolution increasingly favors individuals who learned to lead in nonscholarly roles and sectors. Zavitch argues: "The folks [traditional candidates] that are coming up contemporaneously through the pipeline of presidential candidates, are they really poised to take on such a complex problem? Do they even want to? You would think it's an opportunity of timing for nontraditional candidates."

Fund-raising capabilities, of course, are another must-have in the modern president. Most colleges and universities know their work to bring in more revenues for services will go only so far; to maintain access and affordability, many will become more dependent on philanthropy. Most commentators on presidential searches agree that the main strength hiring boards are trying to spot in candidates is their potential to bring resources, whether through attracting private funds from donors or extracting public funds from state legislatures or winning grant funds from research funders or better management—or, preferably, all four. If this wasn't the overwhelming priority before the 2008–10 financial crisis devastated schools' (and donors') portfolios, it became so after.

As we saw in chapter 3, the reality of a president's life is devoting inordinate attention to this activity. ACE's surveying for its American College President Study series consistently finds it is the area that occupies most of their time—and is the area they admit to being least prepared to address when they began their presidency. Often it is also a task they soon discover they dislike. Rita Bornstein begins her book *Fundraising Advice for College and University Presidents* with an 1847 quote from the president of Randolph-Macon College. In a letter to his wife, he writes of fund-raising: "This is the least agreeable of all my functions—the begging part, I mean."[11]

Do first-time nontraditional presidents tend to have more comfort and competence in fund-raising on day one than their first-time traditional president counterparts? If the individuals I have studied are representative, it would appear that many do. Here, for example, is what Barry Mills of Bowdoin told his school's newspaper: "Raising money is the closest thing to the 'thrill of the deal' that I had as being a lawyer, and it's great fun." Billionaire Stanley Druckenmiller, one of Bowdoin's wealthiest alumni, attests to how good Mills is at it. He told the same reporter that Mills "got more money out of me than any guy who's ever walked."[12] Or take Shirley Ann Jackson, who secured one of the largest gifts to a university in U.S. history ($360 million from an anonymous donor) just two years into her tenure at Rensselaer Polytechnic Institute, and met a later capital campaign goal of $1.4 billion a full nine months ahead of schedule. Asked by C-SPAN's Brian Lamb how she liked raising money, she underscored the importance of the work, then added, "And I've been pretty good at it, so it's fun."[13] It is clear that broad, sweeping generalizations are dangerous. There are both nontraditional and traditional presidents that either excel or struggle with the increasingly important job of fund-raising and securing resources, but this skill seems to have little to do with having come up through the faculty ranks per se.

On the Road Again

Fund-raising may be fun for some people and not for others—but for everyone, it entails travel. And that means hours on the job on top of a higher education leader's already packed schedule of meetings with staff, students, alumni, community leaders, board members, legislators, regulators, and other stakeholders of the enterprise. An unusually *high level of energy* would seem to be required in any viable presidential candidate.

This was a theme that emerged in my conversations with executive search professionals. They clearly see that the lifestyle of a president is increasingly difficult. Shelly Storbeck says she sees many candidates these days opting out of searches after asking themselves: "Can you tolerate not being in your own bed 150 nights a year? Do you mind giving up all of your privacy? Do you mind seven days a week?" Others commented that many qualified candidates see the lifestyles of friends who are presidents and don't want that burden. Richard Ekman, in fact, blames the proximity of faculty to their overworked presidents for the fact that the pipeline of internal talent is drying up. To encourage more of them to step up to administrative roles, he urges presidents when they are criticized for bad decisions not to "defend themselves by emphasizing how difficult and unpleasant their office is, but instead point to its complexity and satisfactions."[14] Unfortunately, that is unlikely to change the perception, much less the reality, that the presidency is, as Anne Coyle called it "just a tough, tough job."

When, after a particularly tumultuous five years at the top of the University of Texas system, the departing Francisco Cigarroa spoke with the *New York Times,* he credited "the countless hours he logged in emergency surgery, which he has continued to perform as chancellor, with giving him the discipline to stay focused on his objectives at his university system post." He told the reporter: "You have to be comfortable in an environment of tension."[15]

Along the same lines, Ken Kring told me that an important personal trait in successful nontraditional candidates "is just energy, and more specifically emotional energy." When he said that, he was thinking of the energy required to counter negative assaults, or, as he put it, "the willingness and temperament to be criticized, to be ignored, to be resisted in ways that are not familiar in nonacademic settings." But the same emotional energy might also be the key to graciousness in interactions with donors and other potential partners, even on long, jetlagged days. In a recent reminiscence about the retiring Barry Mills, a professor at the school marveled at his performance on a whirlwind trip they took together to Sri Lanka: "After he had equipped himself with some local knowledge, I observed him effectively endear the ISLE Program to administrators at the University of Peradeniya and to officials of the US embassy, including the American ambassador."[16]

The Rise of the University Dean

In a chapter otherwise devoted to the attributes of nontraditional leaders, it might seem a strange tangent to devote a few paragraphs to the rise of the university dean. The position of dean, after all, is a step squarely on the traditional pathway to the presidency. Yet their growing success in winning the presidencies of liberal arts colleges in recent years may be part of the same story as the rise of nontraditionals. (In the interests of full disclosure, I do need to repeat here that I am a nontraditional dean, and thus potentially subject to some positionality bias.)

By all accounts, deans of prominent schools are being recruited more because it is being recognized that, in a large university setting, they perform jobs that are very similar to a president's in their mix of duties, even if on a smaller scale. To the extent they are involved in not just academic issues but also fund-raising, brand management, and alumni relations, they are serving, as John Thornburgh of search firm Witt/Kieffer put it to *University Business,* as "mini presidents" already.[17]

John Isaacson explained the phenomenon to me as follows:

> The single biggest trend [in candidate pipelines] is that the American university world has moved slowly but inexorably toward revenue-centered management, in which deans are responsible for the revenue side as well as the expense side of their budgets. . . . Deans are now involved in fund-raising in rather large ways and are attentive to the product mix and how they pull in revenue . . . and highly attentive to enrollment patterns. So a dean in front of a search committee today is a completely different animal. A dean used to be far less attractive . . . [but] the real talent pool [today] . . . is the deans.

My predecessor, Dean Robert Bruner—a traditional leader who came straight from the finance faculty ranks, where he was and is known as one of the best case method teachers in the country—was highly successful and was and is beloved at Darden and beyond after his ten years as dean. So much so, that he was voted the best business school dean in the world in 2011 by Poets & Quants, a respected news website that covers the world of business education. In a recent 2017 article he penned, entitled "The Three Qualities That Make a Good Dean," he argues that the most important qualities involve "readiness, temperament, and purpose"; no mention of traditional or nontraditional. Further, he adds that "general management experience . . . high self-confidence, resilience to failure, humility, and a bias for action" as well as fit with mission and values are the most important qualities that determine a good dean. Much the same may very well be said for the college presidency.[18]

Personally, I can add the following: My own experience at the University of Virginia's Darden School of Business confirms John Isaacson's characterization of revenue-centered management. The Darden School has its own foundation, board of trustees, budget, revenue, fund-raising, hiring, faculty, and administrative functions. In short, it is highly decentralized with modest oversight provided by the university.

The link here to the rise of nontraditional presidents is the similar emphasis being placed on *external-facing duties and skills* and the evident impatience with the idea that they could be learned or grown into on the job. Growing numbers of nontraditional candidates coming under consideration, just like university deans, can be seen not as a necessary concession in a talent-scarce world but as a positive resolve to hire the people best equipped to deal with the greatest challenges institutions face today.

The Business Invasion

I noted earlier that the percentage of presidents who come straight from the private business sector without doctorates as "strangers" is quite small. The occasional appointment of a Bruce Harreld or Lee Todd might garner plenty of headlines and generate attention-getting controversy, but it remains an outlier event. This is perhaps just as well, as earning a doctorate at least familiarizes a candidate with the reality of faculty research, which remains mission-critical for institutions of higher learning.

At the same time, in another sense, the statistics on nontraditional presidents who come from strictly business backgrounds can be deceptively low. Many business-trained and business-oriented presidents are not being counted as "from business" because they learned their management chops within the increasingly administration-heavy education sector. These are the "stewards" Robert Birnbaum and Paul Umbach grouped among the traditional presidents: professionals who previously served in university functions like advancement, development, finance, and student affairs.

In a sense, the infusion of business principles and skills into the presidency has been a steady one made up of multiple streams. We could even trace it back to the 1970s and 1980s, when, while still honoring the tradition of promoting scholars to serve as *primus inter pares* presidents, universities began increasingly to draw from their economics departments. William Bowen is a prime example. His ascendancy to the presidency of Princeton in 1972 came after many years serving on its economics faculty.

The subsequent appointments of economists to the presidency have been many, including Philip Austin at the University of Connecticut (UConn) in 1996; Larry Summers at Harvard in 2001, Christina Hull Paxson at Brown University in 2012, and quite recently, Brock Blomberg at Ursinus College, a 1,600-student liberal arts college in Collegeville, Pennsylvania, in 2015. Economics is, of course, a very scholarly discipline—but it is easy to imagine that, in selecting economists, institutions hope for presidents who are able to bridge between the culture of academe and the bracing realities of succeeding in competitive markets.

Also masking the increasing introduction of business-oriented people into higher education leadership is the common practice of such individuals gaining a foothold in the academy before ascending to the top office. As the *New Yorker* notes, "the highest-profile model of someone with a business background running a university is John Hennessy, the recent president of Stanford."[19] Yet Hennessy manages to have a resume that looks very traditional: after founding the high-tech business that made him prominent, he started teaching classes at Stanford, then became chair of its computer-science department, then dean of the School of Engineering, then provost, before being selected president.

The infusion of business into university presidencies hasn't reached the point that there are many MBAs in the top offices. But, as *Bloomberg Businessweek* points out, "the shortage of MBAs among college presidents shouldn't be a surprise, since most MBAs want to be operators, not academics."[20] Even so, the numbers may be growing. Already they include high-profile leaders such as Drexel University president John Fry; Robert Fisher, president of Belmont University in Nashville, Tennessee; Tulane University president Scott Cowen; Clayton Rose of Bowdoin College; Mildred García of California State University, Fullerton; and others.

More important, the equivalent degree for educators, the master's degree (or doctorate) in educational administration, offers a curriculum that increasingly overlaps with the MBA's. Courses focus on the management of operations, including budgeting and financial, technology, and human resources management as well as theory about curriculum development or the demographics of schools. Thus, the large proportion of nontraditional presidents being drawn from the administrative ranks of colleges and universities should probably be understood as a form of business infusion. Ken Kring confirms that he has seen "an increase in candidates from senior-level staff positions in student and campus life, enrollment management, and development." With administrative staffs growing rapidly relative to faculty ranks, it is a trend that has the power to continue.

More Traditional Women

In my data crunching to discover if there were patterns in the objectively measurable attributes of nontraditional presidents, one trait jumped out more than all others. It's their gender. This finding, for which the statistics were already presented in chapter 1, raises a troubling and vital question: *Why* are nontraditional presidents less likely to be women?

Of course, there are some women, and many of their names have already graced these pages. Janet Napolitano immediately comes to mind. She joined the University of California in 2013 after a career in government, which culminated in her leadership of the Department of Homeland Security. So does Shirley Ann Jackson—who incidentally, as president of Rensselaer Polytechnic Institute, has found herself in the number-one spot in lists of the highest-paid higher education leaders.

Yet the liberal arts college data presented in chapter 1 are clear: women comprise a greater percentage of traditional presidents than of nontraditional presidents. This suggests that, if you are female and aspire to lead an institution of higher learning, you will substantially improve your chances by taking the road more traveled. The ratio of male-to-female liberal arts nontraditional presidents is 4.6:1 versus 2.4:1 among traditional liberal arts presidents.

Judith Rodin's career is a great example of the traditional path. After a short stint at New York University, Rodin joined Yale University's faculty as an associate professor. She stayed there twenty-two years, advancing through the chairmanship of the Department of Psychology and the position of dean of the Graduate School of Arts and Sciences to become provost. From that post she went on to win the presidency of the University of Pennsylvania, making her the first permanent female president of an Ivy League university. Similar trajectories could be traced in the careers of UVA's Teresa Sullivan, Harvard's Drew Gilpin Faust, the University of Pennsylvania's Amy Gutmann, and many others.

Although the cause of the unbalanced ratios is unclear, a few hypotheses can be stated. This might be a reflection of a pipeline issue of one kind or another. For example, it might be that the academy, as the traditional source, prepares a greater number of female candidates, or presents female candidates who are better prepared and/or qualified. The existence of specialized leadership development initiatives, such as HERS (Higher Education Resource Services), which focuses exclusively on preparing women for leadership roles in higher education, is no doubt important—and no equivalent to them exists to encourage and equip women coming from outside academe.

Alternatively, the pipeline might suffer from a dearth of female nontraditional candidates. This seems likely given that, as underrepresented as women are in university presidencies (26 percent), they are even rarer in big corporate CEO positions. Despite now representing fully half of the U.S. workforce, women make up only 4 percent of the CEOs in Standard & Poor's 500 index companies. In that same set of corporations, women occupy only 19 percent of the board seats. Likewise, in politics, only 19 percent of U.S. congressional seats are filled by women. (The 115th Congress convened in January 2017 with twenty-one women senators and eighty-three women in the House of Representatives.) As of 2017, there are only five women governors. Given that nontraditional candidates have usually reached high levels in their careers in other sectors before migrating to academe, this could be a plausible explanation.

Other hypotheses could focus not on the pipeline but on the selection process, in which there might be bias at one or more stage. For some reason, nontraditional female candidates might find it more difficult to be selected. As I suggested in chapter 1, perhaps it is because they are already "nontraditional" by dint of their gender, and for them also to be nontraditional along some other dimension would strain the comfort zones of evaluators too far. Judith McLaughlin recalls a time not so long ago "when I began to study presidential searches, search committee chairs often wondered aloud about whether their institution was ready for a female president." She says now that "Happily, that is no longer a question."[21] But perhaps for some influencers of the process, it is only a question that is no longer voiced.

I look forward to seeing further research on this question, which might start by gauging the available number of candidates and the success rates of nontraditional female candidates. Future research could also study whether the same phenomenon affects the diversity of nontraditional candidates along other dimensions. In 2007, Audrey Williams June wrote in the *Chronicle of Higher Education*: "The remarkable thing about the profile of the typical college president—a married, graying white man with a doctoral degree—is how little it has changed over the last 20 years."[22] As the proportion of nontraditional presidents rises, it would be an irony and a tragedy if that meant presidents looked even more the same.

Please Don't Feed the Stereotypes

In the spring of 2016, the opinion-page editors of the *New York Times* ran a multipart, online "Room for Debate" series under the heading of "College Presidents with Business Ties: Should University Presidents Have to Come from Academia?" In response, one reader posted the following comment: "The business world, and their business school graduates with their 'models' and 'formulas' have done more than enough damage to our country than warrants allowing them to continue to exert their power over our lives. It's time to give other people a chance to make our world a better place. No more lawyers, no more businessmen in charge. Time to let professionals whose training and work require temperaments and personalities who can truly collaborate with others, and work in groups."[23]

And so we come full circle to the stereotype with which we started this chapter. Blanket indictments like this betray what is truly an "anchoring bias" in many constituencies and, most dangerously, among faculty. Having noted the misstep of some business-trained president in the past, they let that initial piece of information serve as an anchor to their thinking on the matter. Subsequent observations can move their judgments only incrementally away from that first impression, if at all. In a liberal arts college setting, the greatest suspicion might be the one noted by James Edward "Jes" Staley (now CEO of Barclays), who chaired the search committee at Bowdoin College that selected the nontraditional president Clayton Rose: "The worry of many in the academy is whether a non-traditional candidate would defend the college (and the classics), or would they capitulate and allow . . . a business major?"[24] Just as often, however, the bias is self-protecting. Faculty typically worry that the arrival of a nontraditional president will mean a diminishment of their academic freedoms, tenure prospects, and shared governance of the institution.

Anchoring biases can quickly turn into confirmation biases, as already made-up minds interpret any ambiguous information in the way that confirms their preconceptions. In other words, a nontraditional president might not be as likely to receive the benefit of the doubt from the faculty. Conversely, some board members may have their own anchoring biases about traditional candidates. At the same time, however, some nontraditional presidents seem determined to perpetuate the stereotypes. By, for example, importing jargon or acronyms from the business world such as B2C customer acquisition, CRM, or balance sheet assets (instead of student admissions, retention, or development and endowment), they reinforce the bias that already exists. Even worse, they can carry over behaviors and skills that, while perhaps problematic in their previous lives, were not career-threatening. They might display too much frustration with the slowness of a shared-governance decision-making process, or too little consideration of the long-term and institutional culture and traditions, or too much orientation to the financial bottom line.

To be sure, more directive leadership is sometimes called for. Sue May's experience is that the type of liberal arts institution that hires a nontraditional is often "a college that is in crisis . . . like Birmingham-Southern, where they hired a former general at a dollar a year in salary." She was referring to Gen. Charles C. Krulak of the U.S. Joint Chiefs of Staff, who became president of that four-year, private liberal arts institution in Birmingham, Alabama, in 2011. Despite its long history of excellence (it was included, for example, in Loren Pope's *Colleges That Change Lives*), Birmingham-Southern College had found itself in financial crisis in 2010. As May sums things up, Krulak "made a lot of really tough calls in the wake of a financial aid kind of scandal there." The result was a stunning turnaround in the college's fortunes. Since May and I spoke, Krulak was elected vice chairman of Sweet Briar College's board of directors—the "rebel" board drafted by alumnae to replace the entire board (and president) that had previously decided to close the college forever. Evidently, Krulak still has a taste for battle.

In most situations, however, the worst thing an incoming president can do is to operate in ways that confirm people's worst fears. The fact that some do, in fact, may be the only thing keeping nontraditionals from getting hired at even higher rates. McLaughlin and others say more nontraditional candidates would prevail if not for pressure on the governing boards by faculty members too quick to assume the worst of them. Nontraditionals (and for that matter, traditionals) who play to stereotype serve up exactly what their detractors need to take them down, and that serves no one well.

5 | Which Schools Break with Tradition?

A S THE 2007–8 school year came to a close, Davis & Elkins was a small college in deep trouble. As the *Chronicle of Higher Education* reported, this hundred-year-old West Virginia institution's annual deficits had touched $2 million on a $14 million annual budget. Having maxed out its lines of credit, it borrowed from its own endowment each semester. Its total operating debt approached a crippling $6 million. Reflecting on the situation later, an English professor at the college, Peter T. Okun, told the reporter the school was in a "death spiral."[1]

Less than a year later, that spiral was reversing and things were heading in a better direction. In November 2009, the *Chronicle* reported a freshman class up by 50 percent, drawn from a pool of applicants more than seven times greater than the previous year's. Thanks to all those applications, Davis & Elkins could be more selective: "In 2007, 42 percent of the freshmen had high-school grade-point averages of 3.0 or better," the *Chronicle* wrote. "This year, it's 63 percent."[2]

What happened to change the school's fortunes? At its lowest point, the school brought in a new president: G. T. "Buck" Smith. He was certainly not inexperienced at college leadership—he had just retired as president of Bethany College and had previously been president of Chapman College. Yet, just as surely, he was cut from different cloth than most of his peers. Lacking a PhD and never a professor, he'd started out in higher education with a successful fifteen-year stint as the College of Wooster's vice president for development. In choosing him, Davis & Elkins had opted to bring in a nontraditional president.

When we look at the colleges that opt for leaders with nontraditional backgrounds, is Davis & Elkins a typical case? There are two ways to go about answering that question. First, we can try to answer it quantitatively, using data to discover if there are common, measurable characteristics of colleges led by nontraditional presidents. Up until now there has been no such quantitative analysis of what types of schools hire nontraditional presidents, for any definition of nontraditional. A big part of my own research has been to find the correlations between institutions' selections of the two types of presidents and other data on institutional size, religious affiliation, endowment, geography, financial metrics and trends, selectivity, yield, public versus private affiliation, and ranking. It is a statistical analysis that cannot claim causality but does reveal clear certain patterns in the schools that select nontraditional candidates.

Second, we can answer the question of what kinds of schools break with tradition by consulting the search firm executives who have a front-row seat to the succession process. Most of the thinking that goes into presidential selections happens outside the public eye and is never captured in the form of data. But outside consultants today are involved in nearly nine out of every ten searches for liberal arts presidential searches and see for themselves the common threads in the deliberations of trustees and search committees. Thus a second line of my research was designed to learn what they believe based on their rich experience in leadership selection.

What the Data Say

Let's start, then, with the numbers — noting again that my definition of non-traditional is more restrictive (i.e., requiring a traditional to be a full professor and or provost dramatically increases the number of nontraditional leaders) and that my research focuses on liberal arts colleges as a subset of the higher education scene. The completeness of the data set regarding these colleges' finances, selectivity, and presidential backgrounds allows for straightforward analysis; reliable information exists and will continue to be tracked over time. Of course, this means the findings reported here can't be assumed to be the same for all institutions of higher education. Remember: there are more than four thousand colleges and universities in the United States, and these data are drawn from only 248 of them. In many respects, however, liberal arts colleges represent a barometer by which to gauge broader trends. In their context, a number of findings become clear.

First, some characteristics one might think to be salient in the selection of traditional versus nontraditional presidents turn out not to be. Take the matter of whether a college is public or private. Public liberal arts colleges are not numerous (in 2014, just under 10 percent of stand-alone liberal arts college were public institutions), yet among them are some of the most elite schools, including the United States Military Academy, the United States Naval Academy, and the United States Air Force Academy. Others are campuses of state systems designated to focus on liberal arts education, such as the University of Maine's Machias campus or the University of Hawaii at Hilo. We should keep in mind a caveat: the small number of schools in the public liberal arts category could challenge the statistical significance of comparisons. Given the data at hand, however, public or private funding seems to have no effect on presidential preferences. One public college, like Evergreen State in Olympia, Washington, opts for a nontraditional leader (Les Purce) from 2000–2015, while another, like St. Mary's College in Maryland, chooses a more traditional resume (Tuajuanda Jordan). No pattern emerges.

Other measurable characteristics turn out to have significant correlations, but with no obvious logic as to why they should. Geographic location is an example. The percentage of nontraditional presidents in the South, for example, is three times higher than in the West (see table 5.1). Yet it is hard to imagine why the location of a college per se could influence what type of president is chosen. Possibly, this is only a correlation reflecting underlying phenomena. We know, for example, that schools in the West are more likely to be highly ranked—and rankings, as we will see below, appear to drive presidential choices strongly. Looking into the thirty-one colleges in the West led by traditional presidents, I discovered that many of them are ranked among the top seventy-five liberal arts colleges in the nation.

For whatever reason it exists, the variation in presidential types by region is striking, with only 14 percent of presidents in the West being nontradi-

TABLE 5.1. Number and percentage of 2014 traditional and nontraditional liberal arts presidents by geographic region

Region	2014 liberal arts traditional presidents (No.)	2014 liberal arts nontraditional presidents (No.)	2014 liberal arts traditional presidents (%)	2014 liberal arts nontraditional presidents (%)
Midwest ($n = 58$)	40	18	69	31
North ($n = 83$)	52	31	62.7	37.3
South ($n = 71$)	42	29	59.2	40.8
West ($n = 36$)	31	5	86.1	13.9
Total ($n = 248$)	165	83	66.5	33.5

Sources: Data from Internet searches and analysis; IPEDS; USNWR Compass 2014 data.

tional, and other regions displaying 2.5 to 3 times that likelihood. On the other extreme, in the South, 41 percent of liberal arts presidents are nontraditional, well above the average. (To the point made already, in the South there is a higher concentration of lower-ranked institutions. Specifically, forty-five of the seventy-one, or 63 percent of liberal arts colleges in the South, are ranked in the bottom 103, or 42 percent, of institutions.)

The Predictive Power of Rankings

The data also reveal correlations that may be easier to interpret. Top among these is the finding that rankings matter. Despite the controversy that surrounds ranking, and the often competing algorithms in use by the various ranking services, the truth remains that a school's ranking serves as a grade on how it is doing. Rankings are routinely consulted not only by students and their parents but by boards, alumni, and in-demand candidates for college presidencies.

Analysis presented in table 5.2 and figure 5.1 clearly demonstrates that a lower ranking has an almost linear relationship with increased likelihood of having a nontraditional president.

Higher-ranked liberal arts colleges in 2014 were clearly less likely to have a nontraditional president than lower-ranked peers. For instance, the

TABLE 5.2. Number and percentage of 2014 traditional and nontraditional liberal arts college presidents by ranking quintile

Rank 2014 USNWR compass	2014 liberal arts traditional presidents (No.)	2014 liberal arts nontraditional presidents (No.)	2014 liberal arts traditional presidents (%)	2014 liberal arts nontraditional presidents (%)
Top 50 highest ranked (n = 50)	42	8	84	16
51–100 (n = 50)	37	13	74	26
101–150 (n = 50)	31	19	62	38
Bottom two quintiles (n = 98)	55	43	56	44
Total (n = 248)	165	83	66.5	33.5

Sources: Data from Internet searches and analysis; IPEDS; USNWR Compass 2014 data.

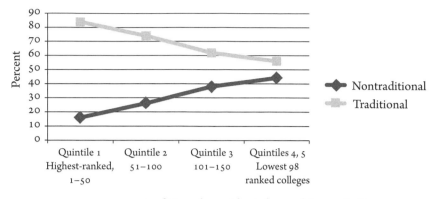

FIGURE 5.1. 2014 nontraditional presidents by ranking quintile

Data sources: Internet searches and analysis; IPEDS; USNWR Compass 2014 data.

bottom two quintiles of schools that represent those ranked over 150, or not ranked at all, are 2.75 times likelier to have a nontraditional president than a top-fifty college.

Why a top-ranked school might be less likely to hire a nontraditional could simply be a function of tradition, inertia, or risk avoidance. After all, it's fair to assume that if a school is highly ranked, it must be doing something right. Remember: nontraditional candidates are often perceived and positioned as change agents—and change is rarely a priority where the status quo is satisfactory. There may be other reasons, too, that highly ranked schools tend to have more traditional presidents. They may have more powerful tenured faculty, for example, who believe in the traditional model and have a strong say in the process. Or, as the traditional talent pipeline yields fewer candidates, they might simply be most attractive to those rare leaders whose resumes "check all the boxes."

This was how executive search consultant Ellen Landers interpreted the rankings correlation. "At the top ranks, they can usually find good traditional candidates who've 'been there and done that' before," she said. "Why wouldn't they go with somebody who's proven in their environment? That's your less risky choice." In the middle to lower tier, she believes, institutions are more "pressed to be creative," both because their choices are constrained and because their situation demands fresh thinking about what they might do differently to change their fortunes. However, both traditional and nontraditional presidents find themselves in the mix at all levels of ranking.

FINANCIAL HEALTH AS A FACTOR

As we've just seen, rankings correlate neatly to presidential selections in liberal arts colleges—but a school's ranking is in itself a hybrid variable. To determine that ranking, *U.S. News & World Report* (whose rankings were used in the above analysis) combines measures of endowment, graduation rate, and selectivity in its algorithm. So let's dig into these factors, starting with endowment—and by extension, the financial health of the institution.

For the purposes of this analysis, I studied three objective markers of financial strength that could result in a different propensity to have a nontraditional president: endowment assets per student, size of total endowment, and the percentage of full-paying students. (These metrics do not measure other sources of financial strain—such as debt, debt covenants, or unfunded pensions and deferred maintenance—or sources of strength such as urban real estate or other valuable items that may appear on the balance sheet at book value such as a Monet painting or land acquired in 1900.)

Overall, my analysis indicates a negative relationship between wealth and the presence of a nontraditional president, with greater resources decreasing the likelihood that a school will look for leadership outside conventional lines. To borrow the phrasing of the American heiress Wallis Simpson, it would appear that an elite college can never be too rich or too traditional.

Endowments are, of course, the most basic measure of institutions' wealth, and because schools come in many sizes, the appropriate metric for ranking purposes is endowment per student. This number provides a more accurate sense of how individual educations might be helped or hindered by available resources. (The highest endowment per student is more than $2.5 million per student at Soka University, a college that opened its U.S. campus in 2001.) The analysis presented in table 5.3 shows that nontraditional presidents are far more prevalent in the poorer half of colleges by this measure (Tiers 1 and 2) than in the richer half (Tiers 3 and 4).

The poorest two tiers of colleges, as measured by endowment per student in 2014, were 78 percent more likely to have a nontraditional president than the two richest tiers.

While endowment per student is the relevant metric for ranking purposes, it is also interesting to look at total endowments when the focus is on leadership selections. Rather than gauging the financial resources that can be brought to bear on a per-student basis, total endowment gauges the absolute scale of wealth a liberal arts college has to draw upon. As seen earlier,

TABLE 5.3. Number and percentage of 2014 traditional and nontraditional presidents by endowment assets year-end 2013 per FTE enrollment

2012–13 endowment assets year-end per FTE enrollment ($K; n = 234)	2014 traditional presidents (No.)	2014 nontraditional presidents (No.)	2014 traditional presidents (%)	2014 nontraditional presidents (%)
Tier 1—smallest (0.044 to 26.3; n = 58)	34	24	58.6	41.4
Tier 2 (27.7 to 60.1; n = 58)	33	25	56.9	43.1
Tier 3 (60.2 to 133.9; n = 59)	44	15	74.6	25.4
Tier 4—largest (135.5 to 2,505.4; n = 59)	46	13	78	22

Sources: Data from Internet searches and analysis; IPEDS; USNWR Compass 2014 data.

total endowments vary enormously. On one end of the spectrum, Williams College in Massachusetts enjoys access to a treasure chest of $2.25 billion. In the same state, but at the opposite extreme, tiny Pine Manor College has an endowment more in the neighborhood of $10 million and has struggled to attract and retain presidents in recent years. My analysis shows that when schools are sorted by their total endowments, as opposed to endowment per student, the tendency of the top tier to stick with tradition in presidential selections is even stronger. Dramatically, only 13.6 percent of the most-well-endowed quartile of schools have nontraditional leaders (for details, see table A.1 in the appendix). Indeed, the likelihood of having a nontraditional president is almost three times higher in the 75 percent of colleges with smaller endowments than in the richest 25 percent of colleges. There appears to be something of a breakpoint whereby liberal arts colleges beyond a certain level of endowment—in the vicinity of $240 million—hew much more strongly to the traditional model.

As with the broader trend in rankings, at least a few explanations are possible. The first is the simple lack of appetite for change. A certain endowment level offers enough of a safety net that financial considerations are not a major factor in decision making about leadership. Another possibility is that richer schools are willing to expend more resources to attract the "best" candidates, leaving poorer schools to make do with less qualified leadership. Alternatively, poorer schools might be displaying a positive preference for nontraditional candidates, believing that new leaders who could fix financial problems would be "best" for them, and seeing more of the skills required to do that in the nontraditional candidate pool. This is a point made by Susan Pierce in her book *On Being Presidential.* She writes that boards of trustees and presidential search committees, facing unprecedented financial pressures, are "sometimes even eager to entertain nontraditional candidates, believing that . . . these nontraditional candidates . . . will possess skills and experiences that Chief Academic Officers may not have."[3]

Before moving on to other components of rankings, we can look at one last indicator of the financial health of different schools and how it affects presidential selections: their percentages of *full-paying students.* Clearly, full-paying students are desirable from a financial point of view. As seen in chapter 2, with its case studies of three colleges' finances, a shift of just a few percentage points of full-paying students to aid-grant students can do substantial damage to financial well-being. My data show that such shifts in full-payers also affect likelihood to hire nontraditional presidents (see the appendix, table A.2). While less dramatic, the pattern of difference still holds. In the top-quartile colleges, 35 percent or more of students are full-paying and receive no discount, and these schools are substantially less likely to have nontraditional leaders.

GRADUATION RATES AS A FACTOR

Financial health is, of course, not the only or even the best way to judge the success of an institution of higher learning. While cash flow is essential to the sustained operation of the enterprise, the real work of the liberal arts college is to enrich minds. One objective way to measure achievement along these more mission-oriented lines is to look at graduation rates. Indeed, one salutary effect of rankings has been to focus more attention on these. As parents and students become familiar with the labels affixed to schools, they also note their differences in graduation rates. Higher graduation rates are found at "medallion" (above 80 percent) and "brand name" (68 to 80 percent) institutions, and lower graduation rates at "good buy" (50 to 68 percent) and "good opportunity" (20 to 50 percent) institutions.[4]

Again, my analysis reveals a broad pattern in presidential choices. Lower graduation rates (and the segment labels associated with them) turn out to be associated with higher selections of nontraditional leaders. In fact, among schools classified as "good buys," there are more nontraditional presidents than traditional presidents (see table A.3 in the appendix for the data). The relationship is not linear; for example, a "good opportunity" college is less likely to have a nontraditional president than a "good buy" college. Still, by combining the top two segments and the bottom two, we find that the colleges with the lower graduation rates ("good buys" and "good opportunities") are 72 percent more likely to have nontraditional presidents than the higher-graduation-rate colleges ("medallions" and "brand names").

Perhaps, then, we should not be surprised that Virginia's Emory & Henry, whose graduation rate of 47 percent helped push its *U.S. News* ranking down to 174, recently chose Jake Schrum as president. Schrum offered previous experience as a university president, having spent the prior thirteen years leading Southwestern University and nine years before that leading Texas Wesleyan University. But he was never a tenure-track professor. He started out in fund-raising at Yale University and advanced from there through administrative ranks.[5] Likewise, even though Hampshire College is in many respects a stronger institution than Emory & Henry, its surprisingly low graduation rate of 64 percent would seem to be in line with its unconventional choice of Jonathan Lash as president. Never an academic, let alone a PhD-holding tenure-tracked one, he came to Hampshire from World Resources Institute, a Washington-based environmental think tank. Earlier he had been a lawyer for the Natural Resources Defense Council, then a public servant as the appointed Vermont commissioner of environmental conservation and later, Vermont secretary of natural resources.[6]

SELECTIVITY AS A FACTOR

Of the three major components of college rankings, selectivity offers the clearest "market signal" of success. It captures the extent to which a school has its pick of the best students. Like financial health and graduation rates, it also tracks with the tendency to hire nontraditional presidents. We can see this in two analyses in particular: of acceptance rates and yield rates.

Schools ranked as more selective have lower ratios of acceptances to applicants, by definition. To be sure, this is not the whole story of selectivity. (Otherwise, tiny Alice Lloyd College in Kentucky would be worldrenowned. Its 7 percent acceptance rate makes it choosier than Princeton, but this a function of free tuition and only enough slots for six hundred total students.) More important in the *U.S. News* rankings are entering freshmen's high SAT/ACT scores and high-school class ranks. Yet acceptance rates generally track with a school's public reputation and reflect large numbers of applications on an absolute basis.

My analysis reveals that acceptance rate is also a differentiating characteristic that maps to the likelihood of having a nontraditional president. Table 5.4 shows the distribution of nontraditional presidents across four quartiles of acceptance rates.

Here again, while the tendency toward nontraditional leadership does not change in a linear way across the quartiles, a difference is strongly evident between the top two and bottom two. Meanwhile, the breakaway difference is in the top quartile—among the fifty-eight liberal arts colleges that accept 41 percent or fewer of their applicants. In contrast to these, schools in the other three quartiles are 88 percent more likely to have nontraditional presidents.

An example of this, taken from the fourth quartile, would be Evergreen State College, the Washington State school mentioned earlier for its choice of Thomas L. (Les) Purce as president. About as nontraditional as leaders come in higher education, Purce spent his early career in the private sector, as a partner in an electrical engineering firm. From there he was appointed director of the State of Idaho's Departments of Administration and Health and Welfare. He also became the first black elected official in Idaho when he took office as a city councilman, and later mayor, of Pocatello. His introduction to the education sector came when he became Evergreen's vice president for advancement in March 1989, after which he served as interim president for nearly two years, and then settled into the role of executive vice president for finance and administration. In 1995, he left for Washington State University and the role of vice president of extended university affairs and dean of academic programs. Five years later, Evergreen called him back to the top post.[7] Purce's fifteen years at the helm have been judged successful along many dimensions, but would the school have been as inclined to install such a nontraditional leader if it were much more selective? (Its 96 percent acceptance rate makes it one of the least selective in the country.) It's impossible to say—but the data suggest not.

Yield rates also factor into selectivity, since both sides of a student-college match must pick each other. A college's "yield" is the percentage of its offers of places in the next freshman class that are accepted in return by students. In decades past, college administrators worried less about yield rates, because they were generally so much higher and more predictable than today. The modern phenomenon of students applying to many institutions and then choosing among the several that accept them (rather than narrowing their choices through careful consideration before applying) has changed

TABLE 5.4. Number and percentage of 2014 traditional and nontraditional liberal arts college presidents by 2013 acceptance rate

Selectivity quartile 2012–13 acceptance rate	2014 liberal arts traditional presidents (No.)	2014 liberal arts nontraditional presidents (No.)	2014 liberal arts traditional presidents (%)	2014 liberal arts nontraditional presidents (%)
1st quartile—most selective (from 6.8 to 41%; n = 58)	46	12	79.3	20.7
2nd quartile (from 41.1 to 62.2%; n = 58)	36	22	62.1	37.9
3rd quartile (from 62.3 to 72.1%; n = 58)	32	26	55.2	44.8
4th quartile—least selective (from 72.2 to 98.3%; n = 59)	39	20	66.1	33.9
Total (n = 233)	153	80	65.7	34.3

Sources: Data from Internet searches and analysis; IPEDS; USNWR 2014 Compass data.

that. Now, colleges track and project yield rates precisely as they seek to send just the right number of acceptance letters to "make the class." They also encourage "early decision" and "early action" applications from students, which have the direct effect of boosting yields.

Given the findings presented already, it will probably surprise no reader to learn that lower yield rates also correlate with greater propensity to choose nontraditional presidents (table A.4 in the appendix presents the data produced by my analysis). Colleges in the bottom two yield quartiles are 51.6 percent more likely to have a nontraditional president than the best two yield quartiles. Colleges in the bottom quartile struggling with low yield are led by nontraditional presidents 49 percent of the time and are 82 percent more likely to have a nontraditional president than the highest two yield quartiles.

Go Big or Go Nontraditional?

So far we've seen that ranking matters to a college's likelihood of having a nontraditional president, along with each of its major components: selectivity, financial resources, and graduation rates. Further analysis of objectively measurable differences among schools reveals that an institution's size is salient, too. The smaller the school, the more likely it is to go nontraditional. This is true whether we define size in terms of number of students, number of staff employed, or total core-expense budget.

The full-time-equivalent (FTE) student enrollments of liberal arts colleges differ by almost a hundredfold from the smallest to the largest institutions. However, as with previous analyses, it is convenient to divide the whole set into quartiles, as shown in table 5.5.

Once again, we observe that the percentage of nontraditional presidents does not uniformly change across the quartiles in this data set—but that the difference from the two smaller to the two larger quartiles is pronounced. The smaller schools (quartiles 1 and 2) are about 35 percent more likely to have a nontraditional president than the larger schools (quartiles 3 and 4).

Similarly, when we shift the definition of size to consider the number of staff employed, the analysis shows a tendency for larger organizations to favor traditional leadership more than their smaller-staffed peers (see table A.5 in the appendix). The data show that, in 2014, the two quartiles representing the smaller institutions, as measured by number of staff, were 31.4 percent more likely to have a nontraditional president than the upper two quartiles' bigger institutions.

TABLE 5.5. Number and percentage of traditional and nontraditional liberal arts college presidents by number of students

Size quartile total FTE enrollment 2012–13 IPEDS	2014 liberal arts traditional presidents (No.)	2014 liberal arts nontraditional presidents (No.)	2014 liberal arts traditional presidents (%)	2014 liberal arts nontraditional presidents (%)
1st quartile—smallest (from 93 to 983 FTE); $n = 61$	37	24	60.1	38.9
2nd quartile (from 989 to 1,646 FTE); $n = 61$	38	23	62.3	37.7
3rd quartile (from 1,647 to 2,316 FTE); $n = 61$	46	15	75.4	24.6
4th quartile—largest (from 2,346 to 7,445 FTE); $n = 62$	42	20	67.7	32.3
Total ($n = 245$)	163	82	66.5	33.5

Sources: Data from Internet searches and analysis; IPEDS; USNWR Compass 2014 data.

Another way to consider size is to examine what we might call the scale of the institution's operations. One metric that can be used to size up schools in this way is core expenses. Core expenses include the operating budget of a school and virtually all salaries and operating expenses; they also include financial aid grants. Given that some colleges have vastly greater endowments and wealth than others, and thus can spend more on salaries and other items, expenses vary even more widely as a measure of size than number of students or staff. In fact, the largest expense budget among the liberal arts colleges I considered is more than 220 times larger than the smallest.

My analysis reveals that liberal arts colleges with smaller budgets are more likely to have nontraditional presidents than their bigger-budget peers (see table A.6 in the appendix). In 2014, the two quartiles representing the smaller institutions, as measured by core expenses, are 42.4 percent more likely to have a nontraditional president than the two quartiles of bigger institutions. Schools with the most expansive operations and biggest budgets are least likely to choose nontraditional leaders.

In some ways, this is a counterintuitive finding. Often we hear that nontraditional candidates are chosen for college presidencies because of their administrative skills—which would presumably be needed all the more in sprawling, more complex, organizations. On this point, we might first underscore the earlier point that the data set is confined to liberal arts colleges. It is possible and indeed quite plausible that the same might not be true of big universities. Meanwhile, earlier interpretations of other correlations might apply here, as well. Schools with smaller budgets might be forced to settle, while institutions with substantially larger resources, particularly from a budgetary point of view, might have more latitude to consider only traditional candidates should they so desire. Or it might be that smaller schools have less empowered faculty. If in a smaller institution the board of trustees has more power, it might more freely choose a nontraditional candidate. Conversely, if a larger institution has more faculty with a say in the presidential selection, a nontraditional candidate might encounter larger hurdles to acceptance there.

Religious and Nontraditional

One last interesting analysis of the data relates to the fact that most liberal arts colleges were founded by religious denominations, back in an era when higher learning was mainly the province of the ministry. John Carroll, for example, the first bishop and archbishop of the Catholic Church in the United States, founded Georgetown College (today Georgetown University) in 1789. Presbyterian ministers Hezekiah Balch and Samuel Doak founded Tusculum College in Tennesee in 1794. Samuel Simon Schmucker, a Lutheran, established Gettysburg College to be that church's first seminary in the United States in 1832. Quakers created Earlham College in 1847 as a boarding school "for the guarded religious education of the children of Friends."[8] Bates College, Baylor University, and Brown University were all founded by Baptists. Later came schools built on non-Christian faiths, such as Brandeis University and Yeshiva University (Jewish) and Brigham Young University (Mormon). Many institutions maintain strong religious affiliations even today, while many others would seem to have no remaining vestiges of their original church ties.

Thus, while just under half of today's liberal arts colleges are identified formally by *U.S. News & World Report* as having a religious affiliation, the degree to which religion infuses the school can vary dramatically. Most are not actually in the business of religious instruction. Very few admit only students from the religion with which they are affiliated; almost all are accepting of students and staff from all walks of life and religious beliefs. Yet in some, the culture and mission of the institution is still strongly influenced and inspired by founding values. It should be noted that variations like these are not captured in blunt designations of whether a school is "religiously affiliated."

Looking at how religious affiliation might be correlated with presidential selections, there is a further wrinkle to consider. For an institution that chooses to emphasize its religious affiliation, the choice of a president with impeccable credentials *relating to that faith* might seem the most "traditional" one to make. Yet if that leader did not previously spend time as a tenure-track professor, he or she counts as nontraditional in this analysis. An example along these lines would be Dr. Rex Home of Ouachita Baptist University in Arkansas. Prior to being president, he was a senior pastor, and prior to that he was president of the Arkansas Baptist State Convention and a trustee at the university.

Undoubtedly choices like these account at least in part for the higher prevalence of nontraditionals in religiously affiliated schools, shown in table 5.6. In some institutions, preference may be given to presidential candidates from a given faith, potentially trumping the preference for academic achievement.

TABLE 5.6. Number and percentage of 2014 traditional and nontraditional presidents by liberal arts college religious affiliation

Liberal arts college religious affiliation? (N = 248)	Traditional president (No.)	Nontraditional president (No.)	Traditional president (%)	Nontraditional president (%)
Religious affiliation (n = 119)	71	48	59.7	40.3
No religious affiliation (n = 129)	94	35	72.9	27.1
Total (n = 248)	165	83	66.5	33.5

Sources: Data from Internet searches and analysis; USNWR Compass 2014 data.

Saint Anselm College's new president stands out, then, for being doubly nontraditional. Steven DiSalvo, while he has a doctorate in educational leadership, was never a tenured professor. He came to the college from Marian University in Wisconsin, where he had been president for three years—but before that he applied his management training as an executive in the philanthropic sector. What makes him most different from all thirteen of his predecessors, however, is that he is not a monk. Reflecting on the choice, the chairman of Saint Anselm's board of trustees told *New Hampshire Business Review*, "Anyone we seriously considered had to have a real strong passion for the Catholic, liberal arts college tradition." At the same time, he said, "We did think fundraising strength was very important. We also thought the economic challenges would make a business background a plus." As the newspaper put it, "For the first time, the letters following the Saint Anselm College president's name include MBA and not OSB (as in Order of St. Benedict)."[9]

Even among religiously affiliated liberal arts colleges, about 60 percent of their leaders are traditional, still the majority. However, the data indicate that, in 2014, religiously affiliated liberal arts colleges were 49 percent more likely to have nontraditional presidents than were colleges without religious affiliation. Interestingly, it turns out that 66 percent of liberal arts colleges in the South are religiously affiliated versus 39 percent in the West. Given the previous analysis indicating geography as a salient characteristic influencing the selection of a nontraditional president, here perhaps is another explanation.

Search Firms See Other Patterns

As with other explorations of emerging trends, not everything about the rise of nontraditional leaders in higher education can be understood through data. To gain more insight into what types of institution choose them and why, I talked with leading executive-search consultants. I began with a simple question: "What kind of college hires a nontraditional president?" One of them, John Isaacson, laughed as he volunteered an answer I'll never forget: "A terrified one." But as the conversation went on, he responded, as did his peers, with a much more thorough and nuanced assessment.

As discussed in chapter 2, search firms are now involved in the vast majority of liberal arts college presidency searches, a trend that has emerged progressively since the 1980s. In a given search, they often help to write the position profile after interviewing stakeholders, receive and sort the various candidate papers submitted, and work intimately with the selection committees and candidates in virtually all stages of the search right through contract negotiation. Selection committees and candidates often turn to search firm executives as a source of outside, objective advice, and to frame choices. The best search executives, behind the scenes, are often counselors to candidates, boards, or presidents and thought leaders on higher education and have closely guarded but extensive Rolodexes of possible candidates.

In asking these professionals my open-ended question—"What are the characteristics of liberal arts institutions that are most likely to hire a nontraditional president?"—my hope was to gain the view from their unique perch. Their responses clustered around a handful of themes: rankings, risk tolerance, crisis, board power, and search committee composition.

DOWN IN THE RANKS

In their responses, all the search consultants went to the topic of rankings, some of them immediately. Interestingly, however, they did not all agree on how rankings related to the likelihood of selecting nontraditional presidents. Shelly Storbeck, for example, was sure there was a linear, inverse relationship. Colleges in the top ten of the *U.S. News* ranking "are really going to push hard to have a traditional candidate," she said. But "if you're in the 10 to 30 range, there's probably going to be a little more variety in the profile. And then when you drift down to 50 and below, you'll see all kinds of candidates." David Bellshaw, however, claimed otherwise. In his experience, lower-ranked schools "are more hesitant about taking a nontraditional candidate, because they are so worried about their reputation that they want a high-flying academic . . . to show they're intellectually making the right moves." He expected to see higher-ranked institutions making the more creative moves in their leadership selections, precisely because they do not have that foxhole mentality.

The data reviewed earlier in this chapter suggest that Storbeck is right, if not down to precise numbers then at least directionally. However, it is possible that Bellshaw's observation identifies an emerging change in behavior or simply what he has observed in his experience. Or it may be that current data reflect not a bias against nontraditionals by elite schools but simply the luxury of not having to choose. Because they are most attractive to candidates, top-ranked colleges might get the best of both worlds: a greater pool of candidates that consistently yield leaders whose resumes have the traditional earmarks but also promise the external-facing strengths or prior credentials such as a presidency that can be hard to find in scholars. Again, schools in all rankings categories had both traditional and nontraditional leaders, just in different proportions.

READY FOR RISK

There may be a better way to think about the differences among colleges that drive them toward varying presidential choices. Comments by some search consultants suggested we might forget about ranking and instead divide colleges into two camps: those with an appetite for risk, and those that prefer to play it safe. Naturally, this is often a matter of whether the people involved in a search process see a need for deep change if not wholesale transformation—or are more or less happy with the status quo.

Anne Coyle's experience has been that "institutions who are anxious enough about their own future, that are willing to take risk, . . . are more likely to hire a nontraditional candidate. Those that are more eager to maintain their good standing, they are likely to go with the traditional candidate that will keep things on the same path and perhaps make incremental, nonpainful changes." Many search executives see in nontraditional candidates a challenge to convention that goes beyond their CVs. Boards of trustees choosing them, they say, are signaling bigger changes to come.

It is understandable that many participants in the selection process would view the choice of a nontraditional president as a risky move. The risks come at the institutional level, as a possibly unqualified leader starts making consequential decisions, and they come at the personal level, as decision makers in the process have their judgment (and sometimes integrity) questioned. Of course, as has often been observed, the most risky decisions in times of trouble are often the ones that involve changing nothing. (As some wise person once said, the definition of insanity is doing the same thing over and over again and expecting different results.) Still, it takes real courage to do things differently than they've been done in the past.

CHALLENGED BY CRISIS

Even an institution that is generally risk averse can make the decision to break with convention in its choice of leader if it finds itself facing a major crisis, whether triggered and defined by a scandal, financial or cultural challenge, or a forward-looking discontinuity. This is related to the previous observation about risk appetite, since a crisis or major uncertainty can represent the burning platform that forces a search committee to make moves it would otherwise resist. There is something else in play, too, however. A crisis not only makes previously intolerable risk more palatable, it provides a kind of proof that the old way of doing things was flawed. Something, in other words, allowed the crisis to occur—and therefore, the old system could not have been perfect. This is the consideration that often sinks the candidacies of any internal candidates for the top job in a troubled enterprise.

For both these reasons, search consultants reported a pattern by which schools in crisis are more likely to appoint nontraditional leaders. Recall how John Isaacson, doyen of presidential searches, put it: the type of college most likely to hire a nontraditional president is "a terrified one." Without doubting the truth of their observation, we might note its counterintuitive aspect. Times of crisis are, in many settings, more associated with retreating to the comfort of the familiar than with venturing into unknown territory.

Yet it is widely understood that leadership matters greatly in times of crisis. When Ellen Earle Chaffee conducted the case research that informed her study "After Decline, What? Survival Strategies at Eight Private Colleges," she found it to be the decisive factor: "I was particularly engrossed by the extent to which quality of leadership seemed to influence the course of institutional experience, before, during, and after a major crisis. I think the readers of these case narratives will largely agree that for small private colleges in trouble, finding an able and dedicated leader is a matter of life or death."[10]

Why a nontraditional president might be better suited to a crisis, strong uncertainty, or a fear-filled situation is unclear from the interviews. One possible reason is that institutions suddenly aware of one type of problem might respond by emphasizing past experience relevant to solving it, above other criteria that would normally take precedence in their decision making. Another is that a big part of dissipating the crisis might be reassuring concerned parties that it is being addressed, for example, by selecting someone who has experience in designing a compelling future strategy. Putting a strikingly different type of leader at the helm might be a way of signaling that the problem is being taken seriously, and things will change.

Still another explanation for why nontraditional leadership choices happen more in situations of crisis focuses on the "supply side" of the hire instead of the demand side. We don't know, after all, what other choices these institutions have in the candidate pool. To overstate things just a bit, maybe the only great candidates interested in stepping into certain crisis-afflicted schools are nontraditional ones.

Of course, traditional leaders may also be just the answer to resolving certain crises, perhaps all the more so if the crisis was caused by a nontraditional predecessor. For instance, if a crisis calls especially for unifying the faculty or re-creating the core curriculum or returning to more traditional values and culture, a traditional leader, even from the inside, may be more likely. Much depends on the background of the candidate. One traditional leader might have already been president for years and seen it all, while another might be a first-time president and product of a tenure track that has not provided the opportunity to face anything like the crisis at hand.

POWERFUL BOARDS

Search consultants also report that the chances of a nontraditional president's being appointed are much greater in an institution where the board of trustees wields more power. Sue May, for example, told me: "A lot of it has to do with the nature of shared governance and the dynamics of the board and the dynamics of the faculty. If the board is running the show, you're more likely to end up with a nontraditional." In many institutions, the board is clearly responsible and accountable for appointing the president; in fact it may be their most important role. The question is then how much of their power they need to share in the selection process to have a process that is viewed as legitimate.

Shared governance is, of course, a great tradition in higher education and calls for constant balancing of the desires of faculty with the desires of trustees (and increasingly, other constituencies). This is a healthy arrangement that ensures that a college both serves its noble mission and survives to serve it longer. At any given time, however, and in any given school, one or the other side may have more influence over decisions than the other. Because faculty tend to prefer appointing "one of their own" to the presidency, nontraditional candidates are less likely to succeed in situations where faculty hold more sway in the decision, search consultants have observed. In schools where that is not the case, for whatever reason, they encounter less resistance. Clearly there are exceptions in either direction.

The moments of crisis discussed above can have the effect of shifting power to boards; indeed, it would seem to be deeply rooted in human psychology that in times of perceived danger, groups defer more readily to focused direction from the top. This is the truth Rahm Emanuel, President Obama's first chief of staff, was observing when he famously commented, "You never let a serious crisis go to waste." He went on to explain himself: "What I mean by that: it's an opportunity to do things you think you could not do before." *New York Times* language columnist Jake Rosenthal helpfully interpreted further: "In a sprawling, contentious democracy, competing interests suspend their antagonisms only when they have to confront an alarming common threat."[11] A college community is no exception. When it is faced with serious threats, whether emanating from shaky finances, exposed scandals, a period of turmoil or mediocrity, or terrifying events, normally noisy debates quiet down.

One interesting question is whether boards have gained relative power in general in recent decades, and whether they will in the future. Search executives describe a strengthening of boards in the midst of the 2008–10 financial crisis that has so far not been followed by a return to the prior balance of power. Some say that by bringing financial concerns to the fore, that crisis changed decision-making processes in an enduring way. Ken Kring, for example, described "a shift in the decision-making dynamics, where boards of trustees are empowered because of financial challenges and are able . . . to step further into succession planning because of the consequences of the financial model being threatening to the institution." Only time will tell if this is a secular or cyclical change.

Another question focuses on whether certain types of liberal arts colleges are more likely to have powerful boards in general. On this point there is no consensus. David Bellshaw's belief is that boards in higher-ranked colleges tend to wield more power in presidential selection decisions because they have generated substantial wealth for the college. In contrast to these powerful rainmakers, he says, "more middle-ground boards may be less prominent, more insecure, more worried about reputation, more worried about what it is that they're signaling to their friends and colleagues." Others, however, note that high-ranked schools also have high-powered faculty with outsized abilities to make their voices heard.

Finally, while noting a general tendency for boards to be more receptive than faculty to nontraditional candidates, search consultants stress that, in any particular case, much depends on the individuals who serve on the search committee. Jackie Zavitch made this point when she told me that the "selection committee profile is key." For an institution to look beyond the conventional profile of a leader, she noted the need for "personalities at the top, and that means the board and the faculty, both to have a willingness."

From Weakness to Strength?

After a chapter's worth of statistics and search firm perspectives, we can answer the question posed at the outset. Is Davis & Elkins, the century-old liberal arts college in West Virginia, typical of the institutions that appoint nontraditional leaders? In virtually every respect, yes. Within its U.S. classification as a southern regional college, Davis & Elkins ranks sixty-third (out of seventy-three colleges ranked). Its acceptance rate tops 57 percent. The school is small by any measure and religiously affiliated (with the Presbyterian Church). Its challenging financial situation has already been noted.

Hiram College in Ohio offers another typical case. For the past few years, the school has found itself on a federal watch list for its financial management.[12] Subject to "heightened cash monitoring" by the U.S. Department of Education, it is under real pressure to boost enrollment and revenue while also reducing costs to improve its financial responsibility score. In 2014, the Hiram College Board of Trustees chose Lori Varlotta to be president of the institution. Not only is she the first woman president in the college's history, she is the first not to have been a tenured professor. Like many colleges in positions of relative weakness and wanting to be strong again, Hiram hired a nontraditional.

Yet there are enough exceptions to the pattern to make one wonder whether it will hold true in the future. Look, for example, at Carleton College in Minnesota. The school is in the winner's circle by every metric (except perhaps its winter weather). Yet in choosing Steven Poskanzer, it opted for a nontraditional president. Poskanzer's resume reveals him to be a strong leader with deep experience in higher education—but with no PhD and very little teaching experience, let alone as a tenure-track professor.[13] Even more strikingly, look at Bowdoin, with its top-five national ranking and 15 percent acceptance rate. Its president, Clayton Rose, elected by unanimous vote in 2015, came from a twenty-year career in the financial services sector by way of a teaching stint at Harvard Business School.

Today, nontraditional leaders are still regarded by many as a "fringe" phenomenon, but, as we've seen, the fringe has grown. In 2014, depending on whose definition of "nontraditional" you use, anywhere from one-third to the majority of liberal arts college presidents are nontraditional. Increasingly, schools have looked to such candidates not as reluctant concessions to thin talent pipelines or trying circumstances but rather as sources of newly important skills and fresh thinking.

Whether more selection committees and boards decide to follow suit will depend on how well nontraditional presidencies are perceived to be working out. An interesting piece of research would be to discover whether schools that have appointed nontraditional leaders have been subsequently convinced that their choice was a good one. In my own analysis, I looked at the level of alternation between traditional and nontraditional leaders—that is, how many schools pick a traditional president after having experienced the leadership of a nontraditional, and vice versa—as an indication of satisfaction. Given the relatively recent emergence of nontraditional presidents during the past few decades, for many institutions it is a measured risk to take the step to head in a new direction. Although this research does not seek to determine whether or not nontraditional presidents outperform their nontraditional counterparts, in some sense a college's selection process of president could be a proxy for satisfaction with a traditional or nontraditional type. In a search to replace a predecessor, some institutions may prefer to continue with a traditional or nontraditional president; some may wish to alternate. Analysis of those liberal arts colleges' current and predecessor type indicate that proportionately 2014 nontraditional liberal arts college presidents are 25 percent more likely to follow a traditional predecessor than they are to follow a nontraditional predecessor, whereas a traditional liberal arts college president is just over 10 percent more likely to follow a nontra-

TABLE 5.7. Likelihood of current traditional and nontraditional liberal arts president to follow traditional or nontraditional predecessor, by predecessor type

Liberal arts college president predecessor type	2014 liberal arts college traditional presidents (%; $n = 113$)	2014 liberal arts college nontraditional presidents (%; $n = 68$)	Total (%; $n = 181$)
Traditional	65	35	100
Nontraditional	72	28	100

Sources: Data from USNWR Compass 2014 data; Internet searches and analysis.

ditional predecessor than to follow a traditional predecessor. Table 5.7 summarizes the analysis.

Thus an analysis of the data does show that a nontraditional president is more likely to follow a traditional predecessor than a nontraditional predecessor; however, that makes sense given the traditionals' sheer numerical advantage. Beyond that, no pattern is visible that would indicate that colleges are systematically unhappier with either traditional or nontraditional leaders. What is clear is that many institutions are alternating between traditional and nontraditional president profiles. Among the 2014 liberal arts college presidents in office, 49 percent alternated from a traditional to a nontraditional president or vice versa, and 51 percent kept the same profile as their predecessor. This may be an indication that many institutions use the selection process to pursue a form of change embodied by the type of president they select, and that this can oscillate back and forth over time. Again, in terms of colleges' experience and researchers' data collection, it is still early days.

The president of Davis & Elkins, for one, thinks that elite colleges may have something to learn from the choices being made by smaller, scrappier schools like his. At a gathering at Lafayette College to discuss challenges facing the liberal arts sector, it was noted that the experience of more threatened institutions could be instructive to others. In classic "canary in the coal mine" fashion, they could be viewed as only the first, and hardly the last, to be hit by challenging trends. As Richard Ekman, president of the Council of Independent Colleges, put it, "some of these issues might be new for them, but they're not necessarily new for small privates." Davis & Elkins president Buck Smith was there and broadly agreed. "We haven't survived with a silver spoon," he said. "Rather we know what it means not to rest on our laurels, but to scrap for every dollar, and then spend it wisely."[14]

In fact, the data suggest something deeper: *the debate should no longer be framed in terms of nontraditional versus traditional candidates.* No matter what college segmentation has been selected, there are examples of traditional and nontraditional presidents that have been selected, have succeeded, or have failed. The choice of president is increasingly about what skill set is needed to solve the problems at hand. The context has shifted, the complexity and associated skill set required to be a successful president has risen, and the pipeline of available candidates seeking the presidency has evolved.

Elite colleges are in many respects leaders, but in some respects might be the last holdouts against changes that are inevitable and might be better dealt with earlier than later. In a roiling environment but with substantial endowments and resources, they have the option to stick with what has worked in the past, whether the topic is business models, curricula, or leader choices. But that could prove to be a dangerous luxury. The biggest risks they take may be in areas where they try to take no risk at all.

6 | Advice to the Ambitious

D EEP INTO MY own candidacy for a presidency I did not ultimately
win, I made a mistake that could have been avoided. Things had
progressed far enough in this liberal arts college's search that I was
invited to fly in for what is known as an "airport meeting." Held off-campus
for the convenience and privacy protection of candidates, such meetings
nonetheless bring together all the constituencies involved in vetting the
choices. After answering the committee's questions that evening, I was invited to pose one—just one—of my own in return. I asked something like,
"How would you describe the values of your college and how they translate
into the kind of president you seek?" and I received an informative response.
A few days after, I learned I was out of the running. When I asked for feedback from the consultant who had brought me into the search, I was given
two reasons: First, "You committed a cardinal sin by not directing your
question to the student in the room." Second, "your comments about not
really having a boss at McKinsey caused some concerns for the faculty—it
sounded like you might be difficult to control." (The irony of the latter was
pointed out to me later by someone who noted that most faculty don't think
of themselves having bosses, either.)

All cultures have their versions of kabuki theater. I now know that everyone else assembled in that airport meeting room expected certain gestures,
in line with an implicit protocol. When the time came for the candidate's
one question, it was only by addressing it to the student representative in
the room, and in particular asking about his or her choice and experience of
the college, that the candidate would display the proper deference and signal
the right priorities. Unfortunately, I didn't know this then.

Insiders in a search process have the advantage of having experienced
and internalized such norms. Outsiders have no such opportunity. And the
insider knowledge doesn't end with manners. Nontraditional candidates
can just as easily be tripped up by their ignorance of other elements. Susan
Pierce lists over a dozen topics that leaders outside higher education often
know very little about: intricacies of shared governance; hiring and tenure;

curriculum reform and its politics; enrollment practices and demographics; financial aid discounting; net tuition revenue; integration of academic and student affairs; interdisciplinary programs; the "amenities war"; athletics; drinking; fraternities and sororities; and new technologies.[1]

This helps to explain why many of today's nontraditional presidents share the experience of having gone through a number of candidacies before getting an offer. "I won't regale you with my stories of failure, but they are numerous," John Fry, for example, told me. "I was at Penn and maybe thirty-nine years old the first time I got a call from one of these places and I got right to the finals. I said to myself, 'Hey, this is easy'—and then I didn't get the job. And then I didn't get the next *six* jobs."

Of course, learning the ways of academe isn't only essential to getting the job of president—it's crucial to doing the job, too. Despite the increase in numbers of nontraditional presidents, the nontraditional pathway is still fraught with difficulties. Pierce notes in general that "the emphasis on process, often at the expense of outcome, will be foreign and often frustrating" to many executives from other sectors, and she bemoans the fact that there are "no programs whose purpose is to prepare people from outside the academy for presidencies."[2] In her own book, *On Being Presidential,* she includes advice well worth reading.

In the same spirit, this chapter shares the perspectives of the experienced presidents, mentors, and search firm executives I interviewed. Having seen many executives succeed and fail as nontraditional candidates, they were collectively able to outline strategies that aspiring presidents can pursue—not only to increase their chances of selection but also to thrive in their new positions and have greatest positive impact as higher education leaders.

Understanding the Odds

Without being too discouraging, it should be noted at the outset that one key to making progress in any endeavor is not to begin by dreaming the impossible dream. Advice to aspiring presidents with nontraditional backgrounds to be realistic in their expectations was a major theme in my conversations. The comments I heard turn out to be well supported by data.

To begin with, we know by looking at the past positions of liberal arts college presidents now in office that there is no one, typical pathway; as table 6.1 shows, presidents are drawn from a diverse set of roles within higher education.

TABLE 6.1. Role from which liberal arts college presidents were recruited

Role immediately before becoming president	Previous liberal arts college president cohort (*n* = 184; %)	2014 liberal arts college president cohort (*n* = 235; %)	ACE college president 2012 data (%)
President	17	16	20
Interim or acting president	2	3	
Chief academic officer or provost	15	19	57*
Other academic officer	22	23	
Nonacademic officer	16	20	
Chair or faculty	7	4	4
Outside higher education	21	14	20

Sources: Data from ACE (2013); Internet searches and analysis; USNWR Compass 2014 data.
*Groups all officer categories.

Reflecting on the long-standing convention by which most presidents arrived in office via the chief academic officer or provost position (part of Michael Cohen and James March's definition of "traditional"), it must be noted how thoroughly times have changed. In 2014, liberal arts college presidents were more likely to ascend from roles as other academic officers (a category that would include, for example, a dean of a school of arts and sciences) or as nonacademic officers (for example, having been dean of students). Adding up the alternatives, 62 percent of the 2014 cohort I studied came from a position other than president, chief academic officer, or provost.

Yet also unmistakable is that liberal arts college presidents overwhelmingly come from roles within higher education. In 2014, fully 86 percent did. While nontraditional presidents are becoming more common in higher education, it remains rare for them to take the top job without having first exercised some on-campus leadership. Indeed, it may be even more rare than these numbers indicate; the data have not been collected to show how common it is for nontraditional candidates to have worked as adjunct faculty or in other higher education roles at some time prior to the post they held when named president. The general observation of people working in the sector is that nontraditional presidents are far more often what Birnbaum and Umbach called "spanners" than they are "strangers." As Storbeck/Pimentel's Anne Coyle observes, "Successful nontraditional leaders [are] not people who move directly from the business world to higher education with no runway in between." She believes, "If you take some guy from Goldman Sachs and just stick him in a leadership position in higher ed, it's not going to work."

We also know, from the data and insights presented in chapter 5, that certain kinds of institutions are more and less likely to install nontraditional presidents. Clearly there are both traditional and nontraditional presidents in every type of school tier, grouping, or segment, but for aspiring leaders, knowing these patterns provides another reality check. Schools are segmented, and the likelihood of a nontraditional president's making a match would appear to be higher among schools that are further down in the rankings, for example, and smaller.

From both the presidents and search consultants I interviewed, I heard how the deliberations of presidential search committees resemble those of college admissions offices. Those at elite schools simply have many more eager applicants. To make their selection task more manageable at the outset, they apply some minimum standards and thresholds—and take special notice of candidates from certain schools. Larry Schall, the nontraditional president of Oglethorpe University in Atlanta, Georgia, told me: "It's very hard to switch segments . . . moving from tier three to tier one would be almost unheard of. Your first presidency is likely to be in the world you know." Again, there are always exceptions to the rule; at certain times the priority may be to bring in someone who fills a specific need. But those exceptions are rarely made for strangers to the institution. An executive is about as likely to gain a plum presidency straight from Wall Street as a student with an English SAT score of 500 is to get into Amherst.

Indeed, some schools are long shots even for proven administrators with deep connections. When I spoke with Schall, the news had just come out that Swarthmore College was embarking on a presidential search. Schall himself is not only a Swarthmore graduate but later served the school as an administrator, eventually reaching the level of executive vice president. Yet even adding his intervening ten years as a liberal arts president, he told me: "If I wanted to throw my hat into the Swarthmore ring, they'd talk to me, I suppose, but I would never get that job."

This isn't defeatism; it is realism. (And in any case, Schall was not looking to make a move.) Other presidents and search firm executives agreed that the top tier of liberal arts colleges are truly distinct from others, both in their priorities and in their conventions and unspoken standards for how to pick presidents. They emphasized that, as Schall noted, "by and large, the first tier is going to hire someone whose life has been spent inside the academy."

Getting into the Lineup

Evaluators of candidates, whether in search firms or search committees, make sense of CVs by looking for some logical progression and theme in a leader's career. It is extremely rare for a nontraditional candidate to simply parachute into a liberal arts presidency as a stranger. With that in mind, a nontraditional candidate should be thoughtful about the story his or her resume tells, and about whether the next step they are attempting will be seen as appropriate and manageable based on their journey so far. This can take many forms, but usually it takes time. A wry comment from Ellen Landers, who specializes in higher education and nonprofit leadership searches at Heidrick & Struggles, hints that she has seen the occasional candidate try to shortcut the process. "Preparedness doesn't just happen in a couple of days before the interview," she said. "What have they done in their career that indicates they have an interest—and this isn't just a way of leaving a corporate job?"

KNOW YOUR STUFF ABOUT THE SECTOR

The challenge begins with building a strong base of knowledge. It would be unthinkable that any candidate for a CEO role in, say, the pharmaceutical or banking industry would not be deeply attuned to how business is done in that sector, the key players in it, and the trends shaping the future. Likewise, in higher education, would-be leaders must go much deeper than a scan of recent content in the *Chronicle of Higher Education* or *Inside Higher Ed* (although those are excellent guides to the topics they will need to master). As much as they may be valued for strengths they gained outside higher education, candidates will be expected to weigh in on affordability and accessibility concerns, strategies for raising graduation rates and degree completions, the promise of new "EdTech" developments, and compliance with Title IX regulations, to name but a few burning topics within it.

Indeed, the questions lobbed at nontraditional candidates might be harder than those posed to sector veterans precisely because, as Jean Dowdall of executive search firm Witt Kieffer says, they "face initial questions of credibility." In *Public Purpose* magazine, Dowdall spoke of the skepticism nontraditional candidates must overcome: "What do they know about higher education? Are they going to bring assumptions about this college as a business as opposed to an educational institution? Are they willing to see the university as fundamentally an educational institution?"[3]

Another area in which traditional candidates' understanding is assumed but nontraditionals' appreciation is often questioned is the academic model of shared governance. As Bornstein puts it, "Power in the academy is distributed differently from the centralized power of the CEO in a typical business corporation, and the president's ability to act with authority and use the power that resides in the office depends much more on the attainment of legitimacy with stakeholders."[4] According to search executives, it is de rigueur that nontraditional candidates not only acknowledge this difference but be clear that shared governance is their own preferred mode for getting things done.

Beyond knowledge of trends and traditions, candidates must display familiarity with the operational issues routinely faced by institutions of higher learning. John Isaacson sees this as the downfall of too many candidates, even in an era where they routinely make it to the short list. "Nowadays every search is interested in nontraditional candidates," he says. "Trustees raise the topic. Faculty resists—but they look at them." The problem comes up later in the process, he claims. "Nontraditionals tend to do rather badly in the interviews. When they're asked questions that are involved in the operations of the place, they mumble."

NARROW YOUR CREDENTIALS GAPS

Presidential aspirants must make the effort to identify the most limiting gaps in their curriculum vitae and, even if it will entail a several-year process, start working to close them. For instance, candidates who have not spent time in front of classrooms might begin teaching as adjunct professors (or, in business schools, "practice professors"). This was a big part of the advice that Ellen Heffernan, a search consultant with Spelman and Johnson Group, offered to chief business officers in a 2012 conference session about reaching the presidency. "If you can teach a class, that helps," she said.[5] Having respect for the academic side of the house can go a long way toward building goodwill among faculty members.

Managers trained in other sectors who can anticipate skepticism about their cultural or operational acumen might plan a first move onto a campus in an administrative role. Sometimes the holes in an otherwise qualified leader's resume can be addressed with special projects or workable adjustments to current roles.

One nontraditional president I interviewed did all these things. After working many years in professional services, he wanted to transition into higher education and could imagine himself rising to the level of president. His first move was into a college administrative role where his deep professional experience would allow him to shine. From there he rose to become vice president for administration. He knew, however, that any presidential search committee would also want to see experience in fund-raising and teaching. "I went about intentionally trying to fill those holes in a way that I could tell two stories in each area," he told me — because after all, "the interview is only going to last so long." Already working in a senior role on campus, he was in a position to ask his college president, "Would you be willing to allow me to go with you on some of your fund-raising visits?" Thus he was able to play a role in securing some large gifts, and when the day came that he was asked about fund-raising experience, "my answer wasn't, 'I don't have any.' I had a couple of stories and that was enough." With equal resolve, he arranged to teach some classes as a side activity to his administrative duties.

This president, in fact, went even further to boost his candidacy by going back to school himself in his forties to earn his doctorate in higher education. The same is true for Bowdoin's recently appointed nontraditional president, Clayton Rose, who earned his doctorate in sociology at the University of Pennsylvania after a highly successful, twenty-plus-year career in finance on Wall Street.

Whether or not other nontraditional candidates must invest in that level of academic degree is a matter of some contention. Sue May of Storbeck/ Pimentel & Associates, for example, considers it table stakes. "If you don't have a doctorate," she says, and "if you haven't worked within academia, faculty are in general highly resistant to the idea of a nontraditional." She and others see the degree as necessary evidence of a candidate's appreciation for the research that the faculty undertake on a regular basis. It also, of course, provides a basis of authority for a decision maker. That was how Dr. John Rudley, the eleventh president of Texas Southern University (TSU), saw things. Rudley started out in financial management at TSU and later became the University of Houston's vice president for administration and finance before returning to TSU as president. He told *Diverse Education*, however, that faculty just didn't give his years of practical experience the same respect they would give to scholarly achievement. "I got sick of them assuming the quality of information I had wasn't worth listening to," he said, so he became a student of his own institution, and in 2001 earned his EdD in administration at TSU. Reflecting on the difference it made, Rudley claimed, "Everyone relaxes when I come into the room because now I'm one of them, as they see it."[6]

One thing is certain: the overwhelming majority of current liberal arts presidents do have some type of doctorate, whether it is a JD, MD, EdD, or PhD supporting their experience. Table 6.2 shows the breakdown by terminal degree for those in office in 2014 and their predecessors. Ninety-two percent of this generation of liberal arts presidents hold doctoral degrees. (Among their predecessors, 89 percent did.) The most prevalent doctorate is the PhD, outnumbering all other doctorates by a ratio of about 3:1.

Gaining a college presidency without a doctoral degree would thus appear to be a difficult feat. On the other hand, we can safely say that only nontraditional candidates have managed it. John Fry, for example, won the top job at Franklin & Marshall with only a master's degree and has gone on to become president of Drexel University since. Richard Hurley, president of the University of Mary Washington since 2010, also stopped at the master's level. He apparently didn't need the extra credibility after succeeding there as executive vice president and chief financial officer and then proving himself as acting president after the abrupt departure of his predecessor. As a way to improve one's odds of advancing in a presidential search, a doctorate is an achievable and advisable step, but for certain people and under certain circumstances, the lack of it may not be a deal-breaker. My own personal experience as a dean candidate at a world-class business school is that my doctorate in higher education management at U Penn was indispensable.

UNDERSTAND THE RECRUITING AND SELECTION PROCESS

A presidential search process can seem mysterious to the uninitiated—and particularly to candidates who aren't themselves products of the higher education world. They typically need to work harder to develop a sense of what to expect and how decisions will be made. The first shock for candidates from the corporate world is typically how prolonged and inclusive a process it is. Rooted in shared governance, like so many other aspects of higher education management, it often takes six to nine months and involves countless interviews by and speeches in front of stakeholders of many stripes.

Even for people (like myself) with family histories in higher education, this can be surprising. Historically, the selection of the college president was the job of the board of trustees—indeed, its most important responsibility. Today, however, it is a project shared by faculty, students, alumni,

TABLE 6.2. Overview of doctorates achieved by liberal arts college presidents

Liberal arts presidents cohort	No. presidents earning doctorate (%)	No. PhD (% of doctorate)	No. JD (% of doctorates)	No. education-related, such as EdD (% of doctorates)	No. other doctorates (%)	No. earning two doctorates
2014 predecessor generation ($n = 187$)	167 (89)	130 (70)	15 (8)	16 (9)	9 (5)	3
2014 presidents ($n = 248$)	227 (92)	178 (72)	14 (10)	8 (3)	19 (8)	2

Sources: Data from Internet searches; USNWR Compass 2014 data.
Note: The "predecessor" generation cannot be labeled with any particular prior; these are all the presidents who preceded the ones in office in June 2014—whenever those transitions took place.

administrators, and professional staff, all jockeying for influence in the choice of successor. Once analogous to a corporate board of directors' selection of a CEO, it has in recent decades come to resemble more a rough-and-tumble political selection. The goal is to arrive at a stronger, consensus-based choice, but sometimes sharp elbows come into play. In the words of Judith McLaughlin and David Riesman, "Many college and university searches have become politicized and factionalized at their very outset by disputes over what constituencies should be represented and in what numbers."[7]

Selection processes often focus on checklists and a detailed set of steps as to how to conduct the search process. One of the early frameworks outlining the process was published by the late John Nason, himself formerly president of Carleton College and also Swarthmore.[8] His essential nine steps include: (1) establishment of search and selection machinery; (2) committee organization; (3) criteria formulation; (4) candidate pool development; (5) candidate screening; (6) candidate interviews; (7) top candidate selection; (8) presidential appointment; and (9) winding down and gearing up.[9] Subsequent process outlines have been provided by James Fisher and James Koch, who spell out a detailed weekly checklist for the search process (and lament that the shared-governance nature of the search process has become more important than the outcome itself); Rita Bornstein, who adds that the search committee's composition is critical to ensuring fit and that the search process gains the legitimacy it requires from the constituencies expecting representation; and the Association of Governing Boards, which offers a twenty-step process with fourteen specific responsibilities divided between the board and search committee.[10]

All are worth perusing by the candidate who needs a sense of what to expect, as are the case studies compiled by McLaughlin and Riesman in *Choosing a College President*.[11] These real-world stories emphasize the importance of confidentiality, specifics on committee composition and modus operandi, the importance of due diligence and background checks, and—to the point we will take up next—the role of executive search firms.

GET TO KNOW THE SEARCH FIRMS

As discussed earlier, search firms are now involved in the overwhelming majority of presidential searches—a fact that does not leave candidates indifferent. As Schall put it: "They're a necessary evil to some extent. But every presidential search uses a search firm. . . . On occasion they add value, and they're very expensive. But it's just part of the business." One of the most emphatic pieces of advice offered by the presidents I interviewed was to build a network with search firm executives.

A typical presidential search results in a flood of applicants, and search firms not only elicit viable candidates from their own networks but also "position" the ones they present to search committees. David Greene of Colby College described the "huge role" they play in these terms: "The thing they do more than anything is to develop the pool. In the end they have some influence, for sure, on who gets into those smaller groups as you move down the road . . . but they'll have a very significant influence on who's in the pool in the first place."

For nontraditional candidates, search consultants can also provide an invaluable service as Sherpas, guiding them through the process and filling in contextual knowledge. John Fry, for example, told me that during the Franklin & Marshall search, he spoke with search executive Shelly Storbeck a number of times about the institutional context and how the search committee was thinking about fit. "Shelly is really exceptional because she can give you those kind of insights," he remarked, with added appreciation that she was "open for these kinds of conversations." People I interviewed, however, cautioned candidates not to assume that such guidance would always be forthcoming. The very nature of the search profession can sometimes make it transactional, given the number of applicants to any given position, the time required to provide one-on-one attention or feedback, and search consultants' general preference for spending that time on persuading already perfect-seeming candidates to toss their hats into the ring. It is not uncommon for a candidate to be buoyed by an intense conversation with a search executive, then have that hope slowly sink across weeks or even months of no contact—and end with the public announcement that a new leader has been chosen.

It is important for nontraditional candidates, I heard, not to conclude that their background is keeping them from making a stronger impression on a consultant. Although a given individual may have a proclivity one way or another, search firm executives have no built-in bias against (or for) nontraditional leaders. As Schall noted: "They succeed when they are able to place a candidate. They don't care where the person is from." Rather, nontraditional candidates (for that matter, any candidates) should make it their goal to be among those limited cases in which search consultants will take special interest. To appear as a brighter spot on their radar from the outset, one search consultant suggested obtaining a nomination written by a respected academic. It is easy to see how that would reduce the search firm's own risk in presenting a nontraditional candidate to a search committee—and intriguing to think about what else one could do with their risk-reduction instincts in mind.

The good news is that the number of executive search firms that place liberal arts presidents is fairly concentrated, reducing the workload this implies. As David Greene put it, "There are only about four search firms out there that actually place the presidents at the top places, and if you knew the top four people in those firms and if those individuals thought you were a credible candidate . . . that is probably the single most important thing you can do." Schall echoed this advice: "As a potential candidate, being well thought of and known by key people of the search firms is critical." Love them or hate them, search professionals are, if not the kingmakers who can place you in your dream job, the gatekeepers who can shut you out. Much of the advice that follows is relevant for any college or university president or dean search.

GET MENTORED

The value of having an experienced party to guide one's initial forays, which surfaced in conversations about search consultants, emerged more generally as a strong theme in interviews with presidents. They pointed out that, almost whatever an individual resolves to do, there are people who have blazed that trail before them. It would be folly not to cultivate relationships with leaders who managed to succeed as college presidents, and ask them to share the wisdom of their experience.

The three nontraditional presidents I interviewed in-depth had worked on campuses prior to their candidacies and had the benefit of mentorship by the college presidents for whom they worked. Whether it was Robert Zimmer helping David Greene at the University of Chicago, Alfred Bloom guiding Lawrence Schall at Swarthmore, or Judith Rodin at the University of Pennsylvania taking John Fry under her wing, excellent executives were generous in sharing what they had learned through their own journeys. Fry, remembering his transition to the University of Pennsylvania from consulting at age thirty-four, recalls: "I began this straight-up-in-the-air learning curve which took a long time, but I had the benefit of an amazing leader who helped me shape what I try to do today."

Undoubtedly, these nontraditional presidents were also regarded more favorably for having spent their apprenticeships at such outstanding institutions, all of them bastions of academic rigor. Mentoring is usually thought of as an interpersonal relationship between a sage veteran and a less-experienced learner, but the knowledge and habits of mind that can be soaked up by working in high-performing organizations also contribute to executives' judgment. Aspiring nontraditional presidents should carefully problem-solve from whom and where they will gain the wisdom they need to become their best selves.

All the more, nontraditional candidates who are not currently working in academic settings must actively seek out mentors. They can increase their understanding of higher education by engaging in regular dialogue with the smart people they already know working in academic environments, and by deliberately expanding their networks to reach the higher education leaders they believe could teach them most.

DON'T BE A STRANGER

Typically, a school that selects a nontraditional president (or leader) has gained a comfort level with that person through some prior relationship. Clearly this is true of the three nontraditional presidents I got to know best through my research. John Fry of Drexel University (and former president of Franklin & Marshall College), David Greene of Colby College, and Lawrence Schall of Oglethorpe University all passed through administrative leadership positions in higher education prior to becoming presidents. Other stories like theirs abound. Mary K. Grant, before becoming president of the Massachusetts College of Liberal Arts (MCLA), was an administrator for the broader UMass system, serving as director of its Center for Social Policy and assistant vice chancellor for administration, finance, and human resources, and leading the team that launched UMassOnline. (And, two decades before becoming president, she graduated from MCLA's predecessor institution, North Adams State College.) Richard V. Hurley, president of the University of Mary Washington since 2010, was formerly that school's chief financial officer and had been at the institution for a decade in various administrative and financial roles. As David Bellshaw of Isaacson, Miller says, "If somebody is a 'stranger to the academy,' they're usually a friend of the institution."

Nontraditional candidates from further afield confront much greater skepticism. Bellshaw continues: "You don't go out and just randomly find some bank executive that's going to run a little liberal college on the east or west coast. It just doesn't work. They have no credibility." There are more exceptions to this than Bellshaw's comment would seem to allow, but it is true that fewer than 10 percent of all higher education presidents were complete strangers to higher education prior to their appointments.

The advice embedded in these comments is to not be a stranger. Non-traditional candidates in particular should try to find ways to make connections to the institutions that interest them most. In fact, looking at 2014 data, just over a third of sitting nontraditional presidents have a previous relationship with the very institution they lead (see table 6.3).

Expanding further on the point about previous relationships, several search executives particularly stressed the credibility that nontraditional candidates gain through board membership. A great example is Barry Mills of Bowdoin, who, long before becoming president in 2001, was a student at the college. Later a successful lawyer in New York, he became a member of the Board of Overseers in 1994 and then subsequently a trustee. Indeed, he was chair of the very presidential selection committee that eventually recognized him as the best man for the job. Likewise, Phillip Stone graduated cum laude from Virginia's Bridgewater College in 1965, then went on to study and practice law. After practicing as an attorney for twenty-four years and along the way joining Bridgewater's board of trustees, he came back to the school for a highly successful sixteen-year term as president. (Having retired in 2010, he was recently coaxed back into action to lead Sweet Briar College out of crisis.) C. D. Spangler, the billionaire businessman who spent an impressive decade (1986–96) as president of the University of North Carolina (UNC), was an alumnus and had served on the UNC Chapel Hill's Board of Visitors.

TABLE 6.3. Previous institutional ties of nontraditional liberal arts presidents

$N = 84$	Previous employment or board member? No. (%)	Alumnus? No. (%)	Both? No. (%)	Either? No. (%)
Yes	17 (20)	21 (25)	9 (11)	29 (34.5)
No	67 (80)	63 (75)	75 (89)	55 (65.5)

Sources: Data from Internet searches and analysis; USNWR Compass 2014 data.

Although just over a third of nontraditional presidents had a previous relationship with the institution they lead, it is equally important to note that 65 percent did not. This means that while a prior relationship may indeed be helpful, it is not a requirement for a nontraditional aspirant. As another way to build a bridge, search executives pointed to classroom contributions as adjunct professors, lecturers, and faculty members in corporate learning environments. Storbeck says, "I always tell nontraditional candidates to get in the classroom; it's an absolute baseline activity . . . to show that you're interested in this space."

Winning the Offer

Once you are in the running for a presidency, the challenge is to survive the pruning process. Obviously, it is essential to prepare by learning what you can about the particular institution. Several search executives point out that selection committees expect to hear insights specifically related to their school's size, programs, strengths, challenges, and traditions—not just generalities that could be true anywhere. They note the advantage they've observed in nontraditional candidates who reached out to students and staff in advance and previously visited the campus. Selection committees further expect a candidate to be able to articulate why their school is especially interesting to him or her, when that interest began, and what about the opportunity makes it a good fit. Such questions are often central to the first round of "airport interviews."

Some of the preparation required is thus long-term, but some is short-term and involves things like crafting an excellent CV and thoughtful cover letter, doing background research on the institution, and connecting with stakeholders. Storbeck acknowledged that a nontraditional "needs to do twice as much homework as somebody who's living inside that environment traditionally."

DISPLAY YOUR RESPECT FOR ACADEMIC TRADITIONS AND PRIORITIES

If you are a nontraditional candidate, it might seem obvious that you have a deep and abiding respect for academic traditions; why else would you divert from an easier path in your current career to be part of them? This, however, is not taken as a given by others; to the contrary, some people's greatest fear is that you will deliberately flout those traditions. Others suspect you will simply not understand how to operate in a culture where faculty are the life-blood of the enterprise. Search firm executives say this is the biggest hurdle to nontraditional candidates' credibility. Notes Coyle, "I'd be hard-pressed to think of a presidential search in recent memory where they didn't express an openness to . . . interview at least one or two nontraditional candidates." But that willingness, she said, "doesn't always get translated into them hiring the nontraditional."

William Bowen's advice for nontraditional candidates is unequivocal: "I would understand the history of the place so that you don't come in as a know-nothing in terms of how the place got to where it is. Respect the history and understand it." Whether it is honor codes, acronyms, mascots, building names, decision-making bodies and their associated processes, try to find out why things at the place are as they are.

Presidents and search firm executives also stressed that vocabulary matters. Every profession has its own vernacular, and when leaders speak off the cuff they tend to revert to the language they find most comfortable. A typical banana peel could be a question such as, "What is your vision for the college?," a question I have received countless times. Bellshaw told me, "It's amazing how poorly candidates do in terms of expressing a vision that is meaningful." Answering such a question well, he explained, means simultaneously expressing a desire to learn from and collaborate with the community to arrive at a vision, and articulating some "notion of what the promised land looks like." For a candidate coming from the private sector, it is doubly hard to offer such a nuanced answer "in academic terms and not business jargon."

It is an understandable difficulty, but any awkwardness in this regard only reinforces a faculty's anchoring bias toward believing a nontraditional candidate does not understand their world. References to, say, B2C customer acquisition, CRM, or balance sheet assets in response to questions about student admissions, retention, or development and endowment only hand ammunition to a nontraditional candidate's detractors, even if the concepts are completely valid and relevant. Ellen Landers warned: "Sometimes we see businesspeople step into these interviews and they're speaking a completely foreign language: wrong terms that aren't typically used in education. There's just a disconnect in the discussions."

Stated in positive terms, the advice to nontraditional candidates is to learn the language of the academy. The effort should go further than using the right operational vocabulary, moreover. In a recent speech to the Council of Independent Colleges' Presidential Institute, Nan Keohane (former president of Wellesley College and Duke University) advised all presidents to use and embody *liberal arts learning* in their discourse, both formal and informal. "If you cite passages of fine literature, draw on instances from history, refer to the arts, and describe learning in the sciences in liberal terms," she said, "you will set an example for others and have an influence greater than you may expect." Such a deeper show of respect (which Keohane jokingly went on to call "larding your language with liberal learning") might be even more noted in a candidate who had never been a tenure-track professor.[12]

PUT THE ELEPHANT ON THE TABLE

John Fry offered a story of his personal experience which resonated with advice from others. It had to do with his own awareness that his CV lacked some lines that search committees typically like to see. After failing to get an offer despite being a finalist in several searches, and doing some soul-searching, Fry realized that faculty members' discomfort with his lack of a doctorate was all the worse for going unspoken.

In the Franklin & Marshall search, Fry took a different tack. Rather than leaving it to others to frame a potential inadequacy and concern when he wasn't there to defend it, he addressed the concern up front in his application letter and also brought it up early in his first interview. He decided, he says, to express: "This is who I am. This is what I believe in terms of my own values from an academic perspective, but I am not [an academic]. So let's get that straight right away." Reflecting on that decision, he is convinced it made all the difference. Without acknowledging the elephant in the room, "I never would have gotten that job," he believes. "I would have gotten all the way to end, and I never would have gotten that job."

In a curious way, explicitly pointing to and embracing the fact that one's background is nontraditional serves a candidate very well. Often, a search committee has an intention to place a nontraditional candidate on its final slate of candidates—but it might also feel that one is enough. If that is true, the nontraditional candidate faces an initial challenge only to beat out other nontraditional candidates. If that sounds easy, however, the challenge that follows is much greater. Once they become the sole nontraditional candidate standing, they have to sell not only themselves but the whole proposition of a nontraditional leader.

Owning up to a CV's downside also serves a candidate well if others perceive that as a sincere intention to build a strong team with complementarity and to rely on others around them to fill in and help close the gaps that matter in practice. Coyle said that leaders with unconventional backgrounds should not only acknowledge the hurdle they face but also display good thinking about how they will get past it. They should "explicitly talk about it . . . acknowledging that the first year will really be spent listening and getting to know people."

SHOWCASE YOUR STRENGTHS RELATIVE TO TYPICAL TRADITIONAL CANDIDATES

While presidents and search executives urged nontraditional candidates to deal with their lack of scholarly credentials head-on, they also made clear there is a difference between acknowledging one's differences and apologizing for them. Seeming too deferential to long-standing customs or too eager to adjust to prevailing norms will only undercut one's perceived strength. Schall points out that liberal arts colleges are under strain, and most search committees see the nontraditional candidate "as an agent of change—because just standing still will bring down most institutions." If you are a nontraditional candidate, this is probably how you have been positioned in the set of choices—perhaps quite explicitly by the search consultant. You should recognize that positioning, and own it.

Remember Jackie Zavitch's comment from chapter 4, emphasizing a similar aspect: "The best candidates I've seen in the nontraditional realm are those that can challenge schools [by saying] . . . have you thought about XYZ? Here are two things I see coming, and these are ways you might address it, understanding you have all these constraints." Any college thinking of hiring a nontraditional leader has some sense that it may need fresh thinking and constructive provocation. Delivering it is the job of the candidate, even though it means "you have to be smarter than the institution," as Zavitch concedes, and "that's a pretty high bar."

This is tricky territory, however. Search executives counseled against getting too prescriptive too early—for example, by sharing ideas for change in cover letters. Even though the nontraditional candidate's outsider view is valued, people don't always appreciate it when a person with limited knowledge of their institution holds forth on not only their need to change but just how they should go about it. In a recent piece for the *Chronicle of Higher*

Education, Allison M. Vaillancourt, a human resources vice president at the University of Arizona, offered unusually frank advice from the perspective of a staffer who has sat on her share of search committees. Under the heading "We may need to be 'fixed,' but we don't want to hear that from you," she wrote:

> Every organization can do better, and search committees are well aware of their institutions' gaps and areas of vulnerability—but we don't want you to embarrass us by talking about how you can save us. One of my colleagues, a woman known for her directness, recently spent two days at what she perceived to be a "lower-tier" institution offering her myriad recommendations for improving rankings, streamlining operations, and enhancing the curriculum. She had done her research and proposed a brilliant five-year plan for achieving the college's aspirations. There was just one problem: This made people resent her. Had she engaged in conversation about the institution's aspirations, asked questions about the trouble spots, and expressed excitement about working together to achieve a better future, she would have been their top choice. Instead, she issued a manifesto and positioned herself as a bossy, know-it-all, institutional savior.[13]

There is a much better way to make a positive impression as a change agent. Rather than coming out of the gate with preformed judgments and solutions, candidates can showcase their capabilities to arrive at them by explaining the process they propose to use, thereby illustrating knowledge of shared governance. They can figure out what a committee suspects is lacking in traditional candidates—often more skill and interest in external-facing and financial stewardship duties—and frame their strengths in those critically important parts of the job.

Demonstrating an understanding of and willingness to address the financial model will usually be important. In many ways a liberal arts college president is equivalent to a CEO in a business. He or she needs to find a way to grow revenue and stay on budget. However, in liberal arts institutions the revenue streams are narrow and come almost entirely from tuition and giving. Nontraditional candidates must demonstrate an understanding of this; as Landers puts it, "a president needs to understand the complexity of the [financial] levers he or she has." Assuming the candidate can reinforce the going-in assumption of financial management skills, he or she will hold an advantage, since "that's not necessarily the skill set of someone who's come up the traditional faculty route."

Based on her experience, Landers also says, "search committees view the reason to go to an external nontraditional candidate is because they will be better in fund-raising." She and other search executives underlined the external orientation of the presidency today, with fund-raising efforts keeping these leaders on the road as many as 150 nights per year. Even at the colleges with the richest endowments, presidents face substantial and unrelenting pressure to raise funds. Recognizing this, nontraditional candidates can showcase their sales experience, success in building trust-based relationships and external networks, or fund-raising experience for nonprofit organizations.

Nontraditional candidates might assume that these aspects of their profile are too obvious to spend time highlighting. They are mistaken, however, if they think that faculty and selection committee members understand where they come from and what they actually did—especially given the difference in terminology across sectors. One solution is to design one's CV to perform the necessary translation—for example, by organizing experience under headings relevant to search committees such as "fund-raising" (in which section the candidate would include sales experience) and "financial crisis management"—and, for that matter, also "publications and research" (speeches and documents authored as an industry thought leader), "faculty experience" (leadership development in the corporation or adjunct faculty experience), and "shared governance" (perhaps as experienced in a law or accounting firm, or less formally in a role requiring balancing of diverse stakeholders' priorities).

The best strategy for a nontraditional candidate might be to point to areas of strength while simultaneously reminding the evaluators that some of these are areas that hold little interest to others. This is my impression of what Patrick Gamble (the nontraditional president of the University of Alaska) was doing when he told *Public Purpose* magazine he had the kind of talents required for "all the mundane stuff" required by a multicampus operating entity, and was happy to respect the "talents of our faculty with regard to what they can do with our specific programs."[14] Recall the finding mentioned earlier by the American Council of Education about the declining interest in the presidential job among chief academic officers (CAOs). ACE's 2009 CAO census found that 66 percent of those surveyed "find the nature of presidential work unappealing."[15] By showing enthusiasm in his interviews for tasks others would consider humdrum, Gamble would have set up a positive contrast.

DEMONSTRATE THAT YOU WILL BE A PASSIONATE ADVOCATE FOR WHAT THE COMMUNITY VALUES

While there continue to be contrasting opinions on the power of the presidency in higher education, everyone acknowledges at least the president's possession of a bully pulpit. People with a say in presidential selection want to see the potential in a candidate to be an effective advocate for the causes they care about most. In a nontraditional candidate, in particular, they need assurance that the new leader will sound the right notes. John Isaacson comments that the nontraditionals who do well often come from government or public service backgrounds that have required them to communicate to complex stakeholder groups. He adds that nontraditional candidates often make the mistake of believing schools want to see their managerial competence and mastery of metrics constantly on display, when in fact, "what goes on in these places is first and foremost inspiration."

Great communicators don't only succeed in broadcast mode; they also rely deeply on their listening skills and abilities to connect with different stakeholder groups, and with students in particular. Landers commented that a common slip-up for a nontraditional candidate is to "show a lack of passion for or understanding of students or the mission (or) to do an interview and never mention the students." As interview processes move to final stages, on-campus interviews allow greater scope for candidates to ask questions. Not only do they need to be able to ask intelligent, open-ended questions, they need to be able to show that they actually listen to the responses.

Nontraditional candidates have a few opportunities to demonstrate that they have the ability to inspire in the process, and they need to make the best of them. On-campus interviews generally afford candidates the opportunity to make opening speeches of perhaps eight to fifteen minutes to groups of faculty, students, and/or administrative staff. Such presentations should be carefully crafted and thoroughly rehearsed for maximum impact. Isaacson recalled one he attended that went especially well, by Jim Yong Kim to the search committee at Dartmouth University. Kim was a nontraditional candidate, having trained as a physician and cofounded and led the renowned nonprofit health-care organization Partners in Health. He would go on to defy tradition even further when his selection by Dartmouth made him the first Asian American president of an Ivy League school. Part of his success, Isaacson believes, is that he "showed up in front of the Dartmouth search committee with the most inspiring speech I've heard." Isaacson elaborates: "He attached Dartmouth's future to the highest possible moral callings and then linked his speech to the sayings and doings of historic Dartmouth presidents. He said we are going to educate the leaders of the world and they must be prepared to do the world's hardest work, and then he launched into what the world's work was and how you inspire students to aspire to that work. Just took them by storm."

Kim's achievement here is of particular note because he powerfully made the case for liberal arts education—a form of advocacy that search executives said was important to many committees. Given the escalating tuitions of many liberal arts colleges, students and their parents are more mindful than ever of the need to see a "return on their investment" and concerned when the hard evidence of higher earnings is elusive. David Bellshaw said he has seen "an increasing desire to find a president . . . who can be a spokesperson and defender of the liberal arts that takes the bully pulpit back." This might not sound like a natural role for a nontraditional president—but perhaps it explains why so many of them are themselves products of liberal arts educations. In any case, a strong sense of the liberal arts mission should be part of the story told by any candidate.

DEAL WITH PRIVACY INTRUSIONS (AND ANY OTHER GLITCHES) GRACIOUSLY

For nontraditional candidates, it often comes as a surprise to discover that their candidacy is something of an open book. As Sue May explains, many aspects of college searches have evolved over the decades, but "the biggest trend has been the flipping around of confidentiality." It used to be that the early steps of the search took place in a "black box," she says, after which committee members "draw back the curtain and three finalists parade in front of the whole community." Today, stakeholders push for more upstream influence over that lineup, and even if an institution tries to protect candidates' privacy, it often doesn't succeed. May points to all the "student newspapers that have Google alerts with the names of every key administrator" as just one of the new realities that mean, if a leader trying to quietly advance his career "sets foot on another campus, he's doomed."

Given the shortages of strong candidates many searches are now witnessing, May believes this might change in the near future. "In the liberal arts realm in particular they're not obligated to be public in the way that public institutions are," she notes, "and they've begun to understand that the best candidates are the ones with the most to lose." Other search executives, too, are urging institutions to give more authority to their selection committees (upon whom the need for absolute discretion can be impressed) and otherwise make their processes more confidential, to ensure that the best candidates are willing to consider their opportunities. For now, however, candidates should be fully prepared for the day when the fact that they are in the running suddenly becomes common, and controversial, knowledge. How they deal with that moment will reveal a lot about them.

SIZE UP THE SELECTION COMMITTEE AND BOARD

One last piece of advice for the nontraditional candidate making his or her way through the process at a particular institution is to understand the key players involved in its search and try to gauge their relative influence. Recall the job description put out by Trinity College that was shown in chapter 2; as discussed there, it calls for a breadth of strengths that perhaps no one could reasonably claim. The implication is that the real requirements must depend on the priorities of the individuals with the most say in the selection.

Coming from the corporate world, it might be easy for a nontraditional candidate to assume that the board of trustees has all of the decision-making power in a liberal arts college or university. Indeed, the trustees have an important role to play and hold the formal responsibility of presidential appointers and evaluators. It may even be, as I heard from some search consultants, that boards have gained influence in the wake of the 2008–10 financial crisis that pummeled so many colleges' endowments. Ken Kring, for example, described "a shift in the decision-making dynamics, where boards of trustees are empowered because of financial challenges . . . to step further into succession planning." His observation was that, more than ever before, financial matters were taking precedence as the greatest threats to the health of many institutions—and that boards are generally thought to know more than faculties about those threats and how to counter them. If true, this might generally bode well for nontraditional candidates.

However, it would be folly to make an assumption that this is the case in any particular search. At most institutions, faculty also play a major role and often comprise up to half of the selection committee membership. While faculty cannot unilaterally select a president, they do often hold a de facto veto, and most boards are loath to override such a veto. Developing an understanding of the committee's composition and its individual members' biases and preferences is therefore important, especially for the nontraditional candidate who has choices to make about how to translate his or her experience into the most relevant terms. The prepared candidate may even choose to direct certain comments toward a selection committee member by demonstrating some knowledge of the committee member's background and context.

Transitioning to Effective Leadership

The focus on landing a college presidency can be so intense that it can be easy to forget that the announcement is really just the beginning of the work, not the end. Like a pie-eating contest where the prize is more pie, the process both reveals and rewards serious appetite for the task. Often, too, it is only once a leader has been chosen and arrives on campus that many of the college's stakeholders have their opportunity to ask questions and form opinions. As a candidate, the nontraditional leader might have gotten a taste of skepticism; in office, it is served up by the plateful.

It is important to manage these early transitional months well because they set the tone for all that is to follow. This is why the literature on leadership in general focuses as much as it does on the topic of "onboarding" and a new executive's game plan for his or her "first ninety days" on the job. Yet very little has been written about how a nontraditional leader in higher education can move from successful selection through productive transition.

Presidents I interviewed named all kinds of imperatives for leaders once they take office, and many of them had to do with achieving the right balance between often conflicting needs. David Greene, for example, noted: "More so than on a university campus, the visibility of the president of a liberal arts college is essential. . . . At the same time, working on development . . . [and] external and board issues, those are also important." The same need to "be very strategic and very balanced" came up in many areas.

PULL TOGETHER THE TEAM THAT
WILL HELP YOU SUCCEED

Getting one's top team sorted out and working productively together is an immediate priority in any new leadership position, and all the more important for a nontraditional candidate who will rely on those direct-reports in more than usual ways. Especially where a president was selected for his or her "outside-facing" skills, there will be a need for a trusted and capable "insider" team, both to cover the areas in which new leaders have relative weakness, and to allow them to double down on the activities where they can add most value. At the dean level, for me this has been my senior associate dean for faculty, Sankaran Venkatramen, a "provost" equivalent at the business school who brings invaluable complementary skills and institutional memory to my team.

Speaking to *Public Purpose* magazine, Weber State University president Ann Millner put it well: "No one brings everything to this role, unless they've been a sitting president," she said. "These are very complex positions. . . . You have to focus on knowing what you're good at and then building the best team that you can build and bringing together the people who have the experience and expertise to collectively provide leadership for the institution."[16] Until they have that strong executive team in place, leaders can't do nearly enough to carry out their institution's mission and keep it running smoothly, so beginning that team-building must be a day-one priority.

DON'T ASSUME LEGITIMACY — EARN IT

An appointment as president far from guarantees that the faculty are energized and enamored with the idea. Every appointment brings disappointment. In many searches, prominent faculty members may have themselves been candidates, or supported a different candidate, and thus suffer wounded pride. Despite official external declarations of "unanimous board support," often mentioned in press releases, the reality facing any new president—but even more so a nontraditional president—is that the journey to win over faculty hearts and minds takes time.

Leadership scholars refer to this as attaining "legitimacy" and see it as crucial to a president's transition into a new role. They hold differing views on how legitimacy is gained. James Fisher and James Koch believe it flows from the transformational power inherent in the presidential position and thus can be conferred only top-down by the board.[17] Others, like Robert Birnbaum, believe that legitimacy can be gained only through interaction with multiple stakeholders. For Rita Bornstein, "to gain legitimacy, a president must demonstrate a leadership style that comports with the culture of the institution."[18]

When I spoke with nontraditional presidents, their first suggestion for a successful transition was to establish rapport and a working relationship with the faculty. They described the investment to establish rapport with the faculty as "not optional" but rather a campaign that should be at the very top of any new president's list of priorities. Remember, they advised, that tenured faculty members have the assurance that they will endure in the organization, and many have seen multiple presidents come and go. Winning them over requires an investment of time and patience, and there is no substitute for a personal approach. One search executive commented that a nontraditional president was very well received when he interviewed every one of the tenured faculty members one-on-one and read their research before meeting with them in the first year.

John Fry related that, in his first months at Franklin & Marshall, he conducted a listening tour, meeting extensively with tenured faculty and other constituents. What he gathered formed the basis for a white paper that he wrote as his New Year's letter. As he put it: "I took my own notes. I did an old-fashioned consulting study where you go and show respect by going to their place and you listen to them." Rather than articulate a key set of imperatives and a to-do list, the note instead focused on summarizing the questions that had been identified in the process and how he felt they should subsequently be tackled. He avoided "hitting the hornets' nest" and instead felt the process "stirred up a lot of relief" by making some unspoken issues more discussible. He continues his efforts to listen in other ways, noting that the role of president in a liberal arts college is "like being the parish priest," where it is all about people and there is therefore no substitute for "building individual and small group relationships." A simple gesture to establish personal rapport that Fry mentioned was inviting everyone from the faculty on the last Friday of each month "for a beer and wine and cheese party at the house . . . open house, no speeches. . . . I was trying to set up a convivial environment."

Once a new president is installed, early decisions will be scrutinized, not only as being right or wrong but in terms of how they are made. Many scholars (at least as far back as Birnbaum, and Cohen and March, in the 1980s) have noted that the leadership styles often found in business—hierarchical, with clear targets and profit orientation, in addition to well-defined processes and accountabilities more associated with top-down decision making—are often incompatible with higher education cultures. This means that any product of that kind of background may have to check his or her instincts. Note how a faculty member praised the approach of one such leader, Patrick Gamble at the University of Alaska: "By bringing the Faculty Alliance on board to work on the academic master plan, President Gamble did a lot to demonstrate he was interested in faculty input and shared governance." He continues: "The alliance had some good ideas about how to bring the document to completion. President Gamble listened and gave us the chance to bring things to fruition."[19]

That sounds completely in keeping with the approach advocated by long-time president and mentor William Bowen. "My advice would be to build alliances with the key faculty, make every effort you can to build friendships and to understand what they're doing," he told me. A president needs "to be willing to say, 'We have to make these choices, and here's the way I see the choices. What do *you* think?'"

CONSTANTLY THWART CONFIRMATION BIASES

The faculty concerns over nontraditional candidates that arise during a search processes do not simply evaporate overnight. For months afterward, people will remain on the lookout for the problems they expected to see. Shelly Storbeck describes the extra burden this creates:

> Every [nontraditional leader] falls and skins their knee . . . in the first year, and usually in a major way. Some horrible thing happens that they didn't anticipate and they don't know how to deal with [it]. . . . The difference with someone who . . . skins their knee from the academy is that somebody's going to pick you up and brush you off and get started again. When you're a nontraditional, they're going to sit back, fold their arms, and they're going to say, "See, I told you he shouldn't have been in this job." It's very unforgiving for somebody who's not a member of the Guild.

Even as this book was being written, a distressingly perfect example of this observation played out in national news headlines. Simon Newman was appointed president of Mount Saint Mary's University in 2015 despite some consternation over his nontraditional background: he was a successful serial entrepreneur and then CEO of a private equity firm before arriving at this small liberal arts institution, the second-oldest Catholic university in America. Newman quickly spotted a way to make a positive difference to the school's retention rate (one factor driving its ranking): he believed that, by surveying entering freshmen during orientation week, they would be able to tell that some of them—perhaps twenty to twenty-five members of the entering class—simply lacked the motivation required to succeed. After all, year after year, it had been the case that some 20 percent of the entering class had washed out. If only the school could spot and act on the least promising cases before late September, Newman explained, the school's admissions mistakes wouldn't have to show up in its officially submitted enrollment data.[20]

The logic was sound enough, perhaps, but the idea of sending students packing so quickly struck many as draconian—and Newman's urgency to carry out the plan felt like an assault to the deliberative decision making to which college personnel were accustomed. Still, Newman might have prevailed if he hadn't made the fatal error of stating his case in the kind of terms he would have used with his private-equity partners. Conferring with a small group of faculty and administrators, he said: "This is hard for you because you think of the students as cuddly bunnies, but you can't. You just have to drown the bunnies . . . put a Glock to their heads." By January, the campus newspaper had put the quote into print; by the end of February, Newman was out of a job.[21]

It's possible that Newman, once he had been formally selected and lauded for just the kind of strategic, financial, and analytical leadership the school needed, believed he was more empowered than he was—and that, in the tradition of business, he could count on his board of trustees to back him up for at least a year's worth of breaking eggs. But the presidents I interviewed spoke of the early transitional months as essentially a continuation of the selection process, with the nontraditional candidate's perceived or real weaknesses still being tested on many fronts. In fact, these presidents specifically told me that new leaders in higher education should resist the temptation to go for the kinds of "quick wins" that are advised in business settings. It is far more important to prove a commitment to collaborative decision making from the start.

The broader implication here is that nontraditional candidates must be especially self-aware and avoid behaviors that might play into their detractors' hands. Search firm executives agree there is often a bias on campuses toward believing that nontraditional candidates will be top-down, directive, authoritarian leaders who issue edicts. Any hints that this may be the case are amplified because they serve to confirm an expectation already in place.

Likewise, if a leader is explicitly brought in as a change agent, people actively look for evidence that, to him or her, nothing is sacred. Most of all, nontraditional presidents are watched for signs that they are opposed to faculty interests. Emphasizing common ground can be a solution. For David Greene, this has meant reminding everyone at the outset of any discussion of change that they all share a profound commitment to "excellence of programs, the quality of faculty and student experience, and the support we provide faculty and students in all kinds of different ways." Once this very fundamental alignment of priorities is established, the search for more effective means to reach those ends can proceed in good faith.

Some search executives compared the president's challenge in office to that of a modern president of the United States: in many ways, it has the executive in constant campaign mode, mindful of future elections. Shared governance results in not only more considered decisions but deeper commitment to carrying them out—and that goes beyond faculty involvement. John Isaacson said, "It's better to think of a broader set of constituents: alumni, board members, parents, prospective students, current students, . . . faculty, the community, . . . staff." He sees a college presidency as analogous to being mayor of "a nice complicated midsize city"—albeit a city "with not a single homogeneous suburb, that has a lot of different people, a decaying infrastructure, and bad economics."

IMMERSE YOURSELF IN THE CULTURE

Of course, it is not always possible to bring everyone around to the same view. There is a reason presidents still exist in even the most collegial contexts: when opinions don't converge, someone has to make the call. Bill Bowen advised "a genuinely collaborative way of thinking, but at the same time retaining the responsibility to decide." He cautioned presidents not to spend too much time "in this, that, and the other effort to find consensus where there may not be consensus."

How can a nontraditional leader know when the time has come to end a debate and make a decision? And how can they be confident their judgment will be accepted? Only by being attuned, I heard from the leaders I interviewed, to the culture of the institution. Every decision made will strike others as either consistent with or in violation of cultural norms. To be sure, knowing the culture might not reveal the right answer itself. "An understanding of organizational culture is not a panacea to all administrative problems," as William G. Tierney of the University of Southern California writes. "An understanding of culture, for example, will not automatically increase enrollments or increase fund raising." What it will do is help a decision be accepted as valid. Tierney argues that "an administrator's correct interpretation of the organization's culture can provide critical insight about which of the many possible avenues to choose in reaching a decision about how to increase enrollment or undertake a particular approach to a fund-raising campaign."[22]

Tierney says administrators must "understand the symbolic dimensions of ostensibly instrumental decisions and actions."[23] Why things get done the way they do in a given college or university often is a result of specific cultural norms and traditions that have grown out of history across decades or even centuries. By the same token, leaders who flout cultural norms in other areas, having nothing to do with key decisions, might be less trusted to make those decisions well—because they don't seem to have become "one of us." Nontraditional presidents might be more advised for this reason to conform on some seemingly cosmetic matters, such as prevailing dress codes; or usual practices in presenting, say, with exhibits, or without notes; or habits of communicating in one format or another.

This doesn't mean that leaders must be thoroughly constrained by cultures. But they should know when they are doing something countercultural, so they can frame their approach. Some presidents I interviewed said they avoided run-ins by spending time up front with faculty, setting expectations and explaining how they like to make decisions. Some took pains to lay out their personal values and signaled how these might color their thinking about some areas of decision making. For example, when John Fry decided to get directly involved in certain aspects of the tenure process, believing it was his fiduciary obligation to do so, he first went to the provost and tenure committee and acknowledged it would constitute a change. "The tradition here has been, the provost comes over to the president's office and presents the package, and the president sits there like a potted plant . . . and [everything] goes to the board of trustees," he said. "Those days are done. I'm going to read the files. I want access to the committee. I want to talk about the cases before they start. I want an interim update and I'll put you on notice that there might be some times when I'm not going to support what you're talking about." He knew this would be uncomfortable for a committee used to viewing the tenure process as its unique prerogative, and because of that he prepared for what he knew would be a series of conversations in advance.

That dialogue proved constructive, Fry says. Undoubtedly it also provided his colleagues with reassurance that in other matters, he would similarly try to avoid surprises.

Learn from the Best

For nontraditional candidates wondering how on earth they will ever be able to successfully transition to a college presidency, there is at least this consolation: by now, many others have done it. Between the presidents now in office or retired, and the search firm executives that helped many of them connect with their colleges and universities, there are plenty of resources to consult about what works and what doesn't. In my own research, I found in many of these people a sincere desire to share their hard-won wisdom. For example, one of the reasons that I included William Bowen in my interviews, despite his being a traditional president, is that he had been a mentor to and keen observer of numerous nontraditional presidents in the variety of influential roles he played in higher education.

Good research also exists on the "derailers" to avoid—in other words, the events and mistakes that most often lead to untimely departures from the president's office. McLaughlin, for example, observes that early exits in failed presidencies can be grouped into three categories: "admissions mistakes," where the suitability of the candidates' intrinsic abilities are questioned; "industrial accidents," where events at an institution spiraled out of control; and "irreconcilable differences" in relationships between the president and stakeholders.[24] Birnbaum explains that, just as exemplary presidents gain and maintain the support of faculty through judicious involvement and acknowledgment of their strengths, failed presidencies typically stem from loss of faculty support.[25]

Finally, any nontraditional candidate would do well to make a study of his or her own unfolding experience. I started this chapter with one of my own learning experiences—it seems only fitting to end with another. Deep into my candidacy for the position I hold now, the deanship of the University of Virginia's Darden School of Business, I found myself making almost weekly trips across the Atlantic from my home and work in Europe—and worse, managing to severely aggravate my lower back into spasms in the process. When the day came that I had my final-round opportunity to address the faculty, I stayed on my feet to present my views from the stage, but as the time came for questions, I eased onto the corner of the table that held the projector and from that semi-seated position started to call on people; my back was killing me.

What I learned later was that, while I was thinking hard about the questions that were posed, a lot of people in that room were thinking about my pose. What did it say about my readiness for a demanding job that I didn't seem to have the stamina to stand up for an hour? The faux pas was all the worse because at Darden, more than most schools, we pride ourselves on high-energy classroom experiences; faculty never sit down, choosing to roam the room working the case method interactive discussion. At the root of the concern was whether a nontraditional candidate like me fully understood the legendary Darden classroom culture and could have a commanding presence.

I give myself some leeway on that experience because I know the pain I was feeling, but I also learned something I won't forget, as leaning on that table almost derailed my candidacy. All of the presidents I met have their similar stories; John Fry eventually concluded that the only way to proceed is to "get in searches and start getting your hands dirty." Just like any industry or profession, higher education has its own specificities, norms, language, and processes that presidents must learn to navigate. Those coming through the traditional path are fully accustomed to many of these norms, but nontraditional candidates will discover many of them only through painful mistakes. In the great words attributed to Will Rogers, "Good judgment comes from experience, and a lot of that comes from bad judgment."

Many of the lessons learned apply to any candidate, it is just that the standard for burden of proof may be more stringent for a nontraditional on some dimensions—something selection committees may want to periodically ask themselves about. At the same time, I am convinced that the absolute number of nontraditional leaders is a clear sign that selection committees are increasingly finding a way to consider the full capabilities of the candidates, nontraditional or not, versus the challenges at hand. Perhaps this is because the context now facing many colleges and universities no longer looks anything like the largely stable, "traditional" context of last century. Traditional or nontraditional? is no longer the right question.

7 | The Right Debate to Have

WHEN DR. MARY JANE England was appointed president at Regis College in 2001, she might have looked like a curious choice. To begin with, the "Dr." in front of her name refers to a medical degree; her first career was as a child psychiatrist, from which she went on to roles in public health administration. Just before arriving at Regis, then a tiny undergraduate Catholic college for women, she'd been program director of the Robert Wood Johnson Foundation's Mental Health Services Program for Youth. But by the time she retired from Regis, a decade later, she was responsible for what the *Boston Globe* called a "remarkable turnaround."[1] Pulled back from the brink of financial crisis, the school had gone co-ed, was granting doctoral degrees, and had a student enrollment more than three times the size it was when she arrived. England might have been a nontraditional choice, but clearly she was a good one.

The task of identifying the right leader to bring about change in a complex institution should never be taken lightly, but perhaps it has been unnecessarily complicated in the world of higher education. Finding the right answer never starts with asking the wrong question, but the people closest to college and university president selection processes have often been doing just that. In search committee deliberations, in press coverage of campus controversies, and in scholarly studies of management, many debates focus on whether schools are better served by *traditional* or *nontraditional* leaders. The implicit belief is that there is some right answer to that question, perhaps based in theory or the preponderance of evidence but in any case applicable to all times and places.

The debate over what constitutes tradition and whether to respect it is the wrong one to have. Not only does it distract from more important questions, but it actually gets in the way of good appointments. In the practical context of searches, the distinction turns out to be more confusing than clarifying.

As we'll see in this chapter, the right debate to have is all about fit—the compatibility of a leader's capabilities and desires with an institution's context and priorities. That is a debate that will play out differently in every setting. Given the diversity of colleges, and the universe of candidates, fit happens on a case-by-case basis, and there is no standard or formula to arrive at it. As McLaughlin and Riesman write, there is no "certain way of knowing how candidates would perform in the presidency of a particular institution. . . . Leadership is always contextual."[2]

The Right Debate Is at the Individual School Level

The first failing of the traditional versus nontraditional debate is that it takes place at a generic level. People ask about the higher education sector as a whole: Is the increased presence of nontraditional leaders a positive trend? Or is it a scourge—the equivalent of barbarians at the gates? This frames the question as something that can be answered in a categorical way, and once answered, remain a settled matter.

Higher education researchers are certainly not alone in this tendency to seek one-solution-fits-all conclusions about leadership. The same kind of debate plays out in corporate settings where, for example, studies try to show that internal versus external candidates for CEO perform better, or that engineers (or marketers, or financiers, or other functional specialists) make the best leaders. Analogous debates focus on whether hospitals should be run by doctors, and whether sports teams are better coached by accomplished players. Amanda Goodall's research touches on all of these macro-level questions. Her PhD work became the book *Socrates in the Boardroom: Why Research Universities Should Be Led by Top Scholars*—and she has gone on to study the correlations between leaders' backgrounds and enterprise performance in several other sectors.[3]

While patterns at the macro level can be revelatory, and are especially valuable for prompting research questions, studies like these are complicated by the fact that individual leaders differ on many dimensions beyond their job histories—and by the fact that no two organizations requiring leadership are alike. Even comparing colleges of similar size, ranking, religious affiliation, and geography, the profile of an effective president can turn out to be very different. The point is well made by comparing King's College of Wilkes-Barre, Pennsylvania, and the College of Saint Rose in Albany, New York, tied for fifty-third place in *U.S. News's* latest ranking of regional universities in the North. At Saint Rose, the situation in 2014 was crisis: the school needed to dramatically cut costs to deal with a $9 million deficit. The board of trustees knew they needed a change agent, and they got one in Carolyn Stefanco. A traditional candidate who had excelled as a professor and program builder in women's studies, she was nevertheless willing to cut twelve academic programs and twenty-three faculty to put the college on firmer financial ground. A combination of tough decisions and innovative moves won her an award from the *Albany Business Review* as one of the top "Disrupters" in its region for 2016.[4] Meanwhile, in Wilkes-Barre, the Rev. John Ryan presides over King's College. Father Ryan is a nontraditional candidate, having started his working life as an accountant and business manager, then become an ordained priest, before being appointed dean of King's business school. As he stepped up to the presidency, the school had already established positive momentum and was seeing record high enrollment. Under his stewardship, it continues to grow, successfully raising capital to take on ambitious building projects, expand athletics programs, and attract ever-greater numbers of international students.[5] These two schools, just two hundred miles apart, are similar in many respects—their religious affiliation, their size, their ranking, and more—yet they face different challenges—and are being led by very different presidents. The same could be said for many state universities' contexts, both within the same state and across states.

For broad findings about nontraditional versus traditional presidents' performance to provide guidance to individual college's choices, it would have to be true that colleges all faced the same challenges. The college setting would have to be called a constant. But to revert to a hackneyed phrase, the only constant in higher education is change. If anything, colleges and universities are becoming increasingly dissimilar over time.

In developmental economics, scholars like to refer to the "great divergence" that happened among nations of the world in the nineteenth century. Thanks to a combination of a few factors in their favor—chiefly their early leads in industrialization—a tiny fraction of economies pulled away from the rest of the world, first gradually and then rapidly. These are the collection of countries that eventually (in the 1960s) started conferring as the Group of Seven, or G7. By analogy, in the competitive world of liberal arts colleges, or top-ranked universities overall, we can see a similar phenomenon playing out. A great divergence is separating the concerns of the highest-ranked schools from those of the rest, and below the level of the elite the challenges are hard to generalize. As F. Scott Fitzgerald so memorably summed things up, the rich "are different from you and me."[6]

In an era of dynamic change, it isn't only that a leader who suits one place doesn't suit another; that leader might be a bad match for the *same* place at a different time. This may be part of why we see many institutions alternating between traditional and nontraditional presidents. When I looked into the predecessor profiles of all the 2014 cohort of liberal arts colleges presidents selected, I found that 49 percent of the institutions had opted to make a shift from a traditional to a nontraditional president or vice versa, while the other 51 percent held fast to the type they'd bet on to win in the last round. Again, there are many attributes that distinguish candidates from each other, and tenure-track teaching is just one of them, but the high degree of oscillation also suggests that search committees and trustees recognize that different times call for different leadership styles and strengths, and use the selection process as a moment to reexamine what is needed next and to recalibrate.

"Fit" Goes Both Ways

Perhaps the fact that colleges' needs are now changing more quickly contributes to the phenomenon cited in chapter 2: the pronounced decline in average presidential tenures. It could be that leaders are right for their times, and when their jobs are done, they ride off into the sunset. Probably at least as much, however, the shrinking tenures reflect many matches that weren't well made in the first place. If there is one consistent theme in the literature about higher education leadership, it is the importance of fit between a person and an organization. According to what is known as Person-Organization Fit theory, when leaders fail, it often isn't because the leader is incompetent or the college is incorrigible; the problem is a lack of compatibility between the two.[7]

Research by Daniel Duke and Edward Iwanicki looked at this in the context of K-12 public school principals, specifically studying cases where principals had been removed from their posts for reasons that could only be characterized as lack of fit. The researchers' conclusion is that fit is a function of the *expectations* of the candidate and the institution; lack of fit occurs when the expectations of stakeholders, which can vary from one group to another, are not met. There is a difference, they point out, between a leader's "received role" (or the set of expectations they must meet) and the role he or she might have expected or wished to play. "Effective principals are good at scanning the school environment and identifying what their constituencies really expect them to do," Duke and Iwanicki write. They need this skill because, unfortunately, "these real job expectations often are not included in the principal's job description."[8]

For Duke and Iwanicki, the implications are clear. The potential for mismatched expectations should be acknowledged and communicated about as soon as possible after a leader takes office. "The earlier principals share the job expectations that they believe are real and important to fulfill, the easier it is to deal with any potential problems of fit," they note. They also believe that, while sometimes the expectations of various stakeholders are so thoroughly incompatible that effective leadership is an impossibility, candidates can nonetheless try to influence the perceptions of fit and make necessary adjustments if they at least acknowledge the existence of fit and try to understand it.

Steve Trachtenberg et al.'s *Presidencies Derailed* is a newer—and very lively—book that translates this argument to college settings. Among the lessons to be drawn from campus flameouts, the authors conclude, "the most notable one is that institutional fit between a president and a university is of paramount importance."[9] Their stories reinforce points also made by Judith McLaughlin and David Riesman; James Fisher and James Koch; Susan Pierce; and Patrick Sanaghan, Larry Goldstein, and Kathleen Gaval.[10]

Much of this work has clarified just why fit is so important: a good fit means increased retention; improved outcomes and success for the institution; higher satisfaction both personally and professionally for the jobholder; and less likelihood of a damaging derailment. For example, when Robert Bretz and Timothy Judge surveyed a large population of professionals all equipped with the same academic degree and working in the same field, they found those experiencing greater person-organization fit to also be enjoying greater job satisfaction and career success. Workers who judged their fit better, on average, earned 20 percent more money, had climbed the organizational ladder 11.6 percent higher, and reported satisfaction higher by 15 percent.[11]

As often as fit or lack of it is cited as a factor in job success and failure, however, it remains an element that is difficult to gauge in advance of an appointment. If we define fit broadly as the compatibility between a person and an organization, then theoretically it would make sense to measure levels of congruence on at least two levels: the match of the individual's capabilities and ambitions with the organization's structure and processes; and the resonance of the individual's values and personality with the organization's culture, norms, and climate. Amy Kristof has thought a lot about the measurement challenges suggested by the pursuit of person-organization fit. For one thing, she cautions, there isn't necessarily much "correlation between perceived versus actual fit assessments." In other words, a good fit might exist between a presidential candidate and institution, without one side or the other sensing that to be the case.[12] Fit can also change dramatically across time. Michael Arthur and Kathy Kram emphasize the idea that individuals want different rewards and experiences from their workplaces in different phases of their careers.[13] Thus "the right fit" is the right person in the right place at the right time. It requires a match along multiple dimensions in the midst of dynamic change.

We also know fit is a mutual phenomenon. Every search process is a two-way street with candidates sizing up the institution while the institution sizes up them. But most research has adopted the vantage point of the institution and focused on the demands of the role. Far less has been written about how individual presidential candidates should approach the process of understanding whether a particular presidency is a good fit for *them*— whether it will fulfill their hopes and dreams or be compatible with their personal and professional profile, strengths, and weaknesses. For example, in the section of her book *On Being Presidential* devoted to "the importance of fit," Susan Pierce writes of what search committees hope to discover from their interviews of candidates: "which ones share their values, understand and honor their culture, and appear to be people with whom they could happily interact." She adds that "this is the most subjective and even intuitive part of the process." But Pierce sees the "fit factor" as an aspect of a search a presidential candidate cannot influence—as indeed the biggest of the "variables they cannot control."[14]

To be sure, presidential searches are competitive, and generally there are at least several candidates under consideration with the qualifications necessary to do the job. Nevertheless, it is important for a strong candidate to understand that he or she is also a "buyer" and should therefore examine each opportunity thoroughly. In seeking to understand the institution fully, candidates need not only to assess whether they are a good fit for the institution but also to discover whether the institution is a good fit for them. Few scholars have offered many suggestions on how to go about doing so.

An important exception is Barbara Moody, who studied how fifteen college and university presidents assessed fit as candidates. She made several observations. First, she discovered that candidates look for different areas of fit particular to them, and, when fit is deemed good enough, a turning point occurs. Second, the desire for a presidency and its prestige often overshadows the evaluation of fit, and in cases where fit is known to be low, some candidates think they can overcome it once in office. Third, some aspects of the process, including the typical lack of confidentiality and very broad participation, actually inhibit an authentic assessment of fit. Fourth, candidates benefit from multiple search experiences, because these hone their abilities to assess fit. Finally, if candidates sense during the search process that fit is strong, they are more likely to have a positive experience as presidents. Moody also offers a framework that could help candidates assess a presidency's fitness for them, outlining seven considerations: (1) personal conditions, expectations, and motivations; (2) job content and demands; (3) timing and readiness; (4) institutional characteristics and setting; (5) fit with institutional needs and expectations; (6) cultural compatibility and fit with institutional culture; and (7) interpersonal chemistry and fit with institutional members.[15]

To add to this line of work, I asked participants in my research about fit, and specifically about how it should factor into nontraditional candidates' deliberations. Like discussions of fit more generally, inquiry into the candidacies of nontraditional college presidents tends to take the point of view of search committees and their considerations of fit. But, given that many such candidates are making changes from successful careers either inside or outside of higher education and are often sufficiently impressive to attract multiple offers of employment, it is also important to consider how they should understand what will constitute a good fit. After all, a candidate is not obligated to accept a presidential offer in the end if he or she is not comfortable. So how have nontraditional candidates thought about whether they like—and should ultimately accept—the presidencies they are considering and offered?

Five Lenses for Fit

My interviews with experienced search executives made very clear that subjective measures deeply influence decision making on both sides. They also confirm that the most frustrating type of feedback a passed-over candidate can receive from a committee is that "the fit wasn't right." Search firm consultants seem to share that frustration, since such vagueness doesn't help them do their job better. John Isaacson expressed the view that "fit is an excuse of not knowing how to talk. If people say it's all about fit, what it means is, they don't know what they're looking for—so they're going to trust their unconscious intuition rather than their conscious intelligence." To Isaacson, that constitutes "irrational, unconscious bias—sometimes useful, sometimes nonsense."

As Isaacson hints, however, fit can be thought about in more consciously intelligent ways. In my interviews with presidents I used open-ended questions to elicit how these leaders went about evaluating fit and how they think other candidates should. I heard about five dimensions on which a particular presidency can be the right match for an individual—mission and values, problems to be solved, authenticity, "chemistry" or an intuitive sense of resonance, and family—and concluded that leaders can make career decisions that are more right for them by deliberately applying these five "lenses." Although the lenses stem from comments about nontraditional candidates, most of the observations are also true for traditional candidates.

MISSION AND VALUES

The first lens focuses the leader's attention on whether the institution's mission and values align with his or her personal values and motivations. This starts at the highest level with passionate belief in the overall mission these places share. Many who pursue a presidency are motivated by the idea of changing students' lives and shaping the next generation of leaders. President David Greene related that, for him, leading Colby and, more broadly, helping liberal arts colleges retain their uniquely important role in society is "a calling." He cares deeply about "transforming the lives of individuals ... [and] democratizing a place like [Colby]" to offer the education to underprivileged students. Fry characterized a liberal arts education as "a gift" that he had received and was dedicated to passing on to others. (In fact, all the liberal arts leaders I interviewed had personally attended liberal arts colleges and had fond memories and deep convictions about how their lives were changed as a result. Some also had children who shared that experience.) Also clear was the message that such beliefs can't be pursued in a relaxed or complacent way. Anyone who imagines that a transition to a liberal arts college presidency—or a university presidency or deanship for that matter—will be a good way to downshift from a corporate or other lifestyle-challenging career will be sorely disappointed. College leadership is an all-consuming task.

Below the level of that shared purpose, institutions definitely vary in their raisons d'être. Some colleges have a religious bent; others are unaffiliated with any faith. Some colleges are very liberal; others, more conservative. Depending on the individual, some differences will be more salient than others. Commenting on how he considered fit at Colby, Greene declared: "It's fundamental that the mission align with my values, that the culture be one that contributes in important ways to the mission of the institution, that there be a desire to move forward. . . . Colby had that."

While a school's formal mission is often prominently displayed on its website, a prospective president might have to do some digging to understand how that mission translates to actual values and culture. Usually the distinctions that really matter between schools' missions are not explicitly stated. But talk to people who have had long exposure to different schools and you hear about them. A tenured professor at a women's college, for example, summed up the difference he saw between Wellesley and Smith: "Both are great at developing women into leaders. But at Wellesley, they are making future CEOs. Smith makes Gloria Steinems."[16]

Executives I interviewed mentioned many sources and ways to find out more about an institution's values, ranging from outright asking about these in interview settings to sifting through announcements, celebrations, and speeches posted on websites, and probing the beliefs and opinions of school representatives they met. The major advice, however, was simply that testing for values fit should be an explicit process, and one that also includes reflecting on and reaching a greater understanding of one's own personal values.

As with every aspect of fit, finding a good match not only makes for greater personal satisfaction; it enables the president to be more effective and allows the institution to thrive. In order to gain support, as Bowen puts it, a president must be "empathetic to the values, historical values, of these smallish places."

PROBLEMS TO BE SOLVED

A second lens for considering fit is to identify the main problems an institution needs to be solved, and how well they match up to the prospective leader's problem-solving experience. Here again, while liberal arts colleges (or, for that matter, larger public or private universities) have many long-term challenges in common, they can also present very different acute issues. One college may face a financial crisis with enrollment challenges and ballooning budget deficits; another may have an especially rebellious faculty; another might have been surprised by a Title IX investigation; and yet others might have disgruntled, disengaged board members or need innovation to generate new revenue streams or need to turn around their health system. One of the presidents I interviewed, John Fry of Drexel University and formerly of Franklin & Marshall, told me that an important item on his mental checklist for assessing fit was simply to ask, "What's the problem? I just want to know what the problem is." Based on information he gathered, he concluded it needed a leader who could redouble its energy and resolve to move forward: "I thought . . . how could this place that had so much momentum and so much resources—why did it lose momentum and how can we think about restarting that?"

Presidents (and a few search executives) suggested that a good place to start is by carefully reading the position description and trying to ascertain if the institution wants change or is happy with maintaining the status quo, or, as Fry and Storbeck put it, "polishing the stone." But distilling an accurate picture from an official job posting by a search firm or on *Inside Higher Ed* might take some deep reading between the lines. Colleges are constantly in the limelight for prospective students and alumni, and standard practice, understandably, is some posturing to put their best face forward. Nontraditional candidates might have a slight advantage in learning what school administrators are really losing sleep over. Given that they are generally perceived to be change agents—rightly or wrongly—their earliest conversation with a search consultant might turn quickly to the pressing issues.

Once he or she has an understanding of the problem to be solved, the presidential aspirant should make a clear-eyed assessment of what it will take to solve it, and what particular capabilities in a leader would prove decisive. Does that align well to the candidate's strengths? Just as important, what will it take beyond what the president can bring to the task—and will it be possible for the college to provide those things? David Greene noted that a make-or-break condition for an effective presidency is "having some resources at an institution to actually do something. It's one thing to want to be better; it's another to have the means to do so."

Along these lines, Lawrence Schall (Oglethorpe College) related that his assessment of the resources required to achieve one ambitious board's vision led to a brass-tacks conversation with the trustees. During the interview process, Schall responded to a problem with which the group rather sheepishly admitted the school struggled. "It's certainly not embarrassing," he assured them, "but if you decide to hire me, it's going to have to change because we can't be successful with the level of support you're providing." According to Schall, a trustee pushed back: "So you're telling us, if we hire you, it's going to cost us money out of our pocket?" Schall's response: "That's exactly what I'm telling you."

THE CHANCE TO LEAD WITH AUTHENTICITY

Ambitious and multitalented leaders are often confident that they can rise to the demands of important challenges. Whatever affect or approach or assets a situation might call for, they believe they can contrive to deliver. Presidents I interviewed emphasized that, to know if a position is really a fit, the question has to go deeper than, "Could I do what it takes to succeed?" A job that really fits can be done while just being oneself. The term that was frequently used was "authenticity."

A leader who is authentically right for a position will not have to spend as much energy on self-monitoring—checking his or her impulses when they run counter to what would be a more productive approach. Neither will they have to make a special effort to engage in situations they would rather avoid, whether they involve schmoozing donors or sharing decision making. Not having to don a mask or play a role to serve the institution well means a leader can get more done and, not unimportant, also have more fun.

The late Warren Bennis, renowned for his writing and teaching on leadership, once wrote a remarkably candid account of his (failed) candidacy for the presidency of Northwestern University, for the *Atlantic Monthly*. The search was hyperpoliticized, with stakeholders waging war for reasons far beyond any differences of opinion they had about presidential candidates, and one ends up feeling sorry for what Bennis experienced as a result. Throughout the process, however, Bennis recognized the most important thing he could do to establish if there was a fit: "My strategy in dealing with search committees," he wrote, "is to be myself, as much as is humanly possible to be oneself with a group of caliper-eyed strangers. If they *really* want someone like me, then there is none better."[17]

Although it is natural in a recruiting process to try to project a persona that conforms to what an institution is signaling it wants, presidents I spoke with also urged others not to conceal their real personalities and leadership styles. By doing so, they might miss the opportunity to gain greater self-awareness. Every candidate, traditional or nontraditional, faces concerns about his or her candidacy. As discussed in chapter 4, every constituency harbors its stereotypes and anchoring biases, some of which are explicitly voiced and others of which are hinted at in more elliptical (if not passive-aggressive) manner. Smart candidates can usually find ways to overcome these. Problems can arise, however, if their focus on "getting the offer" keeps them from reflecting on and expressing their authentic identity.

Thus, when Schall chose to speak candidly to the trustees he met, he recognized the risk—but realized it would be riskier not to let his potential future bosses understand how he would prefer to approach the job. He knew he was the type to challenge the status quo and would find it hard to do otherwise. "If you're looking for someone to come in and be a caretaker of what you've got, I'm just not the right person," he told them. "But if you're really looking for someone to ask really hard questions, to be truthful with you, the board, about what we're doing well and what we're not doing well, then we probably ought to keep talking."

CHEMISTRY: AN INTUITIVE SENSE OF FIT

Very related to the fuzzy territory of authenticity is the fact that sometimes people just feel that there is "chemistry" between them—and often, when there is, it is also evident to others. We don't find it strange when a film critic complains about a lack of chemistry between an actor and actress, for example. However vague the concept is, we all know what the critic is talking about.

Likewise, the presidents I interviewed used the term "chemistry" when I asked them how they ascertained if a certain presidency was a good fit for them. Yes, they tried to assess fit in more logical and strictly rational ways, as noted above. But they also seemed to concede that, when it comes to good matches among people, not everything that matters can be measured. A college presidency demands people-intensive collaboration, and partnerships simply work better when the partners are simpatico.

Interviews did not uncover any rigorous way to test for chemistry; the consensus was that it could only be sensed intuitively, and that one would simply know whether it were present or not. The point was just that it is vital not to dismiss that sense as groundless. President Schall warned, "I think a lot of people, particularly in that first presidency, want to be president so much, [they] have a hard time paying attention to subtle things." He learned this by experience. Years ago, a liberal arts college offered him a position that on objective grounds met all his requirements, yet "there was something going on with the board that just didn't feel right." He ended up walking away from the opportunity—but unfortunately, not until he and the college were at the point of finalizing contract details and drafting the press release. The mistake taught him to pay attention to what his "gut" was telling him sooner rather than later.

The big advice on how to test for chemistry, then, is simply to spend as much time as possible in informal settings with the people who will be colleagues on the job. Usually this is not hard to do; institutions also like to size up candidates in informal settings that may reveal more about their interpersonal skills, points of view, stamina, and even table manners. For that matter, such gatherings allow decision makers to meet a candidate's spouse or partner, who they hope will prove to be an asset (or fear could be a liability). As Greene put it, "They're really testing all the time."

The important thing for candidates is not to forget that fit is a two-way street, and these are also precious opportunities for them to gather impressions of the people with whom they might spend years of their lives. Fry made a point of assigning himself this task and deliberately thinking about questions like: "How did the table feel when I was going through the search, and was it the kind of table that I felt I could have common ground and work with?" If he came away from a conversation thinking "what a bunch of stiffs," he took note of that. The school he remembers feeling the least fit was one where "they didn't ask me any original or good questions. They didn't even care to find out about my wife or my children." Pay attention to cues like these, he says, and "you can just sort of tell."

FAMILY COMPATIBILITY

The final lens used by candidates to understand fit, and it was mentioned by everyone I consulted, is whether a school and its setting is right for their whole family. Of course, job changes that make it necessary to uproot others should always be considered in light of what is best for them, but the special circumstances of college presidencies bring potential problems—and benefits—beyond the usual ones. Consider for a start that many colleges and universities are located in rural environs, and that presidents are often provided with on-campus housing. For loved ones, their new home can quickly take on the character of a fishbowl.

Lawrence Schall put it this way: "These jobs are literally twenty-four hours a day, seven days a week—jobs where there's no line between your personal and professional life . . . so unless it's a really comfortable place to be, life can just become unbearable." For him, that meant he couldn't consider a countryside campus. He and his wife needed a more urban environment where they could be socially and politically active. Each of them, he said, has a "persona that just wouldn't work in a lot of places." But other couples, equally cultured, feel differently. When Sheila Jordan arrived at Kenyon College in 1975 with her husband, former president Philip Jordan, she found a campus quite isolated on a hilltop in Gambier, Ohio, which also had a formal rule by which all faculty had to live within ten miles of campus center. "I liked it," Jordan later reflected, because in a big city, "I couldn't have done what I wanted. I couldn't have been across to an art opening or to a lecture in two minutes from the house."[18]

For John Fry, whose children were still young when he was considering the Franklin & Marshall opportunity, evaluating fit was all about them: "Would my children thrive in the new environment?" He and his spouse placed a great deal of emphasis on evaluating the local schools. Of course, there are other considerations, as well, when it comes to thinking about the effects that a contained and somewhat cloistered community might have on the developing character of a young person. The old saying is that "it takes a village to raise a child"—and the corollary is that the village raises your child whether you want it to or not. In the process of getting to know a school, candidates and their spouses would do well to explicitly ask themselves how much they like the notion of their children—and they themselves—being embraced and influenced by its culture.

DONALD MUNDINGER, WHO studied independent college presidents—and himself spent twenty years as president of Illinois College—saw clearly that "in some situations the desire to become a president is so intense that it interferes with good judgment."[19] The five lenses mentioned in the interviews I conducted are not startling in any respect, but the intent in outlining them here is to provide a framework to help candidates move productively through what is often an implicit process of reflection. This is useful for all candidates, but perhaps particularly for nontraditional candidates who, coming from quite different work settings, may feel less confident that they can trust their gut, or less able to sort out what it is telling them. At the very least, having a framework like this in hand will remind candidates to keep thinking about fit, and reasserting their good judgment.

John Fry, David Greene, and Lawrence Schall all have worked at both liberal arts colleges and larger universities, increasing the relevance of their wisdom to a variety of university contexts beyond the liberal arts. My own experience is that the same lenses of fit are equally applicable to candidates in any higher education presidency or dean search. They certainly were for my selection process.

At the same time, candidates would be well advised to keep their own counsel as they engage in such deliberations. Colleges and universities are well used to thinking in a certain way about the offers they extend. In their student admissions, they don't only ask, "Will he or she succeed here?" An admissions officer—and in the same way, a search committee—must also ask, "If we accept this candidate, how high are the chances that we will be accepted in return?" Thus, candidates who convey high interest throughout the process preserve their options best, while privately reserving their ability to accept or decline, should the offer materialize.

Today's Debate Undermines Excellence

When the debate over presidential selection on a college campus gravitates toward the question of "traditional versus nontraditional," it doesn't just miss the point. It also increases the chances of a suboptimal appointment. This is a difficult point to prove, of course, with data. There is no way of knowing whether search committees less focused on nontraditional strengths would have chosen more enduring leaders than Simon Newman at Mount Saint Mary's or Bob Kerrey at the New School—or if committees less enamored of traditional qualifications could have chosen more effective stewards at many colleges now struggling with budget shortfalls. Yet the logical argument for remaining open-minded about candidates' backgrounds is hard to deny.

When decision makers face situations with many factors to consider, they tend, consciously or not, to use decision trees. That is, they begin with one important question that will substantially reduce the number of options they have to consider, then proceed from there to ask more winnowing questions until finally they arrive at an ultimate, surviving choice. When one of the earliest questions in a presidential or dean selection process is framed as "traditional versus nontraditional?," one or the other set gets almost wholly taken out of the running, even though many of its members might have measured up well on other questions. Applying a screen that arbitrarily reduces one's options only damages the chance of making the best choice, including overlooking a traditional candidate.

By pigeonholing candidates into one camp or other, the traditional-versus-nontraditional debate also causes evaluators to miss the more meaningful and nuanced differences between them. The nontraditional presidents I interviewed felt that the distinction between traditional and nontraditional was increasingly meaningless, particularly in a world where the skill set required to lead as president and to understand higher education can take so many forms. In their cases, they had already been presidents or worked in higher education for decades. Yet, their "nontraditional" status was like a scarlet letter, putting them in a category about which evaluators held certain assumptions.

An unintended consequence of the debate for nontraditional candidates is that they are less likely to make it to the final rounds of selection processes. Although there are exceptions, many committees converge early on a plan by which they will present a range of traditional candidates to their board and then spice up the mix with the inclusion of one, maybe two nontraditionals. Mathematically, that kind of token representation in the finalist pool means many nontraditional candidates are eliminated earlier than their capabilities should merit. It also potentially creates a situation whereby the selection of that one nontraditional would make a kind of statement, and involve a level of drama, that would be unhelpful.

Now consider the impact of all this on capable leaders' enthusiasm for pursuing presidencies or deanships in the first place. Perceiving that they will be stereotyped and subjected to tougher standards, nontraditional candidates might reasonably revise their plans to pursue the highest leadership realms of higher education. That would of course disappoint them, but it would also deprive colleges and universities of their potential contributions.

Again, this is an impact that can't be measured. We will never know how many great leaders never materialized in the higher education sector because they were discouraged from approaching it. We do know, however, that in an era when the job of president has lost its allure to many traditional candidates (recall the data presented in chapter 3), any further discouragement of viable leaders should be resisted.

How Do We Change the Debate?

The alert reader might wonder why a book like this one, and the research project that informed it, is part of the solution. If the problem is too much focus on the "traditional or nontraditional" debate, then writing specifically about that distinction might seem to perpetuate it. The main takeaways from my research, however, show the debate to be rather hollow. First, this work reveals that the distinction between traditional and nontraditional has been too ill-defined to support productive dialogue. One of the ground rules of scholarly discourse is that the community engaging in it agree to use terms with precision, but the defenders and critics of "nontraditional" leaders turn out to be talking past each other, because they have never agreed on what constitutes "traditional." Some may be referring to background credentials, while others may be referring to leadership style. Deeming someone traditional may be a compliment to some, but a criticism to another. Biases can easily prevail.

Second, this research exposes the reality that, even by my conservative definition, nontraditional presidents already make up a large proportion of higher education leaders, both in and outside the realm of liberal arts colleges. Any assertion that a president who did not come up through the tenured faculty ranks is an unusual or especially daring appointment is simply false; recall that almost two-thirds of faculty these days are not on the tenure track and are thus "nontraditional." With almost two decades of presidential searches under his belt, John Isaacson recalls the time that a nontraditional was an "exotic idea." But now it is not so remarkable. Per my Beardsley definition, one-third of liberal arts presidents are nontraditional. Longitudinal comparisons show that the proportion of nontraditional presidents has increased dramatically over time, regardless of how we define nontraditional. Using Birnbaum's definition, it has doubled. (But again, his definition considers anyone whose last two jobs were in higher education to be traditional, narrowing the pool of nontraditional candidates and not requiring any experience on the tenure track.) Using the more stringent Cohen and March definition, requiring experience up the academic ladder to provost, the increase in nontraditional presidents is even more dramatic. They found 10 percent of presidents in the 1980s to be nontraditional; applying their definition to the cohort of liberal arts college presidents in office in 2014, it is 62 percent.

Third, the research shows that, despite plenty of data to crunch about the fortunes of schools led by traditional and nontraditional leaders, no patterns have yet emerged that would suggest that either type is more capable of effective leadership than the other. And this, I believe, is not only the main contribution of this study but the best hope of putting the debate about presidential or other academic leadership selections such as dean on a more productive path: we need more focus on solid data, and on finding any patterns that actually can provide good guidance to decision makers. Meanwhile, deeper examinations of what the most successful leaders are doing differently, regardless of their backgrounds, will help to reveal the capacities schools should be seeking and building in their presidents.

Serving Our Institutions Well

This book will be received by some as pro–nontraditional leadership. Perhaps that perception is unavoidable given my own nontraditional status and recent candidacy. What it means to be, however, is pro–higher education. The interests of the two are intertwined. Although strong traditional leaders are needed as much as ever, more schools will need to move away from traditional leadership, given the pipeline issues. Given William Bowen's proof of a massive reduction in tenured or tenure-track faculty during the past forty years, and the expected continued reduction in tenure-track faculty going forward, it is hard to imagine a future in which the number of nontraditional presidents will decline in the liberal arts or higher education sphere. To be sure, many leaders still want to be college or university presidents or deans. But not everyone does, and the most interested are not necessarily from the same backgrounds that they were before.

Search committees will have to broaden their consideration sets. And boards will need to figure out how to help their new leaders succeed.

Nothing could be more important to a well-functioning society than thriving institutions of higher learning. Thomas Jefferson himself referred to education as the element "which, if the condition of man is to be progressively ameliorated, as we fondly hope and believe, is to be the chief instrument in effecting it."[20] But right now, the sector is challenged in unprecedented ways. The quantitative analysis on the financial situation, including the case studies, shows that the financial parameters and trends facing most liberal arts colleges are challenging. Most are experiencing high and rising tuition discounts resulting from the nonloan merit-aid sweepstakes race, increasing competition for students from public universities, ever-rising list-price tuitions, a value proposition that is increasingly under attack, the emergence of new technologies, the inability of many institutions to increase net revenue, and an inability to control expenses.

Liberal arts colleges are not the only higher education institutions in the United States facing challenges. Ever-rising list tuitions, tuition discounting focused on merit aid at the expense of financial aid, the emergence of new technologies and alternative certificate or competency-based programs, a value proposition under attack, costs rising above the rate of inflation, ferocious rankings-induced competition driving resource intensity, global competition, and record student debt levels describe many MBA programs.

Public universities, responsible for educating the vast majority of students in the United States, are equally under strain. As recalled by a recent report by the Academy of Arts and Sciences' Lincoln Project, the Morrill Act of 1862, signed by Abraham Lincoln to promote public education and build the nation, resulted in the development of public universities throughout the land that "educated and trained members of every profession" and "anchored regional economies." Indeed, they "became a central component of the nation's intellectual infrastructure." Unfortunately, the Lincoln Report goes on to relate that "state funding of public research universities has declined precipitously over the past decade, shrinking an average of 34 percent nationwide [in a trend that] is not sustainable." Among many other recommendations, authors of the Lincoln Report urge leaders of these institutions to establish annual cost and efficiency targets, form alliances with other colleges and universities, explore and pursue new revenue streams, enhance advancement and development activities, pursue private-public partnerships, and provide comprehensive financial aid to low-income, in-state undergraduate students.[21] Large public universities have clear differences from their smaller brethren—for instance, many have large medical schools and health-care systems, and greater state ownership and funding. But most of their challenges mirror those facing liberal arts presidents, albeit at much greater scale and complexity.

The feeling among presidents I have interviewed is that leading liberal arts institutions will not get easier anytime soon. The future will require leaders to pursue innovations such as partnerships, alternative revenue streams, and decreased time to degree through ideas such as a three-year degree, intensified internationalization, and embracing of technology. In selection processes, energy will be better spent on assessing capabilities with regard to the challenges at hand rather than on debating about nontraditional versus traditional backgrounds—with a nomenclature that no one agrees on anyway.

In light of the sector's importance and challenges, higher education deserves and needs to be able to pick its leaders from the largest possible pools of candidates. For those pools to expand, we need to encourage more nontraditional candidates to apply, and equip more of them to succeed. At the same time, given the troubling financial context that so many colleges and universities confront, we need to help traditional candidates shore up their abilities and sharpen their interest in devising the solutions that will put their institutions on more sustainable paths.

In short, no leader who is capable of leading a college or university effectively should be discouraged from considering that career. In a time of turbulent change, new legions of talent should be encouraged and cultivated. Rather than seizing on the dissimilar backgrounds that divide leaders, we should be focusing on the belief in the power of education, and the hope for stronger institutions, that unite us all.

| Epilogue

N
OW THAT I am dean at the University of Virginia's Darden School of Business, I regularly field questions as to how I came to be in this position. I have to smile when the wording of the question implies it was simply a decision I made one day. It's true that throughout my career I have often been goal driven and set my sights on precisely what I wanted, but this journey was not one of them. Making progress in life is as much about remaining open to what each new bend in the road reveals— about the opportunities ahead, and about yourself. As David Brooks puts it in *The Road to Character*: "A person who embraces a calling doesn't take a direct route to self-fulfillment. . . . Such vocations almost always involve tasks that transcend a lifetime. They almost always involve throwing yourself into a historical process. They involve compensating for the brevity of life by finding membership in a historic commitment."[1]

At McKinsey I set out to be elected to the Shareholders Council and was, but I discovered in the process that my calling was to help outstanding people achieve their full potential. Then, the realization came that I might better pursue that calling in a higher education setting rather than a consulting firm—a hope that drove me to get a doctorate in higher education management. As I engaged in the in-depth interviews that were central to my dissertation research, the importance of "fit" came up many times. I arrived at the conviction that as a first step I could contribute most as the dean of a globalizing business school, drawing on my management knowledge, of course, as well as my international experience and networks. (And perhaps I saw, too, that a deanship might be more attractive than what a college or university presidency entails these days, given the challenges of compliance with regulations, lawsuits related to Title IX, the Cleary Act, a greater degree of separation from students, fighting underage drinking, budget cuts, and even more stakeholders.)

If I can offer any lesson to others thinking of pursuing a second chapter, it is that one should not expect a linear, logical process that begins with clear view of the outcome and ends with accomplishing that. It is more like a maze in which you will explore many options, and in which serendipity will play its part. It will require you, yes, to be proactive, but at the same time to tamp down your strong desire to be in control of the future. Instead you must embrace a condition of vulnerability, accepting that your course will be altered as you meet people, listen to their stories and counsel, pursue some opportunities that don't map to the journey you imagined, and learn through the trial and error.

The Transition

One day after my visit to Monticello, where I had stood contemplating the words on Jefferson's tombstone, I went to Richmond with the provost of the University of Virginia (UVA), John Simon (now president of Lehigh University). There we met with various members of the Board of Visitors one by one—it is a peculiarity of public universities' boards that a meeting cannot be held with more than two of them without its being considered a public meeting. Since I had given UVA a deadline to reply by Christmas given other opportunities, John asked where Darden stood among my options. I replied along the lines of, "To use an undergraduate admissions analogy, you should consider that I have applied for Early Decision."

Two days later, John called and said something like, "Your application for early decision has been accepted." I signed my contract on Christmas Eve. On January 8, 2015, the press release was issued—"Scott Beardsley Named Next Dean of University of Virginia Darden School of Business." Two weeks later, UVA president Teresa Sullivan introduced me to the Darden community at First Coffee, a Darden tradition where everyone gathers at 9:30 a.m. to socialize. Although my start date was not until August 1, 2015 (when the previous dean's contract ended), I wanted and felt invited to become part of the community straightaway. I could have resigned from McKinsey and taken seven months of vacation, keeping my distance, but instead my mind-set was that the transition had already begun. I saw that transition as having three stages, actually: pre-August 1, first year, and ongoing.

TRANSITION, STAGE 1

Learning happens every day on a job, but the months before my start date offered a chance to focus on almost nothing but learning. I decided to spend several weeks of personal vacation time at Darden soaking up whatever knowledge I could of the place. My first priority was to learn as much as possible from outgoing Dean Robert Bruner. We spent an enormous amount of time together in private, and he was very gracious and generous with his insights. His own transition into Darden had been rocky, with no smooth process having been provided, and he was determined to make mine as constructive as possible. I asked a lot of questions about strategy, the university, the Business School, personnel, how he spent his time, and what advice he might have for me. He provided invaluable knowledge I could have never gained if I hadn't asked. My view was simple: I would be an idiot not to benefit from the ten years of wisdom he had gained as dean. We maintain a great relationship to this day.

Second, encouraged and enabled by Dean Bruner, I began a listening tour and sought to meet various stakeholders at key events, flying to Charlottesville several times. I came to Darden Days, a cultivation event for accepted students, and took many questions. I participated in the reunion weekend for alumni and made a keynote address, sharing what my values are and attending numerous smaller meetings with key alumni. I attended multiple board meetings, from the diversity board to the board of trustees, and met with many university deans. I listened carefully to what the issues were. When asked for my opinion, I would generally demur and clearly state that Dean Bruner was in charge until I began on August 1. Rather than making a recommendation, I explained how I would go about thinking through the issue.

My dissertation research, review of the literature, advice from mentors, nontraditional president interviews, and wisdom from search firm executives provided clear consensus on one item: the Achilles' heel of many nontraditional leaders is their failure to win over the faculty. I had been told that faculty don't like to be told what to do, and that I should be wary of tenured professors whose lifelong job security has no rival in any profession anywhere in the world. I decided to make the investment of almost three full weeks to sit down and talk with all of the seventy-plus faculty, one on one, in conversations lasting from one to four hours. But my rationale had nothing to do with fear. I was also joining the faculty and genuinely wanted to get to know my new colleagues. I asked open-ended questions about areas of research interest, their views on school priorities and opportunities in the long and short term, institutional strengths that should be protected under all circumstances, and any advice they had for me. Many of them, I knew, had seen multiple deans come and go and had a unique vantage point. Darden's faculty has also been rated the best business school teaching faculty by the

Economist for six years in a row. So it should be no surprise to hear that these interactions proved to be incredibly interesting, valuable, and motivating. One of the most common questions I am asked as a new dean is, "What surprises you the most?" My answer is that the faculty's helpfulness and open-mindedness to my deanship have amazed me, along with the depth of their commitment and caring. I know that faculty can be emotional and opinionated—and Darden is no exception—but I now see that this comes from a place of great caring.

In parallel, I wrapped up several important personal commitments. First, I completed my doctoral dissertation and defense at the University of Pennsylvania. I competed in the International Tennis Federation Senior Individual Championships in Antalya, Turkey, in April 2015, with my friend and coach Cédric Mélot. I transitioned all of my clients and responsibilities at McKinsey, and turned over the reins after many years as chairman of the board of the American Chamber of Commerce, Belgium. We packed a moving van with some belongings and dealt with immigration challenges when our shipment from Belgium was held up for more than a month at the port by Homeland Security. And we took an incredible vacation to the Ecuadorian Amazon and the Galapagos to pause and recharge the batteries.

TRANSITION, STAGE 2

Dean Bruner once referred to an effective dean transition as a sort of relay race where the baton is passed from one leader to the next at full speed. When my "pre-transition transition" ended on August 1, 2015, and my tenure officially began, I truly did feel I was running at full speed.

As I write this, I have just finished my transitional first year and am two-thirds into my second. My focus has been on the long term from the start. One advantage of higher education is that it features annual academic cycles and is not subject to quarterly earnings reports; one can operate with the mind-set that improvement takes time. As in a tiebreaker in tennis, a point gained can matter very much and make the difference between moving up or not. Second, I have continued and expanded my listening tour, meeting stakeholders from students to alumni to boards to members of the broader university community, constantly gathering input. Third, in McKinsey fact-based analysis fashion, I have been analyzing the exact position of the school, looking at its competition and rankings, examining the business model and associated balance sheets and income statements, and getting the input of key stakeholders via a strategy survey. Fourth, I have been assessing the capabilities of the administration team and spending substantial time hiring the next generation of talent in all corners of the enterprise; perhaps most importantly the faculty, where I interview any candidate before they are hired.

In general, I have tried to be externally driven and to get the input of key constituents. I have spent time with current students to find out what they love and don't like about their experience. I have met with many CEOs and senior executives to listen to their observations and to see what their needs are from business schools and how satisfied they are with recruiting. I have had numerous press and media interviews from media outlets all over the world. I have participated in many Darden and university engagement initiatives in global cities, including fund-raising prospects. In so doing, I try to be transparent and to communicate extensively. The intensity of communication required to satisfy all stakeholders as a dean is indeed substantial, and actually quite similar in many respects to that of the presidents studied in this book.

The transition would not be complete without mentioning investing in a life transition from Brussels, Belgium, to Charlottesville, Virginia. We loved Brussels, but Charlottesville is an incredible place; I would have never been able to convince my French wife, Claire, to move if it weren't. For starters, the restaurant scene is a foodies' dream come true, with French patisseries, a wide ethnic variety, and organic farms growing ingredients to please the most discerning palate. Charlottesville has been voted the happiest city to live in the United States and is celebrated for having one of the highest qualities of life. A short distance from Washington, D.C., and Richmond, Virginia, it is nestled at the foothills of the Blue Ridge Mountains and the Shenandoah National Park. Three U.S. presidents (Jefferson, Madison, and Monroe) hail from nearby and were the founding rectors of UVA, giving the region a rich historical tradition. Vineyards and microbreweries populate rolling hills like Tuscany's. No wonder, perhaps, that Charlottesville is one of the top wedding destinations in the country. It has a vibrant music scene, with acts such as Paul McCartney, Elton John, Stevie Wonder, Fleetwood Mac, the Eagles, and Jay Z playing recently. Finally, since tennis is one of my passions, I must mention that the quality of play is high here. It is after all the home of the national championship UVA tennis team, having taken the national team title three of the past four years under Coach Brian Boland's leadership.

TRANSITION, STAGE 3

A final transition priority has been connecting myself and Darden to the broader university community. The University of Virginia is a world-class research university with many leading programs among its eleven schools. The campus, or "Grounds," includes the "Academical Village," the original set of buildings designed and constructed by Jefferson where faculty and students would come together to pursue the life of the mind. Jefferson recognized that an educated public was the key to a well-functioning democracy. Today, the Academical Village is the only university UNESCO World Heritage Site in the Americas (and one of only three modern man-made sites in North America to make that list, the other two being the Statue of Liberty and Independence Hall).

The Academical Village features the school's famous Rotunda and its expansive Lawn, flanked by pavilions—five on the East Lawn and five on the West Lawn. The ground floors of the pavilions were historically used as classrooms, with the professors living upstairs. Between these pavilions today are rows of single-occupancy rooms inhabited by the highest honor students of the fourth-year class at UVA. One must be invited to live in a pavilion; it is a tremendous privilege to live in a museum designed by Thomas Jefferson and be part of the "Lawn room" community. When Claire and I were given the chance to move into Pavilion I, we seized it. Our acceptance of this honor, generally reserved for deans and distinguished faculty, makes me the first Darden dean in fifteen years to live on "Central Grounds."

We have embraced the experience wholeheartedly. The expectation in the pavilions is for them to be used as they were originally intended: as realms of faculty and student interaction and pursuit of knowledge. Seminars and student meetings take place in our pavilion regularly. Thus, NCAA champion tennis coach Brian Boland and I teamed up to teach a class in the Academical Village we called "Maximizing Leadership Potential in Sports and Business."[2] For the 2017 spring schedule I put my name down with UVA professor Ed Freeman's to teach a course in the Rotunda on ethics, stakeholder management, and regulation. Secret societies have held their meetings in our pavilion, and two students successfully proposed to their fiancées in the pavilion garden. UVA is famous for its student-led Honor Committee and honor code, and it is not just a paper tiger; they

Welcoming new Darden students in front of my home, Pavilion I, on the famous Lawn at the University of Virginia. (Photo by Andrew Shurtleff)

have engaged in discussions in Pavilion I. Based on my experience, I can only say that Jefferson's original idea actually works. Beyond the spectacular architecture, the layout of the place creates special interactions. For me, living here also helps the Darden School be more tightly connected to the rest of the university community. In many ways, living on "the Lawn" is magical.

Every risk entails some unforeseen consequences. In the case of my move to UVA, some have been propitious. My brother and sister-in-law (our best friends) are both educators and moved to Charlottesville, where they teach at St. Anne's-Belfield, a top private school. My brother, Andy, is also an inspirational runner and coach who has reunited with our handicapped childhood friend from Alaska, Larsen Klingel, whom he has pushed in local road races, including the Charlottesville ten miler (where they won the age category 50 plus outright) and the Richmond marathon (where they ran a 3:16 despite the two-hundred-pound load).[3] My niece, son, and nephew are first-, second-, and third-year students at the University of Virginia, and my eldest son is dating a fourth-year. After having no extended family for almost twenty-five years in Belgium, it is wonderful to have a support system, and our home filled once again with students.

With Coach Brian Boland after the University of Virginia tennis team won the national championship in Tulsa, Oklahoma, in May 2016. Brian and I teach the leadership course "Maximizing Leadership Potential in Sports and Business" together, and I've served as a guest coach for the team. (Author's photo)

OBSERVATIONS THUS FAR

Given my limited tenure as a dean, I cannot presume to declare success. I have less experience than most others holding my kind of position. Only time will tell whether I am a highly capable leader in higher education. The only victory I can claim now is that I was a nontraditional candidate who beat the odds by finding my way to a great university where I truly believe I fit. To my knowledge, I am the only nontraditional dean currently leading a top-twenty business school (and I am not the first), but there are many in the top one hundred.

Beyond that I can make an honest claim that I bring a fresh and somewhat different perspective to my work, thanks to my background. One of my mentors at the University of Pennsylvania has urged me not to abandon my past life entirely but to keep reflecting on what lessons I can take "from the world of McKinsey into the world of the academy." Of course, the research on liberal arts colleges presented in this book has also yielded many insights I will find ways to apply. With both in mind, I offer a few observations on the trends affecting business schools, and how they might respond.

Many of the challenges I studied in the liberal arts college context have their direct equivalents in the MBA program sphere. Both kinds of schools offer an intense residential experience and the benefit of talented faculty focused on teaching. The typical business school is similar in size to the liberal arts college average; Darden's faculty, for example, numbers around seventy tenured faculty and close to one hundred if we include adjunct and visiting professors and lecturers. Whether you're looking at a top-tier business school or a top-tier liberal arts college, you'll find high fixed costs, with faculty and staff salaries largely fixed, and high capital intensity in the form of beautiful campuses, student amenities, and new buildings. As costs rise well above the rate of inflation, both see their business models severely challenged. Both kinds of institutions have raised their list-price tuitions relentlessly over the past two decades, and therefore both have seen students taking on more debt and have come under greater pressure to show return on investment or else suffer flattening demand. Both realms of education have seen pundits questioning the value they deliver. The long-term survival prospects for many lower-ranked MBA programs, and many obscure liberal arts colleges, look precarious. Business school deans, like liberal arts college presidents, devote substantial efforts to closing the gaps by soliciting philanthropic donations, which as a result have reached all-time highs.

Moreover, all these trends challenge private and public universities, too, on a larger scale—with public universities facing the additional complication of reductions in budget support from cash-strapped state governments with concomitant pressure to not raise in-state tuition.

Competition among business education institutions is intensifying as a result of these factors—and there are more trends, as well. In the United States, many students major in business as undergraduates, making the need for an MBA less apparent. In fact, in 2014, the U.S. National Center for Education Statistics reported that 358,079 business bachelor's degrees were conferred in the United States, up by more than 50,000 from a decade before.[4] Some of these undergraduate business or management degrees are conferred by small liberal arts colleges such as Dickinson College, Franklin & Marshall, or the University of Richmond. Another source of pressure on the traditional two-year degree is a dramatic proliferation of more specialized, one-year master's degrees. For instance, the University of Virginia's undergraduate business school has extended its offerings to include four one-year master's degrees (in commerce, global commerce, information technology, and accounting). Business journalist and education watcher John Byrne recently reported that "half of the top-25 [business] schools have unveiled new specialized master's programs in the past three years—they've been popping up across the country like mushrooms, and attracting huge numbers of applicants." He cites a survey finding by the Graduate Management Admission Council that over 20 percent of prospective business students are considering only such specialized master's programs.[5] Clearly, business education in today's world extends far beyond the traditional MBA.

Further, a market for business education that was once dominated by the United States has become far more global. Impressive international schools such as Tsinghua University School of Economics and Management, India Business School, and INSEAD are making their marks. Tsinghua University, for example, attracted a $300 million gift from Blackstone founder Steve Schwarzman, who didn't even attend the school. Modeled after the Rhodes Trust Scholarship program, the Schwarzman Scholars program allows top students from around the world to study business or international relations in Beijing, all expenses paid.

As any good McKinsey consultant would be quick to point out, in a market so highly segmented, speaking in generalities is dangerous. For example, state universities are subsidized, in the United States and abroad, and are not as caught up in the expensive tuition game seen among elite, highly ranked programs. Yet state-funded schools face their own budget pressures. Governments throughout the Western world, and at all levels, are grappling with budget issues and deficits, often leading to cutbacks in higher education. Interestingly, since about 2000, the University of Virginia's Darden School of Business (as well as the UVA Law School) receives no state funding— making it, in effect, "privatized" (or, in UVA-speak, "self-sufficient"). Tuition and fees in 2016 total about $63,000 per year with just a $3,000 discount for "in-state" tuition. By contrast, MBA tuition at the University Catholic de Louvain (UCL) of Belgium will set a student back just under 1,000 euros per year. In the United States, Arizona State University has started offering a *free* MBA thanks to a large gift.[6] Starting salaries for graduates also vary dramatically, and the program formats and campuses are very different—still, it is hard to argue with a price tag of less than one thousand euros or free.

Competition in a different form comes from professional services firms, whose own very substantial needs to build business capabilities often justify large internal executive education programs. Consider Deloitte's $500 million investment to build Deloitte University in Texas, as well as another large facility in Brussels. Large corporations such as General Electric and Apple make similar investments; famously, Steve Jobs recruited Dean Joel Podolny away from the Yale School of Management to create Apple University. The executive education powerhouse IMD, in Lausanne, Switzerland, is the product of a merger of two business schools, one of which began life as Nestle's corporate training center, and the other as Alcan Aluminum's. Its executive education revenue of around $100 million far exceeds the size of its MBA program.

Technology, meanwhile, is clearly disrupting the traditional MBA curriculum even as it provides business schools with exciting opportunities, too. Here is a clear echo of so many of the consulting analyses I conducted at McKinsey as the age of the Internet dawned. With Moore's Law constantly driving down the costs of connectivity and bandwidth, computing power, and storage, access to business education is being democratized. The hares in the race have been MOOCs (massive open online courses) such as Coursera and EdX, each of which serves millions of users. A basic course is offered asynchronously for free, and students who want a certificate pay only fifty dollars to get verification of course completion. The next level is a suite of offerings called "a sequence"; at Darden, for example, students can complete a Business Strategy Specialization Sequence taught online by Professor Mike Lenox as a five-course module and receive a certificate for $350.

MIT and Wharton have put their entire curricula online for free, and MIT now offers micro-credentials that are "stackable." Harvard Business School (HBS) has likewise launched its HBX offering, whereby a student can take three online, asynchronous courses for $1,950 and receive a certificate of completion. So as not to dilute its brand, HBS offers course credit (for an additional fee) only through the Harvard Extension School and not through HBS itself. What we are starting to see here is the progressive unbundling of the accredited diploma. By tapping into thousands or hundreds of thousands of students willing to pay a few hundred or a few thousand dollars for a credential, technology is providing a new scaling vehicle and important source of new revenue growth.

Other institutions, such as the University of Illinois, are offering full degree programs using the Coursera platform. Some, including the University of North Carolina, offer full online MBAs using the 2U platform. Darden offers an executive MBA using a mix of in-person and synchronous distance platforms that allow for students to have live case discussions and for a professor to "cold call" students online. What is clear is that the proliferation of technology-delivered offerings has just begun. Technology will commoditize basic functional knowledge (driving it to zero-cost and free). It will continue to flip the classroom, allowing class sessions to consist principally of interaction, not lecture. It will allow for stronger global brands to become even stronger as they scale their know-how via technology. And asynchronous components of a course offer the promise of reversing Baumol's Law by reducing the cost of a delivered student credit hour.

The war for top talent is as intense as ever for faculty, students, and administration. First and foremost, this is driven by structural factors. The number of students taking the GMAT has ceased to grow, meaning the applicant pools are not expanding. This may be partially a result of the high prices charged for MBAs, but it is also a result of other degree formats accepting other types of test. Let's face it, it is not fun to take a standardized test such as the GMAT, and it requires time and money to study appropriately to earn one's best possible score. Second, the number of qualified PhD graduates is diminishing relative to the number of MBA programs, meaning that the competition for top tenure-track faculty is rising, especially among the elite schools that depend upon research; lesser-ranked schools do not worry about research and can employ lower-cost adjuncts.

No analysis of the business school landscape would be complete without mentioning rankings. They are annoying because they allow an external entity, and often just one or two individuals, to establish criteria reflecting what they value—often not well aligned with the missions of many schools. Many prospective students simply look at the rankings and, with no idea of how they are constructed, form opinions based on them. Rankings agencies can change their criteria dramatically and randomly from one year to the next, yo-yoing schools up and down the rankings, as *Bloomberg Businessweek* MBA rankings did in 2013, 2014, and 2015. Yet the rankings cannot be ignored; not only students but also faculty and alumni care about them.

One thing rankings certainly reinforce among the elite schools is the war for talent. There are rankings for undergraduate programs, specialty master's programs, MBA programs, and executive education offerings. Almost all MBA ranking methodologies, for example, place heavy emphasis on the average GMAT scores and GPAs of entering students, along with the ratio of students applying to students accepted, and job placement statistics including earning power. Some, such as the *Financial Times*, measure the quantity of faculty research in erudite academic publications, while others, such as *U.S. News & World Report*, generally measure "reputation" by old-fashioned, multiple-choice paper surveys sent in the mail. Thus, if they hope for high rankings, business schools must try to recruit the best students and the best faculty. Those with the greatest resources can provide more full scholarships to top students, pay higher salaries to faculty with large research publication portfolios, and attract top recruiters—and, in a sense, buy their rankings. Just like their liberal arts counterparts, many top MBA (and, for that matter, elite undergraduate business) programs already provide between 20 and 50 percent tuition reductions in the form of scholarships and financial aid grants; this will only rise and continue. Extrapolate this trend to its extreme and, in the elite ranks, it is not impossible that, within twenty years, most top students will go for free, regardless of their ability to pay. (And ideally, they will pay later in the form of philanthropic gifts to their alma maters.)

A common debate centers on which will emerge the winner: the one-year residential MBA degree of Europe or the two-year MBA degree of the United States. The very framing of that debate is deeply flawed. First, the two options are positioned as equivalent means to an end—which can seem plausible when you consider that the two-year degree is actually a four-semester program delivered in about sixteen months of class time. One full year of classes, given a slightly heavier course load, could easily provide a similar number of credit hours. But that fails to recognize an essential experience of the two-year program. At its halfway point, it features a four-month internship, allowing students to try a new kind of work or launch a new venture. (And to be honest, the number of credits and the course hours are also often different, given different standards.) It may be, therefore, that one of these models will appeal to more people than the other—but if so, it should be because they are looking for a different experience, not just a faster or slower process. I expect to see many hybrid options between the executive and residential MBA formats in years to come. In a way, the winner is the students who have an increasing number of business education options every year.

It is true that degrees that look different than those of the past will continue to emerge. They will be delivered via technology synchronously or asynchronously, and in person, and through combinations of both. They will be provided by for-profit and nonprofit educational institutions and businesses. It is true that some people will find it possible to succeed without the liberal arts, or business school, or any higher education. In a world of more than 7.4 billion people, there will always be many variants and pathways to success. But it will also be true, in my view, that an outstanding pathway for decades to come will remain flagship MBA programs at top schools. A key wild card is what employers will value, but, given the talent coming into MBA programs, I remain convinced that elite MBA programs will remain a crucial source of talent for companies for years to come. It is possible that some corporations will decide to fully insource skill building, but this is a very expensive operation and not their core business. Yes, on-the-job training is crucial, and many sector-specific skills are best acquired on the job, but many corporations look for talent to bring their skills to work on day one.

Business schools do a great service deepening knowledge of functional skills. Although many study business as undergraduates or, increasingly, online, the reality is that it takes a while to master the broad array of functional skills needed to run a business. Whether you are a lawyer, a doctor, a business school dean, an entrepreneur, or a manager in a large corporation, it is valuable to know something about strategy, marketing, balance sheets and income statements and the accounting behind them, human resources and organizational models, basic economics, IT, operations, and data analytics—all of it is relevant to the organizational goals you are trying to accomplish. But while these functional skills are important, it is perhaps other skills that the top business programs distinguish themselves by teaching so well. I'm thinking of the ability to synthesize, to think critically, and to operate and demonstrate leadership on teams; the mind-set to be responsible and have strong ethics and business values; the skills to work virtually, manipulate big data, and communicate persuasively both in writing and verbally. Standout students are able to problem-solve diverse cases in different industries; to move effectively across global environments; and to appreciate and understand diverse cultures. They behave entrepreneurially, whether or not they are starting a brand-new business. They know how to make decisions with incomplete information; to ask intelligent questions; to stay abreast of leading business ideas and in touch with the world of practice. These are some of the most important skills honed in a top MBA program, and the capabilities we try to build at Darden.

If some of the skills described above sound like those gained in the liberal arts, it is because they are. Many view studying business as being inconsistent or mutually exclusive with the liberal arts. However, almost any job is part of a business. If you are a university professor or work for Teach for America or help others through the Peace Corps or a charity, you work for a business: a not-for-profit business. If you are a doctor or lawyer or have a small company as an entrepreneur delivering services or making products, it is a business. Knowing how to think critically, speak different languages, understand history, appreciate the arts, analyze complex problems, and communicate cogently is all part of the business world. Steve Jobs, founder of Apple, found that a course he took in calligraphy at Reed College was one of the most important courses he ever took. When combined with functional business skills, it is a powerful combination.

What do I see in the crystal ball for top business school programs? Just as news stories often question the value of a liberal arts degree, stories abound proclaiming the death or lack of utility of the MBA. Sheryl Sandberg of Facebook recently posted a comment on the online forum Quora: "While I got great value from my experience, MBAs are not necessary at Facebook and I don't believe they are important for working in the tech industry."[7] Peter Thiel, the outspoken founder of Palantir and Paypal, accuses business schools of crushing creativity and business school grads of pursuing innovations too late.[8] Some might even go further and claim that because Bill Gates, Steve Jobs, and Mark Zuckerberg didn't finish college, no degree is necessary to be successful. Strictly speaking, it is true. But what if Sheryl Sandberg had not gone to Harvard Business School? Would she have gained those early footholds on the career path that ultimately took her to

Facebook? The question facing people preparing to enter the job market is how to acquire the skills needed to be ready for today's and tomorrow's world, and a forty-five-year career with retirement ages surpassing seventy years old.

My prediction is that the market will continue to assign high value to a business school education. A 2016 survey by GMAC of hiring companies, in fact, shows that the job market for MBAs is better than ever.[9] Thanks to such robust demand, there are now 777 business schools in fifty-two countries and territories having earned full accreditation from the Association to Advance Collegiate Schools of Business (AACSB).[10] Most important, I see MBA programs constantly innovating to stay relevant to an evolving market, adjusting their curriculums to student and employer needs. A number of schools, for instance, have just created new courses to help managers prepare for workplaces increasingly populated by robots and artificial intelligence. (The Kellogg School's, for example, is called "Human and Machine Intelligence.") At Darden, we have recently introduced a mandatory experiential learning component, called IDEA, into the first-year curriculum and offer several courses on data analytics and machine learning. Starting in 2017, Darden and the University of Virginia's Data Science Institute began to offer a two-year dual degree: an MBA and a master's of science in data analytics.

One thing is crystal clear: the world needs more and better business leaders, whether they are in the for-profit or not-for-profit arenas. Enterprises—including universities—must navigate deftly through what military strategists call a "VUCA" world: challenged by increasing volatility, uncertainty, complexity, and ambiguity. Incumbent firms are especially endangered by any leadership capability shortfalls, as immense amounts of capital flow into startups, and rapid technological change unleashes waves of disruption. At an even higher level, the world needs leadership that knows business. In an increasingly interconnected global economy, it is essential to gain a perspective on how national interests are affected and reshaped by geopolitics, religion, immigration, resource constraints, global warming, destabilizing concentrations of wealth, and the temptation of protectionism. Society's implicit and explicit contracts with business in the form of laws, tax rulings, treaties, trade agreements, and regulations are rapidly evolving. Business models, rules of the game, and profit pools of industries react dramatically to the stroke of a pen. Leading effectively in this world—whether in a political, not-for-profit, or for-profit context—will require new heights of knowledge and capability. Universities are not excluded, and it is hard to imagine that having little to no business acumen should be viewed as a plus for candidate leaders in the academy going forward. Equally, having a cursory understanding of higher education and the culture of the academy is not helpful.

A second prediction: For the schools whose mission it is to prepare the next generation of leaders and to develop ideas that change the world through research, scale will matter, as it often does anywhere there are high fixed costs. This is not to say that a bigger classroom with more students is the winning formula. Delivering a great educational experience and career placement will always require individual attention. However, just being small will be a difficult source of sustainable competitive advantage. Not only is technology the ultimate scaling vehicle, but the ability to sustain leading-edge research in multiple disciplines requires a minimum critical mass of faculty, the ability to be global (e.g., brand, admissions, placement) requires resources and size, and the higher utilization of shared services and expensive fixed-cost capital investments in world-class infrastructure and facilities benefit from scale. Perhaps scale is why over time all but one university with business schools in the top fifty have found various ways to combine and strengthen collaboration between their undergraduate, specialty business master's, and MBA programs, the most recent example being holdout Cornell, which unified their graduate and undergraduate business and management schools and programs together in 2016.

The increasing interdisciplinary connections between business functions and other university domains such as medicine, law, life sciences, and engineering will favor larger universities. Interuniversity partnerships will increase, as a mechanism to find smart scale short of mergers, although some de facto mergers may evolve in parts of the business school landscape. Collaboration between business schools, but also with professional service firms and industry, will intensify. Global is here to stay. Being global is no longer an elective; it is core curriculum, as business is truly global. The war for talent will rage, both for top students and top faculty. The need for philanthropy will be higher than ever and will advantage the U.S. schools, where there is a culture and tradition of giving as well as an inheritance and philanthropy tax code to enable it. For example, Harvard Business School just finished raising $1 billion on top of its $3.5 billion endowment and is now extending their campaign; Chicago Booth is raising $850 million on top of its sizeable endowment. Most European business schools by contrast have no such philanthropic tradition or culture or tax code and will find it difficult to keep pace on this dimension, but Asia likely will not. Alternative forms of business education will continue to emerge, with a large array of credentials, certificates, short specialty master's degrees, and customized executive education offerings in an increasingly hybridized blended technology and residential delivered offerings, and be important forms of revenue for top schools.

There will be a shakeout with the strong getting stronger (via philanthropy, the war for talent, and more canny use of technology), and the weaker getting commoditized and closing shop on the traditional MBA program. There are no two ways about it: winning the flagship residential MBA rankings race requires enormous resources given current rankings' algorithms. The top schools with the best global brands and faculty benefit from the ability to scale further.

Meanwhile, like a slain hydra, the demise of some traditional MBA programs will give rise to new variants. As we have seen, business school education is no longer limited to the MBA. Recently, highly respected Wake Forest closed its traditional MBA program after realizing it could not practically move into the top twenty or thirty, instead merging its undergraduate and graduate business schools to get scale and successfully introducing a series of innovative specialty master's degree programs that are more profitable. The University of Arizona recently moved to offer its small full-time MBA program to a maximum of 120 students for free in an attempt to get better students—a signal of how difficult it is to attract top students, and a move that foreshadows the future for many elite programs.[11]

Business schools, like their liberal arts counterparts, will need to address structural business model issues in the years to come. It is simply unsustainable to grow salaries and costs at above the rate of inflation and faster than net revenue. Philanthropists do not want to just plug budget deficits or fund an ever-increasing salary mass, partly driven by escalating "fringe" costs such as pensions and health care, rising central costs driven by regulations such as Title IX or cybersecurity issues, and the fact that most salary costs are fixed, inflexible, and linked to inflation. Expectations need to be reset. The past twenty years have seen top business schools more than triple in price, yet costs have risen even more. Students are graduating from undergraduate programs with unprecedented levels of debt, rendering the return-on-investment (ROI) calculation even more important. Blended learning and the use of asynchronous learning as part of a curriculum holds some promise to rein in the cost of a student credit hour delivered.

I FEEL VERY fortunate to be at the University of Virginia. Since Jefferson's founding of the institution in 1817, it has consistently been one of the United States' top public universities. Among many outstanding schools, UVA's law, education, medical, undergraduate business, and engineering schools are ranked among the nation's very best. Its honor code, excellent high-touch faculty, outstanding sports, affordability, and great academics combine to create an incredible residential experience and fiercely loyal and passionate alumni. Charlottesville, Virginia, is one of the nicest places to live in the world, as well as home to a dynamic local economy. Its metropolitan service area (population 225,000) was rated the fastest-growing venture-capital city in the United States in 2016.

I am particularly honored to be dean at the Darden Graduate School of Business, ranked second among all MBA programs in the world by the *Economist* in 2015. Indeed, the *Economist* has voted it the best educational experience of any program in the world six years in a row. Ours is a transformational program that leaves graduates energized and passionate about the school, making for an incredible network. With more than one-third international students in the MBA program and the vast majority of students having had experience working in more than one country, Darden is globally minded. It is further defined by its intensely collaborative culture of teamwork, by its focus on teaching excellence in the classroom, and by its skillful use of the Socratic case method—a pedagogical approach that does without lectures and instead has professors asking students to consider pivotal decisions real managers have had to make, and to weigh in with their own analyses.

The degree to which schools emphasize, on the one hand, inspiring teaching and, on the other hand, rigorous research is often presented as an either/or tradeoff. And I will admit that it can be hard to excel at both. (I once took a course with a Nobel Prize–winning professor and found it one of the most boring classes I ever endured.) Still, I have always thought that sounded like a false dichotomy, and Darden has shown me I was right. Its tenured professors have outstanding scholarly reputations and publication success but are also rock stars in the classroom. A great professor can be life-changing, and my mission is to make sure Darden stays well-stocked with them.

Darden is tied closely tied to the world of practice and for years has had the top-rated general management curriculum. Part of its edge is a series of course offerings called "Managers in Action" where real CEOs and other "C-level" executives draw the lessons from real-life examples. Darden also has a highly rated entrepreneurship program (ranked number three worldwide by the *Financial Times*) where any student can launch their startup in an incubator and be paid to pursue its development over the summer.

By protecting and building on assets like these, I hope to give to many graduating classes the kind of experience I had personally. Quite simply, the MBA changed my life. As a young engineering college graduate, I had gone to Silicon Valley in one of the early booms. I worked for the darling of the day, Advanced Micro Devices—at the time, the fastest corporation in U.S. history to reach revenues of $1 billion. Many multimillionaires had been minted, and the money and giddy laughter that went along with it at cocktail parties was breathtaking. For a while, I felt like I was king of the world. But when the downturn came, capital dried up, and stock prices crashed, I felt trapped. I was by then firmly branded as a tech engineer, but it turned out I didn't love being one. I was interested in the broader business and frustrated that I wouldn't have the chance to do more.

One of the worst feelings is to give your all to climbing a mountain only to find, when you reach a peak, that you are climbing the wrong mountain. All the worse if, because of financial obligations or because your personal brand is limited to the job you've been doing, you feel stuck there. The MBA was my "get out of jail free" card. Being able to re-create oneself and open life options is inherently valuable. Financial theory shows that the value of options goes up with volatility. The same is true about career options, and in a world where there is huge job volatility and innovation, a quality MBA's value goes up as it creates substantial option value in the mid to long term. In my view, there is no better investment than in one's skills and education.

The MBA continues to change future business leaders' lives every year, although the experience can vary dramatically from one school to another. What a top MBA can offer is the possibility to change trajectory in life—to move from one industry or function or geography to another. It opens up possibilities and options in life. You can go from anywhere to anywhere.

I still have much to learn about higher education and business education. Higher education leaders often face crises not of their own making; the *Rolling Stone* "Rape on Campus" article to which UVA's Terry Sullivan had to respond (despite later revelations that it was based on a fabricated story) is a case in point.

I am sure I will have my share of stumbles, trials, and tribulations. But I resolve to value even them as learning experiences as I strive to do my best in work that really matters. I am determined to honor a calling that I discovered accidentally, but I believe inevitably, after decades spent scaling another peak. If more of the high-integrity, highly capable leaders we need for the future are able to achieve their full potential through my efforts, then it really will not matter whether my apprenticeship in my trade is called traditional or nontraditional. I will have honored those who raised, taught, and influenced me, and fulfilled my own possibilities.

| Appendix

RESEARCH METHODOLOGY AND

ADDITIONAL FINDINGS

THE DISSERTATION I submitted in 2015 to the Faculties of the University of Pennsylvania, in partial fulfilment of my doctor of education degree, presented research designed to explore the following questions:

- What is the context of stand-alone liberal arts colleges today as quantitatively profiled by institutional characteristics such as geography, religious affiliation, graduation rates, selectivity, size, and financial characteristics? By comparison, how do presidents qualitatively perceive the liberal arts context?
- What is the definition of a nontraditional liberal arts college president as seen by search executives?
- What are the number and pathway characteristics of today's nontraditional liberal arts college presidents, and how do the numbers compare with the Cohen and March, American Council on Education, and Birnbaum and Umbach presidential category studies?
- Given the quantitative context above, what are the institutional characteristics (i.e., religion, graduation rates, size, geography, selectivity, financial, ranking) of liberal arts colleges that hire nontraditional presidents, and how do they differ from those hiring traditional presidents?
- How do search firm executives see trends in presidential searches and hiring nontraditional presidents?
- What are search executives' and presidents' views of and lessons learned about how nontraditional presidential candidates may increase their chances of selection?
- How have presidents thought about fit, and what are their lessons learned in the early transition process?

To answer these questions, I deployed a mixed-methods data-collection approach. I gathered quantitative data by building a database of the background and pathways of all current liberal arts college presidents (as of June 2014) and their predecessors (whenever the transition took place). In addition, I captured financial, selectivity, geography, ranking, size, and religion affiliation data on each liberal arts institution. Further, qualitative data were captured via in-depth interviews of three current or recent nontraditional college presidents, one traditional president with expertise in the liberal arts, and eight executive search professionals who have conducted liberal arts college president searches in the past several years. Finally, I collected and analyzed written materials related to the presidents and their colleges, both before and after the interviews.

Although a completely qualitative study might be adequate to provide insight regarding the factors that promote or impede fit of a nontraditional president in the liberal arts context, the reason for a mixed-methods approach was to provide a quantitative and analytical fact base not only about the pathways of nontraditional liberal arts college presidents, but also about the relationship between liberal arts institutions' characteristics and context and the type of president sought. The American Council on Education's *On the Pathway to the Presidency* report (2013) provided only a sampling across all colleges and universities and no complete perspective on the liberal arts. Statistical analysis of the database would explain which types of institutions were most likely to hire nontraditional presidents. The fact base would also allow for an accurate characterization of the liberal arts colleges context overall. To my knowledge, there is no database or analysis of the number of nontraditional liberal arts college presidents, or information on their pathways.

A qualitative approach helped to clarify, compare, and contrast definitions; explain how different stakeholders (i.e., the executive search firm, and the nontraditional presidents) view the liberal arts context and search processes involving nontraditional presidents; compare the view of those responsible for placing liberal arts college presidents with the quantitative fact base of existing presidents and their predecessors; and clarify factors that drive fit.

To clearly delimit the definition of a liberal arts institution, my research used as its sample size the 248 stand-alone liberal arts colleges as defined by *U.S. News & World Report* (USNWR) in its Compass database as of June 2014. The rationale for this is that USNWR is a commonly recognized source. Second, while many larger universities have liberal arts colleges as part of the institution, the research focuses on the challenges of liberal arts institutions as stand-alone entities led by a president. Although there are other classification systems such as Carnegie that include liberal arts colleges as part of other categories such as baccalaureate colleges, the merit of USNWR is that it is a clean list that is well recognized and used. The Annapolis Group list is smaller than that of USNWR. I rejected it so as to increase the sample size, thereby increasing the potential number of nontraditional presidents who could be studied. Further, USNWR provides ranking and a variety of other characteristic data for each institution such as geography and religion, which can be cross-tabulated with other public sources of quantitative data such as the Integrated Postsecondary Education Data System (IPEDS).

To be able to characterize the liberal arts colleges collectively and to segment them along various dimensions to illustrate their diverse starting points and trends, I gathered an array of quantitative data on each stand-alone liberal arts institution. First, basic data are captured by institution from the USNWR college database, as well as from IPEDS, including graduation rate, geography, religious affiliation, size as measured by total staff, total instructional staff, total expenses and number of students (in-state and out-of-state), selectivity as measured by acceptance rate and yield, and ranking. Second, financial data on each institution's endowment and endowment per full-time equivalent (FTE) student are captured from IPEDS. Third, list price tuition and fees (in-state and out-of-state), net tuition revenue and fees (total and per student FTE), the tuition discount rate, total revenues, total core expenses, total and average amount of institutional grant aid received and percentage of undergraduates receiving aid, percentage of full-pay students, and tuition dependency, among others, are captured or derived from IPEDS. I captured the data for the year 2012–13, as that is the last complete year in IPEDS for which data were available as of January 2015, and I also captured it for 2007–8 to allow for trend analysis leading up to the current context.

Additional Tables

The following tables were also included in my dissertation, entitled "The Rise of the Nontraditional Liberal Arts College President: Context, Pathways, Institutional Characteristics, Views of Search Firm Executives, and Lessons Learned by Presidents Making the Transition." All add nuance to the findings reported in chapter 5, on the patterns to be found among the institutions that have appointed nontraditional presidents.

TABLE A.1. Number and percentage of 2014 traditional and nontraditional presidents by endowment assets year-end 2013

2012–13 endowment assets year-end ($K; n = 234)	2014 traditional presidents (No.)	2014 nontraditional presidents (No.)	2014 traditional presidents (%)	2014 nontraditional presidents (%)
Tier 1—smallest (34 to 35,255; n = 58)	34	24	58.6	41.4
Tier 2 (35,526 to 98,752; n = 58)	35	23	60.3	39.7
Tier 3 (100,368 to 240,710; n = 59)	37	22	62.7	37.3
Tier 4—largest (241,584 to 2,025,996; n = 59)	51	8	86.4	13.6

Sources: Data from Internet searches and analysis; IPEDS; USNWR Compass 2014 data.

TABLE A.2. Number and percentage of 2014 traditional and nontraditional presidents by first-year, full-time, full-pay

2012–13 first-year, full-time, full-pay (%; n = 241)	2014 traditional presidents (No.)	2014 nontraditional presidents (No.)	2014 traditional presidents (%)	2014 nontraditional presidents (%)
Quartile 1 — lowest (0 to <1); n = 60)	38	22	63.3	36.7
Quartile 2 (1 to <6; n = 60)	37	23	61.7	38.3
Quartile 3 (6 to <35; n = 60)	40	20	66.7	33.3
Quartile 4 (35 to 100; n = 61)	46	15	75.4	24.6

Data source: Internet searches and analysis; IPEDS; USNWR Compass 2014 data.

TABLE A.3. Distribution of 2014 traditional and nontraditional presidents by graduation rate segment

Segment name (Six-year graduation rate %; $n = 244$)	2014 traditional presidents (No.)	2014 nontraditional presidents (No.)	2014 liberal arts traditional president (%)	2014 liberal arts nontraditional president (%)
Medallion (≥80; $n = 66$)	51	15	77	23
Name brand (68≤ x <80; $n = 60$)	47	13	78	22
Good buy (50≤ x <68; $n = 66$)	32	34	48	52
Good opportunity (20 ≤ x ≤50; $n = 46$)	27	19	59	41
Below segmentation standard (<20%; $n = 6$)	5	1	83	17

Sources: Data from Internet searches and analysis; IPEDS; Robert Zemsky, S. Shaman, and D. B. Shapiro, *Higher Education as Competitive Enterprise: When Markets Matter*, New Directions for Institutional Research (San Francisco: Jossey-Bass, 2001); USNWR Compass 2014 data.

TABLE A.4. Distribution of 2014 traditional and nontraditional presidents by yield rate

Yield quartile 2012–13 acceptance rate	2014 liberal arts traditional presidents (No.)	2014 liberal arts nontraditional presidents (No.)	2014 liberal arts traditional presidents (%)	2014 liberal arts nontraditional presidents (%)
1st quartile—best yield (above 35%; $n = 55$)	39	16	70.9	29.1
2nd quartile (from 28 to 35%; $n = 56$)	42	14	75	25
3rd quartile (from 22 to 27%; $n = 63$)	42	21	66.7	33.3
4th quartile—worst yield (from 9 to 21%; $n = 59$)	30	29	50.9	49.1
Total ($n = 233$)	153	80	65.7	34.3

Sources: Data from Internet searches and analysis; IPEDS; USNWR Compass 2014 data.

Note: Exact quartile boundaries selected to simplify separation.

TABLE A.5. Number and percentage of traditional and nontraditional liberal arts college presidents by number of staff

Size quartile total staff FTE 2012–13 IPEDS	2014 liberal arts traditional presidents (No.)	2014 liberal arts nontraditional presidents (No.)	2014 liberal arts traditional presidents (%)	2014 liberal arts nontraditional presidents (%)
1st quartile—smallest (from 21 to 249 FTE; $n = 61$)	38	23	62.3	37.7
2nd quartile (from 250 to 368 FTE; $n = 61$)	38	23	62.3	37.7
3rd quartile (from 374 to 584 FTE; $n = 61$)	42	19	68.9	31.1
4th quartile—biggest (from 584 to 1650 FTE; $n = 61$)	45	16	63.8	26.2
Total ($n = 244$)	163	81	66.8	33.2

Sources: Data from Internet searches and analysis; IPEDS; USNWR Compass 2014 data.

TABLE A.6. Number and percentage of 2014 traditional and nontraditional liberal arts college presidents by core-expense budget

Size quartile total core-expense budget ($ millions) 2012–13 IPEDS	2014 liberal arts traditional presidents (No.)	2014 liberal arts nontraditional presidents (No.)	2014 liberal arts traditional presidents (%)	2014 liberal arts nontraditional presidents (%)
1st quartile—smallest (from 2.4 to 25.3 FTE; n = 61)	37	24	60.7	39.3
2nd quartile (from 25.4 to 42.7 FTE; n = 61)	37	24	60.7	39.3
3rd quartile (from 42.9 to 73 FTE; n = 61)	43	18	70.5	29.5
4th quartile—biggest (from 73.2 to 532.3 FTE; n = 62)	46	16	74.2	25.8
Total (n = 245)	163	82	66.5	33.5

Sources: Data from Internet searches and analysis; IPEDS; USNWR Compass 2014 data.

ACKNOWLEDGMENTS

THROUGHOUT THE PROCESS of pursuing my second chapter as a business school dean, I proactively sought out a trusted group of advisors, friends, family, and mentors to serve as a sounding board. Their input helped produce the insights in this book just as surely as it helped me find my own way as a professional. To begin with, from my family I sought the opinion of my father, brother, and uncle Bill, who had been a university president. They were brutally honest sounding boards as they know me to the core.

From U Penn, I received invaluable advice from former college president and Professor Mary Linda Armacost. Dissertation advisor Bob Zemsky, who knew something insightful about every opportunity, taught me the essentials of the higher education landscape and was a constructive thought partner at all times. Professor Zemsky provided great encouragement to write this book, for which I am grateful. Professor Matthew Hartley had profound insights on the liberal arts and the literature, and has always been a pragmatic, constructive critic and supporter of the research.

During my research many search firm executives and nontraditional presidents generously contributed their time and insightful perspectives. This book has greatly benefited from their wisdom, and I am very thankful. In particular, I would like to thank the late William Bowen. I had the great privilege of getting to know him during the research. His insights and commentary on leadership in higher education were not only personally very helpful but added tremendously to the research. I am grateful to have met him, and I hope that, in some small way, his voice lives on in this book.

From the world of philanthropy, Joel Fleishman, professor at Duke University and author of the book *The Foundation: A Great American Secret—How Private Money Is Changing the World,* gave me incredible insight on how to think of executive director roles in foundations, and how to think about impact and structure responsibilities with founders.

Trusted McKinsey senior partners and friends Herman De Bode (a Belgian and former office manager of Benelux and Saudi Arabia, and a former McKinsey board member), James Manyika (a Rhodes Scholar and Oxford professor who served as vice chairman of the Council of Economic Advisors for President Obama, and with whom I worked in Silicon Valley for a decade), and Kurt Strovink (senior partner and a Rhodes Scholar with whom

I worked on personnel committees, and in Firm Learning) provided objective advice and encouragement at critical moments, or even on what to say in speeches I needed to make to faculty. Joe Bachelder, a legendary contract lawyer in the United States, provided precise counsel on life as I evaluated various opportunities, some with complex arrangements. Former McKinsey managing director Ian Davis, someone who has been an invaluable mentor over the years, was not only a reference but an insightful sounding board and calibrator who, among others, helped me clearly see that if I wanted a second chapter, I should not wait too long and should pursue it from a position of strength. Fellow McKinsey board member Bill Huyett, who also happened to be on Darden's Board of Trustees, was incredibly helpful in bringing me up to speed once I got involved in the search. Dominic Barton, McKinsey's managing director, provided me with the opportunity to lead "McKinsey University" and with encouragement to pursue my passions, in addition to friendship and mentoring that made me a better person.

I have always been a great believer in seeking the wisdom of my elders, and in the last four months of 2014 I reached out to a person many in McKinsey regard as the wisest of them all, former managing director Ron Daniel, now in his eighties. Ron personifies all that is good about McKinsey. He is selfless, has one of the best professional networks anywhere, operates with scrupulous values, has carried out immense charity and philanthropy work, asks penetrating open-ended questions and listens carefully, and exudes a wisdom born of six decades of seeing McKinsey partners come and go. Once, a family friend struck with cancer expressed a lifelong wish to attend the Masters golf tournament in Augusta. It was Ron who provided the tickets and refused any form of compensation. He became my consigliere and helped me navigate the various opportunities I was juggling real-time in person or on the phone, making himself available at any time in key moments. In a twist of irony and perhaps fate, Ron had decades earlier been a mentor to Ken Kring (the search executive who brought me to Darden), helping the Korn Ferry search executive launch a career with Spencer Stuart when he graduated from the Yale School of Management; however, they didn't speak about me. One of Ron's maxim's is that after working with McKinsey's incredible concentration of talent, senior partners often find the best fit in a new organization that has an extremely high standard of excellence. He had deep insight into each of the opportunities I was pursuing. He also had an incredible regard for the University of Virginia, telling me that if I should receive the offer, mine would be the most prestigious university position to which any McKinsey director (senior partner) would have been appointed. Since he had been treasurer of Harvard University, his words held great gravitas. His counsel was invaluable and gave me confidence at a moment I was unsure.

My second chapter and this book wouldn't have been possible without the inspiration and support provided by so many family members. I have dedicated the book to my grandmother "Nana," Margaret Harriet Whitcomb Beardsley. Growing up, I always wanted to be like her. As an astrophysicist ahead of her time, she taught me the Greek myths looking at constellations in the northern sky, and encouraged me to shoot for the stars. As an educator, she taught me that the power of education can allow someone from anywhere to go anywhere, and gave me the encouragement and self-confidence to try. And as one of the wisest and profoundly positive people I have ever known, her love and values taught me to see the good and the potential in people from all walks of life. She has inspired me to serve others, like she did her whole life. Now that I have come full circle as an educator myself, I am grateful I can follow in her footsteps, helping others fulfill their true potential. This book is for Nana.

To all the family members who have been educators or worked in higher education—Dad, Mom, Nana, Uncle Bill, Uncle Ben, Aunt Betsy, Auntie Bo, sister Katie, brother Andy, sister-in-law Andrea—you were the role models that made me know that higher education was a good pathway. Whenever critics told me faculty would be tough on me, I just remembered that all of you are or have been faculty and we share the same DNA.

To my wife, Claire, and three boys, Edouard, Benji, and Philip, your encouragement, love, patience, and willingness to let me pursue my calling has made it all possible and worthwhile. I could not have done this without you. I am eternally grateful.

In order to inspire others, you need to be inspired yourself. Someone who has always inspired me is my brother, Andy. Andy is a top-notch running coach who won the Chicago marathon for 45 plus. He is also an English teacher in Charlottesville. Another inspiration to me is my quasi-brother, Larsen Klingel, with whom I grew up in Anchorage, Alaska. Larsen has cerebral palsy and has not been able to walk unaided his whole life, yet I have never seen him complain. While writing this book, Andy pushed Larsen in the Richmond marathon on a bicycle weighing almost two hundred pounds so that Larsen could know what it felt like to run. They completed the journey in 3:16 and qualified for the Boston marathon. They have inspired me my whole life, and especially during the writing of this book. They are among my heroes.

As with all journeys, new pathways provide unexpected opportunities and serendipitous encounters. Writing this book I had the great fortune to work in depth over the past eighteen months with Julia Kirby, former managing editor of the *Harvard Business Review* and now a senior editor at Harvard University Press. Her wit, insight, willingness to listen, candor, easygoing manner, and eloquence have been incredible. For someone I didn't know before this project, Julia has synchronized with my way of thinking and writing in a way few have. I am most grateful for having had the opportunity to learn from her. This book has benefited measurably from her expertise and craft.

In my course on leadership, I take a page out of James Loehr's playbook that managing energy is more important than managing time. One of the great sources of energy and pleasure for me has been tennis. While I was making the transition to higher education, I had the great fortune to meet and work with the Belgian tennis coach Cédric Mélot, the runner-up in the 40 plus International Tennis Federation (ITF) Seniors Tennis Championship. He is an incredible coach who inspired me and took my game to new levels in ways that filled me with energy at a time I really needed it. We even played the ITF Seniors Tennis Championships in Antalya, Turkey together. While making my transition to the University of Virginia, I became close friends with the national championship tennis coach Brian Boland, with whom I teach a course. By inviting me to help the world-class program in some small ways, he has made me happy, inspired me, and helped me in innumerable ways. I am so thankful and lucky to have had Cédric's and Brian's support throughout this journey and transition.

At the University of Virginia I would like to thank all of those who have given me a chance to serve, and in particular President Terry Sullivan, who also encouraged me to continue my research. At Darden, I would like to thank Julie Daum, Steve Momper, Eric Fletcher, Dean Krehmeyer, and Sankaran Venkataramen for their steadfast support on this book. Finally, I am very grateful to the team at UVA Press and the reviewers for taking on this project, affording flexibility, and providing constructive and timely feedback.

A Note on Sources

Many of the insights quoted in this book come from personal discussions and interviews conducted in support of my dissertation for the University of Pennsylvania, "The Rise of the Nontraditional Liberal Arts College President: Context, Pathways, Institutional Characteristics, Views of Search Firm Executives, and Lessons Learned by Presidents Making the Transition" (2015). Rather than separately cite every quotation, I am providing here the list of interview subjects. All interviews took place in the period of late August to early November 2014. In some cases, follow-up e-mails also helped to clarify and develop lines of thinking.

EXECUTIVE SEARCH FIRM CONSULTANTS
David Bellshaw, Isaacson, Miller
Anne Coyle, Storbeck/Pimentel & Associates
John Isaacson, Isaacson, Miller
Ken Kring, Korn Ferry
Ellen Landers, Heidrick & Struggles
Sue May, Storbeck/Pimentel & Associates
Shelly Storbeck, Storbeck/Pimentel & Associates
Jackie Zavitch, Korn Ferry (and since moved to Heidrick & Struggles)

PRESIDENTS OF HIGHER EDUCATION INSTITUTIONS
William Bowen, former president of Princeton University
John Fry, Drexel University (and former president of Franklin & Marshall College)
David Greene, Colby College
Lawrence Schall, Oglethorpe University

Prologue

1. See Kahneman's best-selling book *Thinking Fast and Slow* (New York: Farrar, Straus and Giroux, 2011) for an engaging explanation of his theory that we all daily make use of two systems of cognition: the fast, intuitive, and emotional "System 1" and the slower, more deliberative, and more logical "System 2."

2. The concept of positionality bias is an admission that who we are tends to shape the assumptions we make about how the world works, and works best. See, for example, Linda Alcoff's development of it in "Cultural Feminism versus Post-Structuralism: The Identity Crisis in Feminist Theory," *Signs* 13, no. 3 (1988): 405–36.

3. Scott Beardsley and Michael Patsalos-Fox, "Getting Telecoms Privatization Right," *McKinsey Quarterly* 1 (1995): 3–26.

4. Note that any references to specific engagements of McKinsey & Company here are not breaches of the client confidentiality so important to the firm; all have been previously shared publicly through accessible secondary sources.

5. The conference program can still be accessed as of this writing at http://www .oecd.org/internet/broadband/1810983.pdf; and http://www.oecd.org/internet /broadband/dubai20020ecdglobalconferenceontelecommunicationspolicyfor thedigitaleconomy.htm.

6. The *Wall Street Journal* published the content of this July 29, 2008, call as an au-dio recording and transcript. It can be accessed at https://www.wsj.com/articles /SB100014240527023033605045774127707591607112.

7. Bob Buford, *Finishing Well: What People Who Really Live Do Differently!* (Brent-wood, TN: Integrity, 2004), 16.

1. The Rise of the "Nontraditional" President

1. Matthew Hartley, *Call to Purpose: Mission-Centered Change at Three Liberal Arts Colleges* (New York: RoutledgeFalmer, 2002), 6.

2. *Merriam-Webster's Collegiate Dictionary*, 11th ed., https://www.merriam-webster .com/dictionary/liberal%20arts.

3. Thomas E. Cronin, "The Liberal Arts and Leadership Learning," chapter 2 in *Leadership and the Liberal Arts: Achieving the Promise of a Liberal Education*, ed. J. Thomas Wren, Ronald E. Riggio, and Michael A. Genovese (London: Palgrave Macmillan, 2009), 37.

4. Pew Higher Education Roundtable, *Policy Perspectives* (Philadelphia: Institute for Research on Higher Education, 1995), 2A.

5. Daniel H. Weiss, "Challenges and Opportunities in the Changing Landscape," chap. 2 of *Remaking College: Innovation and the Liberal Arts*, ed. Rebecca Chopp, Susan Frost, and Weiss (Baltimore: Johns Hopkins University Press, 2013), 37.

6. Annapolis Group, "Sharing the Value of the Liberal Arts Education," http:// www.annapolisgroup.org/.

7. David W. Breneman, *Liberal Arts Colleges: Thriving, Surviving, or Endangered?* (Washington, DC: Brookings Institution Press, 1994), 4.

8. The phrase is taken from the Annapolis Group's website. For a list of its current members, see http://annapolisgroup.org/members.

9. M. D. Cohen and J. G. March, *Leadership and Ambiguity: The American College President* (Watertown, MA: Harvard Business Publishing, 1986), 20.

10. Sue May of Storbeck/Pimentel was one of several professionals I interviewed personally as part of my dissertation research. Henceforth, quotes from these subjects will not carry distinct endnotes. Please refer to "A Note on Sources" for details of when interviews took place and with whom.

11. Robert Birnbaum and Paul D. Umbach, "Scholar, Steward, Spanner, Stranger: The Four Career Paths of College Presidents," *Review of Higher Education* 24, no. 3 (Spring 2001): 203–17.

12. Reeve Hamilton, "After Gains and Discord, U.T. Chancellor Moves On," *New York Times,* March 22, 2014, https://www.nytimes.com/2014/03/23/us/after -gains-and-discord-ut-chancellor-moves-on.html?_r=0.

13. American Council on Education, *On the Pathway to the Presidency,* 2nd ed. (New York: TIAA-CREF Institute, 2013), 5.

14. Birnbaum and Umbach, "Scholar, Steward, Spanner, Stranger," 205–6.

15. American Council on Education, *On the Pathway to the Presidency,* 5.

16. American Council on Education, *The American College President Study: Key Findings and Takeaways; Supplement,* Spring 2012, para. 10, http://www.acenet.edu /the-presidency/Pages/Spring-Supplement-2012.aspx.

17. University of Chicago News Office, "Dean David Oxtoby Named Pomona College's Ninth President," February 11, 2003, http://www-news.uchicago.edu /releases/03/030211.oxtoby.shtml.

18. Alan Finder, "A College President Whose Credentials Stress Taking Care of Business," *New York Times,* March 5, 2008, http://www.nytimes.com/2008/03 /05/nyregion/05face.html?_r=4&.

2. A Transformed Context

1. Russell Westerholm, "Swarthmore President Rebecca Chopp Surprises School Community with Resignation," *University Herald,* June 12, 2014, http://www .universityherald.com/articles/9901/20140612/swarthmore-president-rebecca -chopp-surprises-school-community-with-resignation.htm.

2. National Center for Education Statistics, Fast Facts, Institute of Education Sciences, https://nces.ed.gov/fastfacts/display.asp?id=75.

3. Victor E. Ferrall, *Liberal Arts at the Brink* (Cambridge: Harvard University Press, 2011), loc. 187. (References to "loc." in these notes signify "location." Sources with this designation were accessed using a Kindle Paper White Model EY21.)

4. Sarah E. Turner and William G. Bowen, "The Flight from the Arts and Sciences: Trends in Degrees Conferred," *Science* 250, no. 4980 (October 26, 1990), 517–21, https://eric.ed.gov/?id–EJ417318.

5. Pew Higher Education Roundtable, *Policy Perspectives,* 2A.

6. Michael S. McPherson and Morton Owen Schapiro, "The Future Economic Challenges for the Liberal Arts Colleges," *Daedalus* 128, no. 1 (Winter 1999): 47–75. Later collected in *Distinctively American,* ed. S. Koblik and S. R. Graubard (New Brunswick, NJ: Transactions, 2000), 49–50.

7. Robert Zemsky, *Checklist for Change: Making American Higher Education a Sustainable Enterprise* (New Brunswick, NJ: Rutgers University Press, 2013), 126.

8. Breneman, *Liberal Arts Colleges,* 21.

9. "Top of the Class: Competition among Universities Has Become Intense and International," *Economist,* March 28, 2015, http://www.economist.com/news /special-report/21646987-competition-among-universities-has-become-intense -and-international-top-class.

10. American Academy of Arts and Sciences, "Public Research Universities: Recommitting to Lincoln's Vision: An Educational Compact for the 21st

Century," Cambridge, MA, 2015, 7–8, http://www.amacad.org/content.aspx ?d=22174.

11. See, for example, this commentary for *Forbes* by Richard Vedder, Distinguished Professor of Economics Emeritus at Ohio University and director of the Center for College Affordability and Productivity: "Are State Universities Being Privatized?," Forbes.com, January 26, 2012, https://www.forbes.com/sites/ccap/2012 /01/26/are-state-universities-being-privatized/#79444b961db5.

12. Institute for Research on Higher Education, "Resurveying the Terrain: Refining the Taxonomy for the Postsecondary Market," *Landscape, Change,* March/April 2001, http://web.stanford.edu/group/ncpi/documents/pdfs/lndma01.pdf.

13. William G. Bowen and Eugene M. Tobin, *Locus of Authority: The Evolution of Faculty Roles in the Governance of Higher Education* (Princeton, NJ: Princeton University Press, 2015), 152.

14. Benjamin Ginsberg, "Administrators Ate My Tuition," *Washington Monthly,* September/October 2011, http://washingtonmonthly.com/magazine/septoct-2011 /administrators-ate-my-tuition/.

15. Amy Scott, "To Compete for Students, Colleges Roll out the Amenities," National Public Radio, December 25, 2013, http://www.marketplace.org/2013/12/25 /education/compete-students-colleges-roll-out-amenities.

16. Breneman, *Liberal Arts Colleges,* 3.

17. Zemsky, *Checklist for Change,* 127.

18. Ferrall, *Liberal Arts at the Brink,* 57.

19. Hartley, *Call to Purpose,* 143.

20. Ferrall, *Liberal Arts at the Brink,* loc. 295.

21. Loren Pope, *Colleges That Change Lives: 40 Schools That Will Change the Way You Think about Colleges* (New York: Penguin, 2006), 3.

22. Bryan J. Cook, "The American College President Study: Key Findings and Takeaways," *The Presidency,* Spring Supplement 2012, para. 18, www.acenet.edu /the-presidency/columns-and-features/Pages/The-American-College-President -Study.aspx.

23. University of Iowa chapter, American Association of University Professors (AAUP), "Press Release on Presidential Search," September 23, 2015, http://blog .aaup-uiowa.org/2015/09/press-release-on-presidential-search.html.

24. AAUP, "College and University Governance: The University of Iowa Governing Board's Selection of a President," December 2015, https://www.aaup.org/report /college-and-university-governance-university-iowa.

25. Patricia Sellers, "The Unluckiest President in America," *Fortune,* March 25, 2015, http://fortune.com/2015/03/25/uva-president-teresa-sullivan/.

26. Ferrall, *Liberal Arts at the Brink.*

3. New Pressures and Pathways

1. J. B. McLaughlin and D. Riesman, *Choosing a College President: Opportunities and Constraints* (Princeton, NJ: Princeton University Press, 1990), 227.

2. Marcus Lingenfelter, "Presidential Search Consultants in Higher Education: A Review of the Literature," *Higher Education in Review* 1 (2004): 38.

3. American Council on Education, *The American College President Study*, para. 14.

4. Association of Governing Boards, https://www.agb.org/store/presidential-search-overview-board-members, *AGB Presidential Search: An Overview for Board Members* (Washington, DC: AGB, 2012), 71.

5. Ted J. Marchese, "Search from the Candidate's Perspective: An Interview with Maria M. Perez," *AAHE Bulletin* 42, no. 4 (December 1989): 5.

6. Susan R. Pierce, *On Being Presidential: A Guide for College and University Leaders* (New York: Wiley, 2011), 171.

7. American Council on Education, *On the Pathway to the Presidency*, 1.

8. Rita Bornstein, *Legitimacy in the Academic Presidency: From Entrance to Exit.* (Westport, CT: Greenwood, 2003), loc. 3388.

9. Jack Stripling, "College Headhunters, Accustomed to Secrecy, Find Themselves under Scrutiny," *Chronicle of Higher Education*, June 20, 2014, http://chronicle.texterity.com/chronicle/20140620a?pg=3#pg3.

10. James Finkelstein, "Executive Search Firms and the Disempowerment of Faculty," AAUP Annual Conference on the State of Higher Education," Washington, DC, June 2016. The research has not been published as of this writing but has been reported on extensively. See, for example, Jillian Berman, "This Is How Much Colleges Spend Just Searching for a New President," *MarketWatch*, June 21, 2016, http://www.marketwatch.com/story/study-raises-questions-about-the-way-college-presidents-are-hired-2016-06-17.

11. McLaughlin and Riesman, *Choosing a College President*, 252.

12. Ibid., 226.

13. Ibid., 294.

14. American Council on Education, *On the Pathway to the Presidency*, 10.

15. Peter D. Eckel, Bryan J. Cook, and Jacqueline E. King, *The 2009 CAO Census: A National Profile of Chief Academic Officers* (Washington, DC: American Council on Education, 2009).

16. Trinity College (2013), pp. 25–28, http://www.trincoll.edu/presidentialsearch/Documents/TRINPresident%20Prospectus%20REV2.pdf.

17. Richard A. Kaplowitz, "Selecting College and University Personnel: The Quest and the Questions," ASHE-ERIC Higher Education Report No. 8, Association for the Study of Higher Education, 1986: 13, http://files.eric.ed.gov/fulltext/ED282488.pdf.

18. American Council on Education, *The American College President Study*, para. 11.

19. Karen Doss Bowman, "The Presidential Pipeline: Nontraditional Candidates Often a Natural Fit for Campus Top Spot," *Public Purpose*, Summer 2011, 17, http://www.aascu.org/uploadedFiles/AASCU/Content/Root/MediaAndPublications/PublicPurposeMagazines/Issue/11summer_presidentpipeline.pdf.

20. Kevin Simpson, "Chancellor Rebecca Chopp Charts New Direction for University of Denver," *Denver Post*, September 20, 2015, http://www.denverpost.com

/2015/09/19/chancellor-rebecca-chopp-charts-new-direction-for-university-of
-denver/.

21. Stephen Joel Trachtenberg, Gerald B. Kauvar, and E. Grady Bogue, *Presidencies Derailed: Why University Leaders Fail and How to Prevent It* (Baltimore: Johns Hopkins University Press, 2013), vii.

22. Cohen and March, *Leadership and Ambiguity*, 9.

23. American Council on Education, *The American College President Study*, para. 5.

24. Kevin Kiley, "Searching for an Answer," *Inside Higher Ed*, October 4, 2012, www .insidehighered.com/news/2012/10/04/major-turnover-research-university -presidencies-could-lead-unconventional-picks.

25. Kellie Woodhouse, "A Controversial Search," *Inside Higher Ed*, September 2, 2015, www.insidehighered.com/news/2015/09/02/changing-search-process -and-nontraditional-candidate-rankle-some-university-iowa.

26. Susan Frost and Shelly Weiss Storbeck, "Using Governance to Strengthen the Liberal Arts," chap. 4 of *Remaking College: Innovation and the Liberal Arts*, ed. Rebecca Chopp and Daniel Weiss (Baltimore: Johns Hopkins University Press, 2013), 61.

27. Stephen G. Pellietier, "Structuring Boards to Capitalize on Technology's Power," *Trusteeship Magazine*, November/December 2013, www.agb.org/trusteeship /2013/11/structuring-boards-capitalize-technologys-power.

28. Cohen and March, *Leadership and Ambiguity*, 205.

29. Robert Birnbaum, *How Colleges Work: The Cybernetics of Academic Organization and Leadership* (New York: Wiley, 1988), 29.

30. James L. Fisher and James V. Koch, *Presidential Leadership: Making a Difference* (Phoenix: Oryx, 1996), loc. 63–64.

31. McLaughlin and Riesman, *Choosing a College President*, 4.

32. Trachtenberg, Kauvar, and Bogue, *Presidencies Derailed*, 1.

33. James C. Turpin, "Executive Search Firms' Consideration of Person-Organization Fit in College and University Presidential Searches" (PhD diss., College of William and Mary, 2012), https://eric.ed.gov/?id=ED550877, available from ProQuest Dissertations and Thesis Database (UMI No. 3537424).

4. A New Breed

1. Richard Ekman, "The Imminent Crisis in College Leadership," *Chronicle of Higher Education*, September 19, 2010, http://chronicle.com/article/The -Imminent-Crisis-in-College/124513.

2. Holly Madsen, "Institutional Decision-Making in Liberal Arts Colleges Led by Nontraditional Presidents" (PhD diss., Harvard University, 2004), https:// scholar.google.com/scholar?q=Holly+Madsen%2C+%E2%80%9CInstitutional +Decision-Making+in+Liberal+Arts+Colleges+Led+by+Nontraditional +Presidents%E2%80%9D+%28PhD+diss.%2C+Harvard+University&btnG =&hl=en&as_sdt=0%2C47, available from ProQuest Dissertations and Theses Database (UMI No. 3134491).

3. Qtd. in Kellie Woodhouse, "Unpopular Pick," *Inside Higher Ed,* September 9, 2015, https://www.insidehighered.com/news/2015/09/04/appointment -businessman-bruce-harreld-next-u-iowa-president-upsets-faculty.

4. Richard Ekman, "The Imminent Crisis in College Leadership," *Chronicle of Higher Education,* September 19, 2010, www.chronicle.com/article/The -Imminent-Crisis-in-College/124513.

5. "Oglethorpe President Takes Hands-On Approach to Sell College, City," *Atlanta Journal-Constitution,* May 27, 2009.

6. William G. Bowen, "Costs and Productivity in Higher Education," Tanner Lectures on Human Values, delivered at Stanford University, October 10–11, 2012, http://tannerlectures.utah.edu/Bowen%20Tanner%20Lecture.pdf.

7. Stein noted later that this proposition, "arising first in a discussion of the [1980s] balance of payments deficit, is a response to those who think that if something cannot go on forever, steps must be taken to stop it or even to stop it at once" (Herbert Stein, *What I Think: Essays on Economics, Politics, and Life* [Washington, DC: American Enterprise Institute, 1998], 32).

8. Bowdoin Says Goodbye to Barry Mills after Fourteen Super Years," *Bowdoin Magazine* 86, no. 3 (Spring/Summer 2015), https://issuu.com/bowdoinmagazine /docs/bowdoin-vol-86-no3-springsummer2015.

9. Qtd. in Lydia Lum, "Under New Management," *Diverse Issues in Higher Education,* November 13, 2008, http://diverseeducation.com/article/11945/.

10. Bowman, "The Presidential Pipeline," 17.

11. Rita Bornstein, *Fundraising Advice for College and University Presidents* (Washington, DC: AGB, 2011), 1.

12. Nick Daniels and Zoe Lescaze, "The Evolution of a Leader: Barry Mills as President," *Bowdoin Orient,* December 10, 2010, http://bowdoinorient.com /article/5878.

13. Brian Lamb, "Q&A with Shirley Ann Jackson," C-SPAN December 10, 2004, https://www.c-span.org/video/transcript/?id=7939.

14. Ekman, "The Imminent Crisis in College Leadership," 1.

15. Reeve Hamilton, "After Gains and Discord, UT Chancellor Moves On," *New York Times,* March 22, 2014.

16. Daniels and Lescaze, "The Evolution of a Leader."

17. Melissa Ezarik, "Paths to the Presidency," *University Business,* March 2010, https://www.universitybusiness.com/article/paths-presidency.

18. See http://www.chronicle.com/article/The-3-Qualities-That-Make-a/238883 ?cid=trend_right_a.

19. Vauhini Vara, "Do Businesspeople Make Good University Presidents?" *New Yorker,* September 10, 2015, http://www.newyorker.com/business/currency/do -businesspeople-make-good-university-presidents.

20. Patrick Clark, "MBAs Don't Get Much Love (or Money) from the Ivory Tower," *Bloomberg Businessweek,* January 6, 2014, www.bloomberg.com/news/articles /2013-12-18/mbas-don-t-get-much-love-or-money-from-the-ivory-tower.

21. Jill Anderson and Matt Weber, "The Growing Number of Women College Pres-

idents," August 18, 2014, Harvard Graduate School of Education website, http://www.gse.harvard.edu/news/14/08/growing-number-women-college-presidents.

22. Audrey Williams June, "Presidents: Same Look, Different Decade," *Chronicle of Higher Education,* February 16, 2007, http://chronicle.com/article/Presidents-Same-Look/19958/.

23. The comment was made by "WI" specifically in response to Benjamin Ginsberg's essay "College Presidents Should Come from Academia," March 3, 2016, http://www.nytimes.com/roomfordebate/2016/03/01/college-presidents-with-business-world-ties/college-presidents-should-come-from-academia.

24. Jes Staley, "Lessons from a Search," *Bowdoin Magazine* 86, no. 2 (Winter 2015): 14–15.

5. Which Schools Break with Tradition?

1. Scott Carlson, "Turnaround President Makes the Most of His College's Small Size, *Chronicle of Higher Education,* November 15, 2009, http://chronicle.com/article/Turnaround-President-Makes-the/49138/.

2. Ibid.

3. Pierce, *On Being Presidential,* 145.

4. Robert Zemsky, S. Shaman, and D. B. Shapiro, *Higher Education as Competitive Enterprise: When Markets Matter,* New Directions for Institutional Research (San Francisco: Jossey-Bass, 2001).

5. Details about Jake Schrum's career are from the "President's Biography" on the Emory & Henry College website, http://www.ehc.edu/about/office-president/about-president/presdents-biography/.

6. Details about Jonathan Lash's career are from his biography on Hampshire College's website, https://www.hampshire.edu/presidents-office/jonathan-lash.

7. Details of President Purce's career are from his biography on the Evergreen State College website, http://evergreen.edu/president/history/purce.

8. John William Oliver and Charles L. Cherry, *Founded by Friends: The Quaker Heritage of Fifteen American Colleges and Universities* (Lanham, MD: Scarecrow, 2007), 45.

9. Brandon Gee, "Q&A with Saint Anselm College President Steven R. DiSalvo," *New Hampshire Business Review,* November 15 2013, http://www.nhbr.com/November-15-2013/Q-A-with-Saint-Anselm-College-President-Steven-R-DiSalvo/.

10. Ellen Earle Chaffee, "After Decline, What? Survival Strategies at Eight Private Colleges," NCHEMS Executive Overview, National Center for Higher Education Management Systems, Boulder, CO, 1984, http://files.eric.ed.gov/fulltext/ED253131.pdf.

11. Jake Rosenthal, "A Terrible Thing to Waste," *New York Times,* July 31, 2009, http://www.nytimes.com/2009/08/02/magazine/02FOB-onlanguage-t.html.

12. Goldie Blumenstyk, "Dept. Names More Than 550 Colleges It Has Put under Extra Financial Scrutiny," *Chronicle of Higher Education,* March 31, 2015, http://chronicle.com/article/%E2%80%A8Dept-Names-More-Than-%E2%80%A8550/228957/.

13. Details on President Poskanzer's career can be found in his CV posted online, https://apps.carleton.edu/campus/president/assets/SP_CV_April_2010.pdf.

14. Kevin Kiley, "Welcome to the Party," *Inside Higher Ed,* April 19, 2012, https://www.insidehighered.com/news/2012/04/19/less-elite-colleges-well-versed-confronting-problems-think-they-can-teach-elites-few.

6. Advice to the Ambitious

1. Pierce, *On Being Presidential,* 158–59.

2. Ibid., 165.

3. Bowman, "The Presidential Pipeline," 16.

4. Bornstein, *Legitimacy in the Academic Presidency,* loc. 590.

5. Kevin Kiley, "Meet the New Boss," *Inside Higher Ed,* July 31, 2012, https://www.insidehighered.com/news/2012/07/31/business-officers-might-be-next-pipeline-college-presidents.

6. Lydia Lum, "Under New Management," *Diverse Issues in Higher Education,* November 13, 2008, http://diverseeducation.com/article/11945/.

7. McLaughlin and Riesman, *Choosing a College President,* 57. Susan Pierce elaborates on this point in *On Being Presidential.*

8. John Nason, *Presidential Search: A Guide to the Process of Selecting & Appointing College & University Presidents,* 1984, https://eric.ed.gov/?id=ED247877.

9. The phrasing here is from a summing up by James C. Turpin, "Executive Search Firms' Consideration of Person-Organization Fit in College and University Presidential Searches" (PhD diss., College of William and Mary, 2013), 29.

10. Fisher and Koch, *Presidential Leadership;* Bornstein, *Legitimacy in the Academic Presidency,* loc. 3394; Association of Governing Boards, *Presidential Search: An Overview for Board Members.*

11. Additional research underlining the role and importance of boards in conducting the search for presidents and chief executives can be found in Birnbaum, *How Colleges Work;* C. B. Neff and B. Leondar, *Presidential Search: A Guide to the Process of Selecting and Appointing College and University Presidents* (Washington, DC: Association of Governing Boards of Colleges and Universities, 1997); and Pierce, *On Being Presidential.*

12. Nannerl O. Keohane, "The Liberal Arts and Presidential Leadership," *Carnegie Reporter* 7, no. 3 (Winter 2014), http://higheredreporter.carnegie.org/wp-content/pdf/HigherEdReporter.pdf.

13. Allison M. Vaillancourt, "What Search Committees Wish You Knew," *Chronicle of Higher Education,* January 2, 2013, http://anthropology.tamu.edu/images/Special_Report_Academic_Jobs.pdf.

14. Bowman, "The Presidential Pipeline," 17.

15. Susan Resneck Pierce, "Producing Academic Leaders," *Inside Higher Ed,* January 26, 2011, https://www.insidehighered.com/advice/2011/01/26/producing-academic-leaders.

16. Bowman, "The Presidential Pipeline," 19.

17. Fisher and Koch, *Presidential Leadership,* loc. 391.

18. Bornstein, *Legitimacy in the Academic Presidency,* loc. 632.
19. Bowman, "The Presidential Pipeline," 17.
20. Katherine Mangan, "A President's Plan to Steer Out At-Risk Freshmen Incites a Campus Backlash," *Chronicle of Higher Education,* January 20, 2016, http://www.chronicle.com/article/a-presidents-plan-to-steer/234992.
21. Yonette Joseph and Mike McPhate, "Mount St. Mary's President Quits after Firings Seen as Retaliatory," *New York Times,* February 29, 2016, https://www.nytimes.com/2016/03/02/us/simon-newman-resigns-as-president-of-mount-st-marys.html.
22. William G. Tierney, "Organizational Culture in Higher Education: Defining the Essentials," *Journal of Higher Education* 59, no. 1 (January–February 1988): 2–21, http://faculty.mu.edu.sa/public/uploads/1360751907.3479organizational%20cult10.pdf.
23. William G. Tierney, *The Impact of Culture on Organizational Decision-Making: Theory and Practice in Higher Education* (Sterling, VA: Stylus, 2016), chap. 3.
24. J. B. McLaughlin, *Leadership Transitions: The New College President* (San Francisco: Jossey-Bass, 1996), 10–11.
25. Robert Birnbaum, *How Academic Leadership Works: Understanding Success and Failure in the College Presidency* (San Francisco: Jossey-Bass, 1992), 96, 98.

7. The Right Debate to Have

1. Steve Maas, "A Remarkable Turnaround at Regis College," *Boston Globe,* April 26, 2015, http://www.bostonglobe.com/business/2015/04/25/remarkable-turnaround-for-regis/AzfSnRJYeP86grC4qmceXO/story.html.
2. McLaughlin and Riesman, *Choosing a College President,* 306.
3. Amanda Goodall, *Socrates in the Boardroom: Why Research Universities Should be Led by Top Scholars* (Princeton, NJ: Princeton University Press, 2009).
4. Ellen Wexler, "Cutting Faculty Jobs Brings President Award," *Inside Higher Ed,* February 29, 2016, https://www.insidehighered.com/news/2016/02/29/president-wins-award-cutting-tenured-faculty-jobs.
5. Mark Guydish, "King's College Looks for More International Students and Offers More Sports, School President Says," *Wilkes-Barre (PA) Times Leader,* March 16, 2016, http://timesleader.com/news/522048/kings-college-looks-for-more-international-students-and-offers-more-sports-school-president-says.
6. It was in "The Rich Boy," one of the short stories in *All the Sad Young Men* (New York: Scribner's Sons, 1926), that Fitzgerald included his now-famous observation: "Let me tell you about the very rich. They are different from you and me. They possess and enjoy early, and it does something to them, makes them soft, where we are hard, cynical where we are trustful, in a way that, unless you were born rich, it is very difficult to understand."
7. For an overview, see Amy L. Kristof, "Person-Organization Fit: An Integrative Review of its Conceptualizations, Measurement, and Implications," *Personnel Psychology* 49 (1996): 1–49.
8. Daniel L. Duke and Edward Iwanicki, "Principal Assessment and the Notion of 'Fit,'" *Peabody Journal of Education* 68 (1992): 31.

9. Trachtenberg, Kauvar, and Bogue, *Presidencies Derailed*, 48.

10. McLaughlin and Riesman, *Choosing a College President*; Pierce, *On Being Presidential*; Fisher and Koch, *Presidential Leadership*; Patrick H. Sanaghan, Larry Goldstein, and Kathleen D. Gaval, *Presidential Transitions: It's Not Just the Position, It's the Transition*, Ace Series on Higher Education (Lanham, MD: Rowman and Littlefield, 2009).

11. Robert D. Bretz and Timothy A. Judge, "Person-Organization Fit and the Theory of Work Adjustment: Implications for Satisfaction, Tenure, and Career Success," *Journal of Vocational Behavior* 44, no. 1 (February 1994): 32–54.

12. Amy L. Kristof, "Person–Organization Fit: An Integrative Review of Its Conceptualizations, Measurement, and Implications," *Personnel Psychology* 49, no. 1 (1996): 1–49.

13. Michael B. Arthur and Kathy E. Kram, "Reciprocity at Work: The Separate, Yet Inseparable Possibilities for Individual and Organizational Development," in *Handbook of Career Theory*, ed. M. B. Arthur, D. T. Hall, and B. S. Lawrence (New York: Cambridge University Press, 1989), 292–312.

14. Pierce, *On Being Presidential*, loc. 2930.

15. Barbara C. Moody, "The Question of Fit: How Candidates Assess Individual-Institutional Fit before Accepting a College or University Presidency" (PhD diss., Harvard University, 1997), available from ProQuest Dissertations and Theses Database (UMI 9734813).

16. The comment was made in private conversation in April 2016 and related to me by Julia Kirby, whose daughter was at the time faced with a decision between the women's colleges that had offered her a place.

17. Warren Bennis, "Searching for the 'Perfect' University President," in *The Essential Bennis* (New York: Wiley, 2009), 73.

18. Sheila Jordan's comment was made in response to a question about Kenyon College's long-standing "ten-mile rule" compelling faculty to live within that distance of the rural campus's center. It appears in a 1999 "oral history" project by the Women's and Gender Studies Feminist Methodologies class, Kenyon College, http://classprojects.kenyon.edu/wmns/Wmns31/Housing/debate.htm.

19. Donald C. Mundinger, "What a Presidential Candidate Needs to Know," *AGB Reports* 24, no. 2 (March–April 1982), 45.

20. Citing the source of this oft-quoted sentiment is complicated. It is found in Jefferson's letter to French Revolutionary Marc-Antoine Juliien dated July 23, 1818, but included there as a direct quote from what Jefferson claims was a prior letter to Mr. F. I. DuPont of September 9, 1817. See *The Works of Thomas Jefferson: Published by Order of Congress from the Original Manuscripts Deposited in the Department of State*, vol. 7, ed. Henry Augustine Washington (New York: Townsend MacCoun, 1884), 106, https://books.google.com/books?id=_PpFAQAAMAAJ&pg=PA106&lpg=PA106&dq=Jefferson#v=onepage&q=Jefferson&f=false.

21. American Academy of Arts and Sciences, *Public Research Universities: Recommitting to Lincoln's Vision: An Educational Compact for the 21ˢᵗ Century*, a publication of the Lincoln Project (Cambridge, MA: American Academy of Arts and

Sciences, 2016), 5, 29, http://www.amacad.org/multimedia/pdfs/publications/researchpapersmonographs/PublicResearchUniv_Recommendations.pdf.

Epilogue

1. David Brooks, *The Road to Character* (New York: Random House, 2015), 46.

2. See http://uvamagazine.org/articles/business_anyone.

3. See http://www.newsplex.com/content/sports/Crossing-the-finish-line-together-for-STABS-Beardsley-415917333.html.

4. National Center for Education Statistics, Digest of Education Statistics 2015, "Figure 16. Bachelor's Degrees Conferred by Postsecondary Institutions in Selected Fields of Study: 2003–04, 2008–09, and 2013–14," https://nces.ed.gov/programs/digest/d15/figures/fig_16.asp?referrer=figures.

5. John A. Byrne, "Should You Get a One-Year Master's Degree in Business?," LinkedIn post, December 9, 2015, https://www.linkedin.com/pulse/should-you-get-one-year-masters-degree-business-john-a-byrne.

6. Lindsay Gellman, "The Price of an M.B.A. at Arizona State University's Business School? Free," *Wall Street Journal,* October 14, 2015, https://www.wsj.com/articles/the-price-of-an-m-b-a-at-this-school-free-1444867124.

7. The comment was widely reported in the business media. See, for example, Richard Feloni, "Facebook's Sheryl Sandberg Says You Don't Need an MBA to Be Successful in Tech," *Business Insider,* December 17, 2015, www.businessinsider.com/sheryl-sandberg-says-mbas-arent-necessary-in-tech-2015–12.

8. Natalie Kotroeff, "Peter Thiel on Creativity: Asperger's Promotes It, Business School Crushes It," *Bloomberg Businessweek,* October 7, 2014, https://www.bloomberg.com/news/articles/2014-10-07/peter-thiel-criticizes-harvard-business-school-praises-aspergers.

9. 2016 GMAC Corporate Recruiters Survey, June 2016, http://www.gmac.com/market-intelligence-and-research/gmac-surveys/corporate-recruiters-survey.aspx.

10. AACSB International, "AACSB-Accredited Schools Worldwide," www.aacsb.edu/accreditation/accredited-members.

11. Ryan Lasker, "Arizona State Announces Free MBA Program, Seeks to Increase Diversity," *USA Today,* October 21, 2015, http://college.usatoday.com/2015/10/21/arizona-state-free-mba/.

Books on Leadership in Higher Education

Birnbaum, Robert. *How Academic Leadership Works: Understanding Success and Failure in the College Presidency.* San Francisco: Jossey-Bass, 1992.

Bornstein, Rita. *Legitimacy in the Academic Presidency: From Entrance to Exit.* ACE/Praeger Series on Higher Education. Lanham, MD: Rowman and Littlefield, 2003.

Bowen, Willliam G. *Lessons Learned: Reflections of a University President.* Princeton, NJ: Princeton University Press, 2010.

Bowen, William G., and Harold T. Shapiro, eds. *Universities and Their Leadership.* Princeton, NJ: Princeton University Press, 1998; paperback ed., 2016. Includes an essay by Shapiro (former president of Princeton University and of the University of Michigan) entitled "University Presidents, Then and Now," which the publisher says blends "personal insights with a historical account of changes over time in the roles of university presidents."

Cohen, Michael D., and James G. March. *Leadership and Ambiguity: The American College President,* Brighton, MA: Harvard Business Publishing, 1986.

d'Ambrosio, Madeleine B., and Ronald G. Ehrenberg, eds. *Transformational Change in Higher Education: Positioning Colleges and Universities for Future Success.* Northampton, MA: Edward Elgar, 2008.

McLaughlin, Judith Block, and David Riesman. *Choosing a College President: Opportunities and Constraints.* Princeton, NJ: Carnegie Foundation for the Advancement of Teaching, 1990.

Nelson, Stephen. *Leaders in the Labyrinth: College Presidents and the Battlegrounds of Creeds and Convictions.* ACE/Praeger Series on Higher Education. Lanham, MD: Rowman and Littlefield, 2007.

Padilla, Arthur. *Portraits in Leadership: Six Extraordinary University Presidents.* ACE/Praeger Series on Higher Education. Lanham, MD: Rowman and Littlefield, 2005.

Pierce, Susan R. *On Being Presidential: A Guide for College and University Leaders.* New York: Wiley, 2011.

Trachtenberg, Stephen Joel, Gerald B. Kauvar, and E. Grady Bogue. *Presidencies Derailed: Why University Leaders Fail and How to Prevent It.* Baltimore: Johns Hopkins University Press, 2013.

Books on the Challenges Facing Liberal Arts Colleges

Breneman, David W. *Liberal Arts Colleges: Thriving, Surviving, or Endangered?* Washington, DC: Brookings Institution Press, 1994.

Chopp, Rebecca, Susan Frost, and Daniel H. Weiss, eds. *Remaking College: Innovation and the Liberal Arts.* Baltimore: Johns Hopkins University Press, 2013.

Ferrall, Victor E., Jr. *Liberal Arts at the Brink.* Cambridge: Harvard University Press, 2011.

Zakaria, Fareed. *In Defense of a Liberal Education.* New York: Norton, 2015.

Books on Career Transitions and "Second Acts"

There are numerous career advice and self-help books aimed at professionals who either are in transition to a work in a new sector or occupation or would like to be. The smattering of titles below does not imply direct competition with *Higher Calling* but rather speaks to the constant hunger for such content.

Ben-Shahar, Tal. *Being Happy: You Don't Have to Be Perfect to Lead a Richer, Happier Life*. New York: McGraw-Hill Professional, 2010.

Brooks, David. *The Road to Character*. New York: Random House, 2015.

Buford, Bob P. *Finishing Well: The Adventure of Life beyond Halftime*. Grand Rapids, MI: Zondervan, 2011.

————. *Halftime: Moving from Success to Significance*. Grand Rapids, MI: Zondervan, 2008.

Christensen, Clayton M., James Allworth, and Karen Dillon. *How Will You Measure Your Life?* New York: Harper Business, 2012.

Gongwer, Todd. *Lead . . . for God's Sake! A Parable for Finding the Heart of Leadership*. Carol Stream, IL: Tyndale House, 2011.

Hoffman, Reid, and Ben Casnocha. *The Start-up of You: Adapt to the Future, Invest in Yourself, and Transform Your Career*. New York: Crown Business, 2012.

Ibarra, Herminia. *Working Identity: Unconventional Strategies for Reinventing Your Career*. Brighton, MA: Harvard Business Review Press, 2003.

Kelley, Katie C. *Career Courage: Discover Your Passion, Step Out of Your Comfort Zone, and Create the Success You Want*. New York: AMACOM, 2016.

Pollan, Stephen M., and Mark Levine. *Second Acts: Creating the Life You Really Want, Building the Career You Truly Desire*. New York: HarperResource, 2002.

Seligman, Martin E. P. *Authentic Happiness: Using the New Positive Psychology to Realize Your Potential for Lasting Fulfillment*. New York: Simon and Schuster, 2004.

Zander, Rosamund Stone, and Benjamin Zander. *The Art of Possibility*. Brighton, MA: Harvard Business Press, 2000.

Books on the Inner Workings of McKinsey & Co.

There are a couple of recent books purporting to give a behind-the-scenes view of "the most respected and most secretive consulting firm in the world," although none is authored by a true insider.

Bower, Marvin. *Perspective on McKinsey*. New York: McKinsey & Company, 1979.

McDonald, Duff. *The Firm: The Story of McKinsey and Its Secret Influence on American Business*. New York: Simon and Schuster, 2013.

Raghavan, Anita. *The Billionaire's Apprentice: The Rise of the Indian-American Elite and the Fall of the Galleon Hedge Fund*. New York: Business Plus, 2013.

Page numbers in italics indicate illustrations. Page numbers with appended t or f indicate tables or figures.